ALSO BY PHYLLIS ROSE

*Woman of Letters: A Life of Virginia Woolf*

*Parallel Lives: Five Victorian Marriages*

*Writing of Women: Essays in a Renaissance*

*Jazz Cleopatra: Josephine Baker in Her Time*

*Never Say Goodbye: Essays*

*The Norton Book of Women's Lives* (editor)

*The Year of Reading Proust: A Memoir in Real Time*

# THE
# SHELF

# THE
# SHELF

*From LEQ to LES*

PHYLLIS ROSE

*Farrar, Straus and Giroux*
*New York*

Farrar, Straus and Giroux
18 West 18th Street, New York 10011

Grateful acknowledgment is made for permission to reprint
the following illustrations:
p. 240: Photograph of Etienne Leroux copyright © David Goldblatt.
p. 242: Photograph of girls playing mah-jongg in pool
courtesy Library of Congress, Prints and Photographs Division.
p. 251: Weeded books, photograph by Adina Hoffman.

Library of Congress Cataloging-in-Publication Data
Rose, Phyllis, [date].
  The shelf : from LEQ to LES / Phyllis Rose. — First edition.
    pages   cm
  ISBN 978-0-374-53536-0
  1. Rose, Phyllis, 1942—Books and reading.   2. Books and reading—
United States.   3. Authors, American—20th century—Books and
reading.   4. Reading interests—United States.   5. Fiction—History
and criticism.   6. New York Society Library.   I. Title.

Z1003.2 R67 2014
028'.9—dc23

                                                              2013034092

Designed by Jonathan D. Lippincott

Farrar, Straus and Giroux books may be purchased for educational, business,
or promotional use. For information on bulk purchases, please contact the
Macmillan Corporate and Premium Sales Department at 1-800-221-7945,
extension 5442, or write to specialmarkets@macmillan.com.

www.fsgbooks.com
www.twitter.com/fsgbooks • www.facebook.com/fsgbooks

To Annie Dillard
*lector prodigiosa*

In the vast Library, there are no two identical books.

—Jorge Luis Borges, from "The Library of Babel"

# CONTENTS

# THE
# SHELF

# THE EXPERIMENT BEGINS

T HIS BOOK RECORDS THE HISTORY OF AN EXPERIMENT. Believing that literary critics wrongly favor the famous and canonical—that is, writers chosen for us by others—I wanted to sample, more democratically, the actual ground of literature. So I chose a fiction shelf in the New York Society Library somewhat at random—it happens to be the LEQ–LES shelf—and set out to read my way through it, writing about the experience as I went. I had no reason to believe that the books would be worth the time I would spend on them. They could be dull, even lethally so. I was certain, however, that no one in the history of the world had read exactly this series of novels. That made the project exciting to me.

I thought of my adventure as Off-Road or Extreme Reading. To go where no one had gone before. To ski fresh powder in the backcountry of the Rockies. To hack through a Mexican jungle and discover a lost city. To be the first to cross Antarctica, reduced to eating the sled dogs, leading my men through the frozen wastes, across the Strait of Magellan, and over the treacherous mountains of South Georgia Island. To be the first. However, I like to sleep under a quilt with my head on a goose down pillow. So I would read my way into the unknown—into the pathless wastes, into thin air, with no reviews, no bestseller lists, no college curricula, no National Book Awards or Pulitzer Prizes, no ads, no publicity, not even word of mouth to guide me. In the fifteenth century, Poggio Bracciolini, a Vatican secretary, spent his leisure time combing monastery libraries for texts of antiquity. He located them, copied them in his own beautiful hand or caused them to be copied, and made them known to other humanists. I read about Poggio in Stephen Greenblatt's *The Swerve*, and I envied that Renaissance geezer. I would have loved to spend weeks going through unexamined scrolls and codexes and to stumble upon Lucretius's masterpiece, *De Rerum Natura*, which no one had read in fifteen hundred years. This was my kind of exploration.

Usually we choose our reading from a preselected list of books, compiled by reviewers, awards panels, librarians, teachers, and professors, and these reading lists are remarkably resistant to change. Occasionally an intellectual movement comes along, feminism for one, that opens up our sense of what is major and what is minor, enlarging the pool of books read, but this does not happen often. And then the upstarts themselves have a way of becoming canonical, unquestioned, and a new generation considers *Mrs. Dalloway* or *The Harder They Come* essential reading. What about all those books that are never read at all, never even considered? Who speaks for them? Arbitrary choice is the most radical response to conventional judgment. Let me, I thought, if only for a change, choose my reading almost blindly. Who knows what I will find?

Not all my friends saw the potential of this idea. How many books were on a shelf? Maybe thirty. How many writers? Maybe ten. "So you will write about ten randomly chosen unknown writers?" they said, smiling with feigned enthusiasm. "No," I replied. "Something more organic. It will be more like a travel journal." "But you're going to discover a great writer who lived in obscurity without the recognition he or she deserved, right?" Well, maybe, but that wasn't the point.

My generation was shaped by an approach to literature that began with the Romantics, was codified by Matthew Arnold, and reached its peak through a broad group of critics that included Lionel Trilling and F. R. Leavis. It believed that literature was an instrument of moral education. It imbued literature with depth and urgency, what we did not hesitate, as late as the 1960s, to call relevance to life. It believed that novelists and poets were special beings, "unacknowledged legislators," people who taught and enlarged us. Through them we might investigate every important issue. No matter what future you imagined for yourself—as a doctor, a lawyer, a banker, a cabaret singer—engaging with literary texts in your student days would benefit you. Therefore, for a while, the study of literature moved to the center of the liberal arts curriculum. Many of us became "English majors."

This approach had flaws, of course. It always risked becoming moralistic, and it elevated certain writers over others, writers whose works were considered especially meaningful. By the last quarter of the twentieth century, a reaction had set in. Any attempt to justify literature as giving the reader something became suspect. We had known for a long time not to seek a simple message in literature. But under the influence of French criticism, we were led to believe that there was nothing there at all. Everything we thought we saw in fiction, we ourselves brought to the text. A text was a culturally produced set of markers, no more, and the author's role in producing the text was very small. Nothing could be more ridiculous than to discuss what he or she was trying to say. That nothing lay at the heart of the literary experience—no author-intended meaning or even set of concerns—was, temporarily, refreshing.

We English majors, despite our military epithet, never understood that we had to fight for the literature we so much enjoyed. Its study seemed so well-entrenched, we took it for granted. When the Trojan horse arrived, in the form of clever, infinitely sophisticated professors of literature from France, we accepted their delicious gifts of irony, novelty, and nihilism and did not see the danger. Now, a generation later, the edifice that took a hundred years to put in place, and that spread a kind of enlightenment over America, is gone. We have to do all over again the work of proving that there is any point to reading a novel besides making time pass more quickly. This book is my way of making amends for not fighting when I should have. I thought the problem would go away if I waited, and eventually it did. But, as with a tsunami engulfing a city, when the waters receded, the city was gone.

My project began with a storm. The entire Northeast was about to be hit by Hurricane Irene, which was expected to be historically destructive. I was vacationing in a rented house on Martha's Vineyard as we all waited, terrified, fearing we would be washed out to sea as people were by the hurricane of 1938. I searched my landlord's collection of books for appropriate reading and found it in *The Last Voyage of Columbus* by Martin Dugard.

Columbus was trying to locate the western passage to India when he arrived in the Caribbean on his fourth and last voyage. Superb seaman that he was, he sensed an extraordinary storm in the offing. He sought shelter in the harbor of Santo Domingo on the island of Hispaniola, but the governor, jealous of Columbus, found a reason not to let him bring his ships in. Columbus begged the governor to detain the treasure fleet that was about to set sail for Spain, but the governor would not do that either. Denied shelter in the harbor, Columbus led his ships northwest to relative safety and rode out the storm. The treasure fleet headed northeast, into the path of the hurricane, and no one survived.

This was perfect reading for a tense moment. As I was definitely on Columbus's side, I knew I would be safe. And so I was. Irene passed, doing no harm to New York or the Vineyard, though much to inland parts of New England. I was able to return to New York City, where I would spend the rest of the summer.

Two weeks after my return, hurricanes were still on my mind. The papers were still filled with hurricane news. I went to my local library to find *Hurricane*, a novel by Charles Nordhoff and James Norman Hall, recommended by a friend who knew I shared her enthusiasm for Nordhoff and Hall's *Mutiny on the Bounty*. My friend and her husband, dedicated readers, had set out to read everything Nordhoff and Hall had written and so had discovered *Hurricane*. I found the volume in the stacks, experiencing that rush you get when you find the title you want, and put it in my tote bag to check out. But at the same moment, I realized I had no desire to read it. I had had enough of hurricanes.

What, then, should I read? I was surrounded by thousands of books, but I had no reason to head toward one letter of the alphabet rather than another.

The library was the New York Society Library on East Seventy-ninth Street in New York, a magnificent lending library where one can browse in the stacks and take several books home to read at a time. Only members can check out books, but anyone can use the reference room and can become a member by paying a fee, currently $225 per year for one person or $275 for a household. This is the oldest library in New York, in existence since 1754, founded by a group of young men who believed that a library would help the city prosper. They called themselves the New York Society. To belong to the library is to join a self-selected family of readers stretching back to the Founding Fathers. George Washington borrowed books from this library—and, some say, failed to return them. Later, Thoreau and Audubon, among others, roamed its hospitable stacks. Later still, Truman Capote and Willa Cather both used the library and became friends as a result. Originally in the Wall Street area, it moved uptown over the years, first to Leonard Street and Broadway, then to University Place off Union Square, and then, in 1937, to its current location on Seventy-ninth Street just off Madison Avenue, where it has become, with the 92nd Street Y, the greatest center of literary activity on the Upper East Side.

The building had been a private home, built in 1917 for the John S. Rogers family. The mansion was extensively reconfigured to become a library, but many of the original features survive—the stately Renaissance Revival limestone façade, the elegant stone staircase to the second floor, the coffered ceilings, the carved wooden arches. These give the building an aura of privilege and of Gilded Age splendor. At the back there are twelve floors of stacks to hold the collections and at the front, on the second floor, a gracious, light-filled room where a member can sit in a comfortable chair and read in quiet. From the moment the massive street doors open for me and I ascend the entrance stairs with their polished brass banister, I feel privileged. I have entered Edith Wharton's New York—a grandfather clock opposite the checkout desk in the lobby, ancestors' portraits in the stairwell. The Old Ones believed in dignifying the life of the mind with marble, murals, and mahogany, creating such grand spaces as the Widener Library at Harvard, the New York Public Library, and, on a more intimate scale, this jewel on Seventy-ninth Street. It may be the cheapest luxury in New York.

I was still standing in front of the books by Nordhoff and Hall, of which there was a huge number. As I looked around—and this was only one of two floors in the stacks holding fiction—I saw many long runs of books by one author. It was disconcerting. Often, I knew authors by only one book, as I had known Nordhoff and Hall by *Mutiny on the Bounty*. But each writer had spent a lifetime writing. What were the other books like? Who were all these scribblers whose work filled the shelves? Did they find their lives as writers rewarding? Who reads their work now? Are we missing out? I wonder if, at some point, all readers have the desire that I had then to consume everything in the library, but it is a desire no sooner formulated than felt to be impossible. One shelf, however, might be read, a part to stand for the whole. Even that would take time and perseverance.

Thus I came to the idea of choosing a shelf at random and reading my way through it to find what I would find. I suppose my friend's gallant and reckless gesture of reading everything by Nordhoff and Hall was in my mind. But the moment I had this idea I realized that wholly random would not do. If I whirled around and pointed to a shelf, it might be the shelf containing Nordhoff and Hall, which would contain little but Nordhoff and Hall—or, if I moved down a few shelves, Kathleen Norris. So I created a rule: I would not read a shelf that contained more than four books by one author. This eliminated many shelves because writers, if they have any success, are unlikely to stop with four books. The shelves were filled with the work of writers who had published dozens: Stuart Woods, Sinclair Lewis, Louis L'Amour, to say nothing of Trollope, Dickens, and Walter Scott. The inner stacks in the New York Society Library are nine shelves high, with eighteen of them per floor, six shelves wide, making 972 shelves on each floor. The outer walls have another 277 shelves. I sampled dozens without finding a shelf that held fewer than four books by one author. So I revised my rule. There had to be several authors represented on the shelf, and only one could have more than five books. Of those five I had to commit myself to reading only three. In addition, there had to be a mix of contemporary and older works, and one book had to be a classic I had not read and wanted to.

This mixture, too, was surprisingly difficult to find. Sometimes a shelf caught my eye, seeming, at first, varied and nicely balanced, but as I made my way from left to right, I found myself facing the monumental oeuvre of some vastly successful author of a century ago. Or I found a nicely balanced shelf, but there was no classic. Many shelves were filled with the popular entertainments, especially the detective stories, of another age. As for the entertainments of today, I had already read the ones I cared to. I had read almost every Elmore Leonard, Sarah Paretsky, and Alexander McCall Smith. This experiment was not about my learning to love Jodi Picoult or Danielle Steel, worthy as these writers may be.

As I surveyed shelf after shelf, I had to formulate other rules—for example, I could choose no shelf that contained work by someone I knew. This was occasioned by a tempting *W* shelf that held five novels of Katharine Weber, who is a friend of mine and who is not, to my mind, widely enough known. It would give me the greatest pleasure to write about her work and explain its many virtues. But that would bias the project and also make me watch what I was saying more than I wanted to. So, no friends.

At last, after looking at perhaps two hundred shelves out of some thirteen hundred on this floor of the stacks (remember that fiction continues onto a second floor) I found a classic that I had not read and wanted to—Lermontov's *A Hero of Our Time*. This seminal work in the history of the Russian novel, which I had managed to live my life without reading, shared a shelf with another book I had heard of as an English major but never read, *Gil Blas*, the granddaddy of picaresque fiction. There were also works by a writer called James LeRossignol, whose name intrigued me, and two books by an immensely prolific writer named William Le Queux, which had spilled over from a previous shelf and gave me the chance to sample this evidently popular Edwardian novelist. Visually, the shelf I had focused on was a pleasing mix of old-style bindings, gold-stamped library-bound hardcovers, and modern books whose colorful jackets were wrapped in Mylar.

I was hoping I had found the goal of my quest. But as I moved right, tracking titles with my finger, I came to a big block of books by the same author, old books in purple bindings with gold stamping. The author was Gaston Leroux, and one of his books was *The Phantom of the Opera*, but there were many, many others. To add to the problem, I could see another big block of books up ahead of me in the paper jackets and plastic protectors that signaled contemporary works. These novels proved to be by John Lescroart, whose oeuvre, after depositing six books on my shelf, cascaded over in a mighty flow onto much of the next. Well, who was setting the rules? Who was writing the algorithm? What was the point of this activity if not to assert my own freedom? Without rules, there is no forward movement, but the rules themselves are malleable. Creativity can be thought of as a stone you roll down a ramp that you yourself built. The ramp and stone are imagined; what's real is the energy created by the imaginary stone hurtling down the imaginary ramp. That energy enables people to get things done, books written, companies founded. So I devised a new rule that if the shelf was well-balanced overall, especially if it included some women if it was mostly men, or men if it was mostly women, I could include not just one but two longer runs, of which I had to read only three books in each run. Now the shelf LEQ–LES, running from William Le Queux to John Lescroart, by way of Rhoda Lerman, Mikhail Lermontov, Lisa Lerner, Alexander Lernet-Holenia, Etienne Leroux, Gaston Leroux, James LeRossignol, Margaret Leroy, and Alain-René Le Sage, would do just fine. More than fine.

The instant I selected my shelf, I felt an immense tenderness for it. As when a puppy is put into your arms for the first time, or even more so, too much so, a child. The sense of pure potential might be depressing, your sense of your own responsibility exhausting, but it is not. It is exhilarating. You are at the start of something together. You are moved by the bond.

•

I allowed myself complete freedom to choose the order in which I approached the authors on my shelf and, within each author's work, freedom to determine the order of the novels. Something led my eye and hand to begin with *One for the Devil* by Etienne Leroux, a South African writing in the 1960s in Afrikaans. If one of my tasks, perhaps the simplest, the book reviewer's task, was to decide if a book, however much its author had invested in it, deserved anyone else's time to read, this one presented particular problems. It turned out to be a kind of novel that requires special standards of judgment. I had not heard of *One for the Devil*, but this English translation, published in 1968, featured an equivocal blurb from Graham Greene, who said that Leroux's novels were too original ever to be very popular. "They tease, they trouble, they elude." Other blurbs promised wit and a penetrating examination of life in South Africa.

I liked the writing from the start. The proprietor of a great estate in the South African wine country, Mr. Jock Silberstein, is out walking his property with his wife, always called " 'slim' Mrs. Silberstein" to distinguish her from her mother-in-law. Above a series of spillways, elaborately conceived and described, in which water courses from one level to another through the mouths of carved, masklike faces down to a large pond, their dog, a setter, suddenly points. He raises his forepaw and stiffens into "the catatonic posture characteristic of its breed." The prey he has located turns out to be a plastic swan that has blown off the swimming pool. The Silbersteins would always remember this moment as "a piece of *kitsch* on the mantelshelf of their memories."

My enthusiasm for the prose style was quickly extinguished by some annoying, if minor, stylistic traits, just as someone who makes a good first impression at a party may turn you off within minutes by referring to himself in the third person or peppering his speech with French phrases. Leroux really did *always* call his character " 'slim' Mrs. Silberstein," and when he introduced a policeman, he was *always* called "Detective-Sergeant Demosthenes H. de Goede." This Demosthenes had a severe stutter that prevented him from uttering a word. Was this the promised wit?

Then too, and worse, Leroux had no interest in narrative. People went here and there across the estate, Welgevonden, had this and that sighting or encounter, spoke, largely in eccentric monologues on very deep themes, and never did anything, until the final scene, when they did so much at once—a wrestling match, a dance, a bullfight, for goodness' sake—that I had to suspect a symbolic intent. This, then, was one of those novels, once proudly called "experimental," in which the reader was led in one direction or another only to be deprived of the expected resolution, while at the same time he or she was assaulted with meaning through analogy and equivalences. Like the setter pointing to a plastic swan when you thought he was pointing to the body you knew would be discovered floating in the pool, the book was always sending you on a wild-goose chase and asking you to be pleased by the plastic swan you found at the end of it.

Detective-Sergeant Demosthenes H. de Goede tries to find out who killed Lila, the girl whose body is floating in the swimming pool—a loose girl whom everyone, literally, had loved. There is a prime suspect, the retarded and giant grandson of the Silbersteins, Adam Kadmon Silberstein. But so far as I know, and I did finish the book, we never find out if the giant whose name invokes the first man and the first English poet really did kill the girl whose name is close to Leda, the woman raped by Zeus in the form of a swan, and if so, why, and if so, what significance the murder has. Indeed, on my own, unaided, I was unable even to guess what this book was about.

Certain genres hold themselves cheap. However good they are, however deeply they may affect us, they do not present themselves as more than entertainment. But some kinds of literature demand to be treated respectfully. The obligation is on the reader to live up to them and not so much on them to entertain the reader. What we call literary fiction is a genre with great aspirations. If a novel presents itself as serious, judging it becomes more complicated. That it isn't enjoyable does not immediately disqualify it from having succeeded. Literary fiction can say, "You will learn to love me in time. My difficulties are there for a reason. They will challenge you, but you will learn from them and be changed for the better." At first I did not realize that this was the case with *One for the Devil*. I thought it was a country-house mystery, a genre familiar to me—and beloved—because of Agatha Christie. But I was wrong. It was Serious Fiction. How did I know? Because nothing made sense. I did not have a clue what the author was going on about.

Who was Etienne Leroux? Why was Graham Greene his booster? The question was, of course, a sign of failure in itself. Both mine and the text's. The text was supposed to be sufficient in itself. I was not supposed to have to go outside it for satisfaction. Nor, in the pre-Internet past, would one have been so readily tempted to look beyond the text for analysis or information. Such research would have involved a physical trip to a fairly large library and a tedious search in archived magazines and newspapers, encyclopedias, or such printed databases as *Contemporary Authors*. Now *Contemporary Authors* is online, and I can access it from home via a university library website. It took a little more Internet time than usual to find my guy because Etienne Leroux, it emerges, was a pseudonym. His real name was Stephanus Petrus Daniel Le Roux. Furthermore, although I know he died in 1989, Gale Research, which produces *Contemporary Authors*, does not, and considers him still alive in 2001, when his entry was last "updated." Therefore a search by death date and name was ineffective.

In fact, *Wikipedia*, available with no special access, is more helpful in placing Etienne Leroux than *Contemporary Authors*. It tells me he was an influential Afrikaans author and a member of the Sestigers literary movement. Sestigers is hyperlinked, so I quickly learn that it refers to a group of writers in South Africa in the 1960s that included André Brink, Breyten Breytenbach, and Chris Barnard. What exactly did the Sestigers stand for as a literary movement? For that I have to go back to the university online library and *Encyclopaedia Britannica*:

> **Sestigers** ("Sixtyers," or writers of the 1960s), whose declared aim was "to broaden the rather too parochial limits of Afrikaner fiction." In essence, this meant depicting sexual and moral matters and examining the **political system** in a way that rapidly antagonized the traditional Afrikaner reader.

I could see why Leroux's writing antagonized traditional Afrikaners. It was artsy, self-conscious, pretentious, and—call me Philistine—it antagonized me. *Wikipedia* insisted on the importance of the Azazel myth in *One for the Devil (Een vir*

*Azazel* in Afrikaans). I had no idea what the Azazel myth was. I'd assumed "Azazel" was the Afrikaans word for "devil," but clicking on the hyperlink, I discovered that it refers to the rite of the scapegoat in rabbinical literature. According to Leviticus, on the Day of Atonement, the high priest, along with observing other rituals seeking God's forgiveness for sin, chose two goats. One was for the Lord, and one was for Azazel. The one for the Lord was sacrificed in the temple, but the other one (known as the scapegoat) was elaborately endowed with all the sins of the people and then sent away to die in the wilderness. How did this apply to *One for the Devil*? Was Lila the offering for the Lord? Was Adam Kadmon Silberstein the scapegoat? Were the sins to be atoned for the sins of apartheid? No idea. Could this precious, labored novel really be politically motivated? More research was in order.

A typical entry in *Contemporary Authors* provides the facts about a writer's life (dates of birth and death, list of publications with dates, and so on) followed by a section in which critical opinion on the writer's work is summarized, often with quotations from contemporary (that is to say, ancient) reviews. The entry on Leroux quoted a review by Charles R. Larson, an American scholar specializing in African fiction, from 1969. Writing in the *Saturday Review*, Larson explained that Leroux's social protest had to be allegorized, "steeped in mythology, and tortured with symbolism just obscure enough to prevent his works from being banned in a country where title alone has frequently been sufficient to lead to a book's being censored."

Here was the perspective I sought. Expecting political fiction to depict conflict realistically, as in Malraux or Steinbeck, I was confused by Leroux's work, which is not like that at all. Mr. Larson helped me by pointing out that it was produced in a country that was virtually a police state, at a time of violence and fierce divisions in the culture. The evasiveness and portentous symbologizing, the refusal to depict a real place at a real time, which so grated on me, might be the author's way of presenting unpopular views in a climate so hostile that he could have been punished for them. Obfuscation has political uses, and aggravating the middle class has often been a political tactic. In that way I could see the stultifying *One for the Devil* as an attempt "to broaden the rather too parochial limits of Afrikaner fiction." I was in a world of secret messages and hidden meanings, people tapping in code on the walls of their prison cells, whereas I had expected to find myself in an Evelyn-Waugh-meets-Agatha-Christie country-house-weekend murder mystery. Moreover, I was back in the 1960s, when I was an undergraduate reading John Hawkes and John Barth outside of class. Cutting-edge fiction was highfalutin. The whole pop culture revolution, which legitimized enjoyable fiction—doing in "experimental" writers like Barth and Hawkes and preparing for Jonathan Franzen and Jeffrey Eugenides—had not happened yet.

As I learned about Leroux from outside sources, as I tried to see his work in historical perspective, I gained a respect I did not have while reading it. Here was a writer trying to breathe life into a traditional and close-minded culture. He did that by invoking, however ham-fistedly, great themes of Western civilization—the nature of evil, the force of guilt—and by using myths and structures he thought had the power to transcend banal circumstance and to ally his native culture with the ancient Greeks. If that is a tacky thing to do, it's the same tacky thing James Joyce was doing in *Ulysses*.

The Leroux novel I had chosen to start with, perhaps attracted by the word "Devil" in the title, turned out to be the second of a trilogy. Reluctantly, knowing already that I would not enjoy it, I began the book that preceded it, *Seven Days at the Silbersteins*. Again, the narrative started well, with a young man, Henry van Eeden, of good but impoverished family, being selected to marry Salome Silberstein, an only child and heir to the Silberstein fortune. He is an appealing, well-meaning, but untried and somewhat naïve person who arrives at Welgevonden for a seven-day visit during which he will meet and get to know his bride-to-be. But day after day passes, each day ending with an elaborate party involving a different segment of the local population—the landowners and farmers, the intellectuals and artists, the workers—and Salome never appears. Each day follows the same pattern. Henry rises and bathes, walks the property with Jock Silberstein or someone else or by himself, has lunch, at which improbable monologues on stately themes are delivered, and whiles away the afternoon until the set-piece evening party, for which he almost invariably wears the wrong clothes.

By day three, I was skimming and skipping. I got it that he was not going to meet Salome. That was disappointing. But even more was the knowledge that I would have to go through the same sequence of rising, lunching, walking, and partying seven times. Even in my own life I do not have to endure that kind of routine. Why should I in a novel? Detective-Sergeant Demosthenes H. de Goede with his tiresome speech impediment was blessedly absent from this book, but the monologues his silence evoked in *One for the Devil* from a voluble friend of his were here in force.

I skimmed every chapter to see if Henry met Salome. I skimmed to see if anything happened. I read the set pieces. I kept dipping into the disquisitions on philosophical subjects to see if they would begin to interest me. That was the nature of my reading of this book.

We give the name "reading" to many different activities, and the only one that matters to me is the one in which attention is fiercely focused, each word has weight, and each sentence makes me more aware of the world I am reading about than the one in which I actually live. In this sense every successful reading experience for me is escapist. The word has no negative meaning. Reading Etienne Leroux, I was always aware of myself reading, constantly asking myself how much more I had to read. As I was the one making the rules—no one was standing over me forcing me to read Etienne Leroux—this involved an uncomfortable struggle with myself, between my will and my purpose (to read the whole library shelf) and my principal virtue, my ability to acknowledge and obey my own sources of pleasure.

From my point of view, the only bright note was a comic character, old Mrs. Silberstein, usually called the Duchess because of the airs she gives herself, who wanders about muttering Yiddish insults at Henry but finally embraces him and wishes him mazel tov. What was the significance of the Silbersteins' being Jewish? I had no idea. Did Leroux mean us to see them sympathetically, as outsiders of some sophistication and culture in a world of yahoos? Or were they meant to epitomize the materialism of a materialistic culture? Or was it of no consequence, just a fact? Try as I might, I could find no internal evidence that directed me one way or another in this important question of how to view the Silbersteins' Jewishness. Even by consulting *Wikipedia* and *A History of Afrikaans Literature* online, I still did not know.

My chosen shelf contained the last volume of Leroux's trilogy *The Third Eye*, but nothing could induce me to read it, not even the knowledge (gleaned somewhere off the Internet) that Demosthenes H. de Goede is cured of his speech defect in this volume. And certainly not *Newsweek*'s Jack Kroll opining forty years ago, as quoted in *Contemporary Authors*, that in this novel Leroux rose above the trilogy's previous treatments of South Africa's social problems and racial tensions to deal with "the condition and ultimate destiny of human society." I had not gotten all I might have out of Etienne Leroux, but I had given as much of myself to him as I was going to. No more of my life would be spent reading his work. I would have liked to know more about the man and more about South Africa, especially the effect of apartheid on literature, but that was a different thing from reading his books.

The first thing I learned from my experiment—aside from the weakness of my will or, by the same token, the strength of my impulse toward enjoyment—was that in the age of the Internet, it is very hard to stick with a book without consulting an outside source. Reading is more centrifugal than it used to be. Because the material is so readily available, you want to see the author's biography and read the reviews of the work. You are even tempted to contact the author, who is only a Google search and some keystrokes away.

From time to time people contact me by Internet about something I've written. If they offer praise and thanks, I am happy. More often, however, the e-mail begins, "My discussion group is reading your book and I have been assigned to lead the discussion." What follows is a request to suggest topics or to restate the book's conclusions or to explain its personal meaning or, most often, to detail how I got the idea for it. This upsets me. Didn't I write the book precisely to have conversations that transcended actual contact? Nevertheless, I found myself itching to contact someone about Etienne Leroux. No one I knew had read him, and in good conscience I could not ask anyone to. There was, however, Charles R. Larson, who in 1969 (when I had recently graduated from college) had reviewed *One for the Devil* for the *Saturday Review*, a magazine that ceased publication more than a quarter of a century ago. I googled Charles Larson and was amazed and happy to find that he was still teaching African literature at American University in Washington, D.C. Shamelessly, I e-mailed him. Kindly, he replied. He had not read Leroux in thirty years and didn't remember the book he had reviewed. He certainly could not comment now on its importance. Kindly, too, he did not ask me what I was reading in 1969 and what I thought of it currently.

And now, in another of its manifestations or epiphanies, the Internet threw in my way an incredible document, which drew me closer to Leroux than either of the novels I had read. This was a YouTube film clip of his funeral in 1989, broadcast in Afrikaans on South African television. That I understood not a word of the broadcast did not matter. His death was TV news. The man meant a lot to South Africans. The images spoke for themselves: his study, lined with books; the covers of his novels, many translated into foreign languages; a page of manuscript in his handwriting, greatly worked over. Then, the funeral: his grieving family arriving at the church; other famous South African writers coming to pay their respects; black workers arriving in a segregated mass, one woman still wearing the gray-and-white uniform of domestic service. To my astonishment, the camera left the church and followed the coffin as it arrived at Leroux's bleak ancestral homestead. Pallbearers carried the plain wooden box up a hill, where, their graves covered in shiny black granite, his parents already lay. The camera followed as the coffin was lowered into the grave and his family and friends threw in flowers. I was shocked to find myself, a stranger—a stranger who didn't even like his writing—at the man's graveside. The intimacy was terrifying and carried responsibility. Never again could I mention Etienne Leroux without feeling that I had been at his funeral and that I had a special relationship with him. If the quality of a work of art is measured by the quality of the experience we have encountering it, Leroux's work was not worth much to me. I would never go back to it, I would never recommend it, whereas I have looked at that film clip more than once on the edge of tears.

Merely the fact that I checked out Leroux's novels has changed their fate. Since almost all formulas for deciding whether to keep or discard books in a library depend on how often a book is taken out and when it was last removed from the stacks, my interest alone will give these volumes another five years or so of life in the valuable real estate of a Manhattan lending library. Leroux deserves at least that. I am not the one to rescue him from obscurity, however, and neither is Charles Larson, who had been so enthusiastic about him once. Does some future literary critic exist who can resurrect these books? Or will they sink back into the abyss of unread literature? After all, it has been only forty-four years since they appeared. When you think of Lucretius waiting for fifteen hundred years to be rediscovered, that does not seem long at all. On the other hand, some books have an impact at the moment of their publication and for their immediate audience that they can never have again. I suspect that is the case here. Politically, South

Africa has moved on, and so has literary fiction. The shock of the new becomes the schlock of the familiar. But in a larger sense, so what? In his time, in his homeland, Leroux was revered and beloved. What difference does it make to him now, next to his parents, under black granite on a windswept hill, whether he is immortal?

*Two*

# THE MYTH OF THE BOOK:
## *A HERO OF OUR TIME*

I WAS EAGER TO READ LERMONTOV. AFTER ALL, HE WAS the principal reason I had chosen this shelf. *A Hero of Our Time* is a touchstone of Russian literature, a novel I had heard of since college but never read, and I was particularly happy with the copy available, a small Doubleday Anchor Original from the 1960s (price $2.50), the text translated by Vladimir Nabokov in collaboration with his son, Dmitri. What could be better than to read a great Russian novel in a translation by a great writer who was a master of both Russian and English? Moreover, I loved the book as an object. Its very size, the modest dimensions of yesteryear, produced nostalgia. Its appealing cover, designed by Edward Gorey and dripping with his personality, shows tiny travelers on horseback on a ridge below an even higher mountain in an ink-and-wash drawing based on a painting of the Caucasus by Lermontov himself. The title in typical Gorey typography floats over the mountains on a lime-green sky. It is a small masterpiece of graphic design.

Many people claim deep attachment to the feel of traditional books. They say they like holding books in their hands. They like the smell and feel of the paper. They like turning pages. But the opposite is possible. The physical book can come between you and the text you are trying to appreciate. This is what happened to me with *A Hero of Our Time*. The print was too small. The pages were yellowed and unpleasant to touch, rough yet fragile: they crumbled as I read. The cover felt greasy from use. People who rhapsodize about the pleasure of physical books, do they not have these problems? Do the books in their library never age? I have carried some of mine with me from home to home since college, paperbacks with a price of 95 cents on the cover, filled with my underlinings and embarrassing comments: "good/evil theme" or "flower imagery" or "cf. Faulkner." When I look at them objectively, like a child looking at the tented skin of a beloved grandparent, I must admit that they are not physically attractive.

*A Hero of Our Time* is actually a slim collection of short stories tied together by a location, the Caucasus, and by three characters: the unnamed, unknown narrator; a rough man-of-the-people soldier named Maxim Maximich; and the romantic—that is to say, world-weary and cynical but supposedly appealing—hero, Pechorin, an officer demoted to duty in the Caucasus. Pechorin keeps a journal, the manuscript of which he gives to Maxim Maximich, who in turn gives it to the narrator, who publishes it as much of the book you are reading.

In the first story, "Bela," Pechorin kidnaps a Circassian girl and keeps her captive, hidden from her family, plying her with gifts until she agrees to "be his wife." She dies shortly after, but not before realizing he has tired of her. There is also a great deal about stealing horses.

Maxim Maximich is devoted to Pechorin and thinks they are friends. In a touching story that bears his name as its title, he and the narrator run into Pechorin at a remote outpost in the mountains. Maxim Maximich looks forward to a warm reunion, but Pechorin snubs the old man.

In "Princess Mary," the longest and most absorbing story, Pechorin, stuck in a tedious provincial spa town, wins an aristocratic young lady away from his friend Grushnitsky just to amuse himself. Then he drops her. Along the way, he kills Grushnitsky in a duel.

In the last story, "The Fatalist," a Serbian officer bets Pechorin that predestination exists. This is taken to mean that if he shoots himself, he will not die, because it is not his time to die. Pechorin takes the bet because he sees death on the man's face. The Serb shoots himself in the head, but the gun malfunctions and does not fire. So he wins the bet. But later that evening the Serb is killed in the street by a drunken Cossack.

This book, which is considered the first prose narrative in Russian literature, was written by Lermontov in 1839, when he was twenty-four. Like Pechorin, he served as an officer in the Caucasus. Like Pechorin, he was sent there as a punishment for bad behavior in the city. Like Pechorin, he fought duels. But, unfortunately for him and for Russian literature, Lermontov died in a duel in the Caucasus at the age of twenty-six, not long after writing a preface for a new edition of *A Hero of Our Time*, with its account of the duel Pechorin wins and its fatalistic conclusion that when your number is up, it is up. The relationship between the writer's life and work in this case immensely glamorized the work and helped raise it to its position of importance in literary history.

Generations of Russian schoolboys read this monument of romanticism and saw themselves in Pechorin, the way American youths once saw themselves in James Dean's rebel or in John Wayne's cowboys. One of those schoolboys was Vladimir

Nabokov. In 1958, at the time of his translating *Hero*, he had metamorphosed into an adult of immense stature—a father, a professor, an entomologist, the author of four novels in English, including *Lolita*, as well as many in Russian. Nabokov's preface to this wild and woolly work focuses cerebrally on narrative structure. This is not a book about combat or exiled officers or affairs of honor; it is a book with three narrators, a tale within a tale within a tale. What may have been narrative clumsiness and the jerky invention of an inexperienced novelist becomes, through Nabokov's ironic intervention, a piece of literary cubism. Inevitably, he implies that his own work on the text makes him a fourth narrator.

For Nabokov, previous translations of Lermontov's novel have merely been paraphrases. He dismisses them all. The translator's task, he argues puckishly, is not to smooth out the text and make it lovely, but to reproduce its exact texture, whatever its inadequacies. The stock phrases and stagy gestures of a hasty author must exist in the translation as irritatingly as they exist in the original text. "Dull pallor" must spread across faces at crucial moments, and a hand must "tremble slightly" to indicate agitation. It is the translator's duty to render as faithfully as possible this absence of elegance in the prose. The argument cunningly turns the old ideal of a translation as a pane of glass upside down. If the translation is not to come between the reader and the text, it must risk alienating the reader by reproducing the text's infelicities. "His Russian is, at times, almost as crude as Stendhal's French," Nabokov writes of Lermontov, killing two bards with one barb. "His similes and metaphors are utterly commonplace; his hackneyed epithets are only redeemed by occasionally being incorrectly used."

About the disillusioned, cynical, impulsive, and proudly

selfish hero, Nabokov writes that nothing need be said. Then he says a lot. Of all the nonsense written about Pechorin, he tells us, some was by Lermontov himself in his own introduction to the novel, "a stylized bit of make-believe in its own right." Lermontov claimed that Pechorin was a composite of "all the vices of our own generation." Actually, says Nabokov, "the bored and bizarre hero" is the product of several generations, some of them not Russian at all: Rousseau's Saint-Preux, Goethe's Werther, Chateaubriand's René, Constant's Adolphe, and Byron's Giaour and Corsair, to say nothing of Pushkin's Eugene Onegin, a whole line of bored, scornful, dashing heroes before Pechorin. But Lermontov's incarnation of this figure—with his "romantic dash and cynicism, tigerlike suppleness and eagle eye, hot blood and cool head, tenderness and taciturnity, elegance and brutality, delicacy of perception and harsh passion to dominate, ruthlessness and awareness of it"—has proved of lasting appeal, especially to young readers. Indeed "it would seem that the veneration elderly critics have for *A Hero of Our Time* is rather a glorified recollection of youthful readings in the summer twilight, and of ardent self-identification, than the direct result of a mature consciousness of art."

Take that, Lermontov: grown-ups do not like your novel; what we like is our own remembrance of our experience of reading it when we were young.

Eventually Nabokov lands the cruelest blow of all. *Hero*, he suggests, would be of little interest if it did not present a duel in the Caucasus that anticipates Lermontov's own death in a duel in the Caucasus three years later. As Nabokov puts it, "Much of the novel's poignancy and fascination resides in the fact that Lermontov's own tragic fate is somehow superimposed on that of Pechorin."

Nabokov's preface shaped my experience of *A Hero of Our Time*. I could not find excitement in the narrative of the Russian soldiers in the wild mountain landscape, the kidnapped girl, the stealing of horses, so aware was I of the ridiculous eavesdropping, the clunky stage gestures, the stock phrases. And as if that wasn't enough, there were footnotes, intrusive little numbers superimposed on the text, which felt, as I was reading, as though a bell tinkled and a message played "Excuse me, we would like to interrupt your reading for a word from Mr. Nabokov."

"I was traveling post from Tiflis.[4] All the luggage in my small springless carriage[5] consisted of one valise stuffed half-full of notes on my travels to Georgia.[6]" This is the opening of the novel in Nabokov's translation. Some of the information in the footnotes is interesting, on the gradual annexation by the Russian Empire of the Caucasus states from the early eighteenth to the mid-nineteenth century. Some is detailed description of the narrator's route, and some is pedantic quibble about the Russian word that signifies "small springless carriage," which others translate simply as "cart." And that is just the first two sentences. If you read *A Hero of Our Time* in this translation along with all the footnotes, you will know a great deal more than when you started about Russia in the early nineteenth century, you will know the difference in social status of being in the Guard and being merely in the army, you will understand the nature of the fighting in the Caucasus and what it meant for an officer to be sent there, and you will understand Lermontov's place in Russian literary history as the heir of Pushkin, but it will be hard for you to get caught up in the story. Footnotes point out all the glitches: "This theme is not followed up." "Here and elsewhere the listener's eagerness is a little overdone." "The whole interplay between Grushnitski and the Captain of the Dragoons is extremely unconvincing." "Odd behavior! Should we believe that Pechorin, a fashionable man, had remained seated after Mary had come in?" Nabokov is always with us as we read, judging and correcting, commenting and recasting, creating a very different text from the one Lermontov presumably intended. Lermontov writes: "In simple hearts, the sense of beauty and grandeur of nature is a hundred times stronger and more vivid than it is in us, enthusiastic tellers of tales." Nabokov replies, "This is, of course, a romanticist notion. It is completely untrue."

Reading *Hero* in this edition was like watching two literary men in combat, one long dead, a naïve but energetic writer with a young man's passion and love of posturing, and the other wily, learned, subtle in two languages, a genius who turns everything he touches into his own substance. Of course victory goes to the one who has the last word. The dry, witty, learned, infinitely sophisticated translator captures the young man's Byronic tale and turns it into something else, a match between youth and age, narrative innocence and narrative sophistication, impetuosity and pedantry.

Where have we seen before this rivalry between author and commentator, this meta-narrative created in the act of reading? It is so—well, so Nabokovian. It may seem familiar if you have read *Pale Fire*, in which the scholarly Charles Kinbote transforms John Shade's Wordsworthian poem of the unfolding of the self into a tale about the deposition and exile of a northern monarch who may be Kinbote himself. Kinbote's loony commentary is not only more interesting than the text it purports to illuminate, its fantasies and paranoia are the real subject of the novel. Kinbote overwhelms Shade as Nabokov overwhelms Lermontov. "Let me state that without my notes Shade's text simply has no human reality at all since the human reality of such a poem as his . . . has to depend on the reality of its author . . . a reality that only my notes can provide. To this statement my dear poet would probably not have subscribed, but, for better or worse, it is the commentator who has the last word."

In *The Anxiety of Influence*, Harold Bloom changed the way we look at writers' relations with their predecessors, pointing out the resemblance to an Oedipal drama, with strong writers engaging with strong predecessors and critically misreading them, recasting them into something they were not in order to serve the later writer's own identity. The son murders the father in order to become himself. Wordsworth misreads Milton in order to become Wordsworth. Nabokov corrects and undercuts Lermontov and Pushkin in order to make himself Nabokov. This is a crude summary and cruder application of Bloom's theory, but my point is to suggest that a writer's relationship with a previous writer he or she admires is not a clear-cut case of influence, in which the later writer takes from the earlier one something admired and carries on with it, but a more complex inheritance tinged by resistance and combat. It is questionable whether all writers behave as Bloom imagines them doing. It has been argued that especially with women writers, gay writers, and other marginalized groups, literary influence can operate in a less combative fashion and writers gain strength from their predecessors without some quasi-Oedipal rebellion. Still, Nabokov seems at times to provide magnificent proof of Bloom's theory—one writer swallows and digests another in order to create himself. Read this way, Nabokov's translation of *A Hero of Our Time* is as amusing—and as Nabokovian—as *Pale Fire*.

•

I had had a stimulating encounter with Nabokov, but I felt I still had not read *A Hero of Our Time*. The English translation available on my e-reader was the oldest, dating back to 1853, by Marr Murray and J. H. Wisdom. This was one of the translations Nabokov dismissed as mere paraphrase, so my expectations were low. But as soon as I started reading it, I felt I was in another world from his. I was free to follow the cart up the mountain without the nagging, nit-picking, show-off footnotes distracting me with information I did not need. "I was travelling post from Tiflis. All the luggage I had in my cart consisted of one small portmanteau half filled with travelling-notes on Georgia." It proved to be perfectly possible to follow this without knowing exactly where Tiflis was, or who built the highway through the mountains, or the history of Georgia's absorption into the Russian Empire, or that "portmanteau" was an archaic word for suitcase.

I did not mind the absence of paper and pages. I did not miss the yellowed paper of an ancient paperback crumbling in my hands as I turned pages. It actually helped to weld this somewhat disjointed narrative together to have the bland screen flick to the next block of text without a constant numerical assessment of my progress. The ideal of translation as a pane of glass becomes embodied when you read on a Kindle or a Nook. Nothing comes between you and the text, certainly no object reminding you distressingly of age and decay.

I was on my own now with *A Hero of Our Time*, and my first reaction was to be horrified by what I read about the kidnapping of the Circassian girl. It was like reading the story of the sexual predator who kept a girl in a shed in his backyard for eighteen years—forcing her to bear him two children—from the point of view of the predator, who thinks himself a pretty cool guy. This cad who woos lovely Princess Mary only to dump her—how could I find anything redeeming or appealing about him? Is this what young men fantasize about? Mistreating women?

There is no way to read a text putting aside who one is and what one has experienced. In this sense, as many twentieth-century literary critics came to understand, *every* reading of a book is the creation of a new book. Every reading is a misreading. Nabokov read *A Hero of Our Time* as a Russian and as a writer, vexed as a prose stylist by the way Russian schoolchildren had had this book held up to them as a model, vexed as a novelist by the sloppiness of the construction, and inspired as a genius who saw in the engulfing of the text by a reader's imagination a potential model for a great work of art.

I reacted first as a woman, distressed by the stories being offered as adventure. I was also an ex–English major, a student of late-eighteenth-century and early-nineteenth-century literature, and so, like Nabokov, I saw Pechorin as a literary construct, a product of his times and the successor of other literary heroes. I knew that when I encountered the phrase "romantic hero," it didn't mean Brad Pitt, but a literary figure from the early nineteenth century, someone difficult but attractive, tempestuous, tormented, often cruel, but with his own compelling sense of honor, like Mr. Rochester, Heathcliff, Eugene Onegin, or Pechorin. In my time in college and graduate school I had met them all except Pechorin, so I knew what to expect. But I had never really liked any of them. I did not identify with them or see the heroines' attraction to them as anything but self-destructive. In real life, I would have gone out of my way to avoid such a man. As an example of romantic (that is, early-nineteenth-century) literature, I could see the interest of *A Hero of Our Time*. But it did not speak to me. It would never make it to that inner shelf of books that affected my life.

Still, I wanted to give it every possible chance, and so I turned to yet another edition, another version, and the most modern translation I could find, that of Marian Schwartz, published in 2004 in the Modern Library Classics paperback series, with an introduction by Gary Shteyngart. Now, I may be exaggerating a little, but only a little, when I say that I consider Gary Shteyngart the most interesting novelist at work in America today. His *Super Sad True Love Story* is certainly one of the best novels about American life published in the last ten years. Its protagonist is a Russian immigrant, like Shteyngart himself, who is making his way in a future (but not so future, as it has turned out) version of New York.

Everything about this new translation of *A Hero of Our Time* was young and hip, starting with the cover, which featured a photo of a young man in sunglasses pointing at us in a gesture dripping with attitude. Pechorin, it said, was not a long-dead guy, but alive and among us. The translation read well. Where Nabokov felt it was his job to point out the inadequacies of Lermontov's Russian, Schwartz feels it is her duty to enable English-speaking readers to understand why the book is a masterpiece. Shteyngart's introduction is equally upbeat and enthusiastic:

> *A Hero of Our Time* is one of the most exciting, innovative, and engrossing novels ever written. It is a sensual

pleasure, elegantly proportioned, clearly structured, and, despite its easy categorization as both adventure and romance, endowed with an existential question in its final pages—"If predestination truly does exist, then why are we given free will and reason? Why must we account for our deeds?"—that magnifies the entire work, unites it, and bestows upon it the immortality it deserves.

Shteyngart compares *A Hero of Our Time* to the film *Pulp Fiction* in its use of fractured narrative and its concern with predestination and accountability.

For the third time, I began the novel, ready to appreciate its offbeat narrative structure and its weird existential depth, trying to see Pechorin as the cool guy in sunglasses on the cover. I had bought this copy online from AbeBooks.com, used. I had wanted this edition and no other because of Shteyngart's preface as well as the new translation, and this was the only copy available. It arrived with a sticker identifying it as having come from the University of San Diego bookstore. It was not in great shape—some underlining in the first story, but none after that. (I supposed whoever started reading the book had not finished it.) But the size was nice, and the book felt better, newer, cleaner than the Doubleday Anchor Original I had taken out of the library.

"I was traveling post[1] from Tiflis." The footnote explained "traveling post": "On long journeys, travelers changed horses at regular intervals along their route. This was known as 'traveling post.'" But in my copy, someone had printed in red ballpoint "TRADING POST" over the word "post." I was stopped cold. I could not even make it to "My cart's entire load consisted of one small valise which was half filled with travel notes about Georgia." I could make no sense of "trading post." Was that the previous reader's guess at the meaning of "traveling post"? "I was traveling by trading post from Tiflis." Influenced, perhaps, by westerns, did the previous reader imagine that "traveling post" was a misprint for "trading post"? I wanted to contact the previous reader and correct his understanding, making sure he knew what it meant to "travel post" and that "trading post" had nothing to do with it.

Instead, I made myself move on into the vivid opening scene in which the narrator has to hire a team of oxen to pull his cart up the mountain's icy roads. He meets Maxim Maximich, a staff captain, whose own cart is more heavily laden but is being pulled more easily by fewer oxen. Maxim, long in the Caucasus, explains how the locals will fleece inexperienced travelers any way they can. "You'll see, they're going to get a tip from you as well."

On this exchange, the previous reader had commented, "talking about servants 'they' = deceitful." And a few paragraphs later, after a lovely description of day turning suddenly to night in the mountains and about how light is reflected from the snow, the two men with their carts descend the mountain, and what the staff captain predicted came true. "The Ossetians had gathered volubly around me and were demanding tips, but the staff captain shouted at them so menacingly that they scattered instantly." The previous reader's sympathies are with the Ossetians. "Treated inhuman" is inscribed in the margin.

The Previous Reader, my predecessor, is developing a strong interpretation of the novel. It is about Russian prejudice against the oppressed native peoples of the Caucasus. The narrator calls them "a pathetic lot!" The captain replies, "A very stupid nation . . . Would you believe it? They don't know how to do anything, they're incapable of any kind of education!" The Previous Reader sees in this exchange "no respect for inhabitants." And so it goes throughout the text. Outraged accusations batter the margins: "stereotypes," "discrim.," "inhumane description," "RACIST," or "Circassian racial comment." I cannot tell if the Previous Reader is angry at the characters or at the author. I wonder if, however strong in their defense, he or she (I am guessing "she") knows who Circassians are. I am pretty sure she is not as up on the geography, religions, and races of the Caucasus as Mr. Nabokov would have wished. For the Previous Reader, reading a novel is an exercise in spotting bias, and she is good at it.

If anything was needed to finish off this novel, I found it at the end. The "Reader's Guide" or "Guide for Discussion" or, in this case, "Reading Group Guide" has become a standard feature in paperback publishing.

> 1. The five related stories that comprise *A Hero of Our Time* are presented out of chronological order. Why do you think Lermontov chose this arrangement, and what is gained by the unconventional structure? What is the proper chronological order for the stories?
> 2. According to Lermontov, *A Hero of Our Time* offers "a portrait composed of the sins of our entire generation in full flower." What are Grigory Alexandrovich Pechorin's vices? Does he have redeeming qualities as well? How would you compare him to today's youth?

I closed the book, having made it only as far as the Previous Reader, and looked again at the cover: a twenty-something white guy in white T-shirt and tailored jacket, long-haired, not American, with a wispy mustache and traces of a goatee, eyes concealed by cheap sunglasses, pointing at us in that challenging way. Rather than finishing the novel for a third time, I researched this terrific photo. It was credited to Roger Wright of Getty Images, so I went to the Getty Images website and tracked it down: *Young Man in Street Wearing Sunglasses, Pointing.* The meta-tag keywords were Aggression, Well-dressed, Casual Clothing, Confrontation, Confidence, T-shirt, Road, Square, Looking at Camera, Waist Up, Outdoors, 20–24 Years, Close-up, Jacket, Sunglasses, Mustache, Blond Hair, Serious, Pointing, Day, One Person, Button Down Shirt, Color Image, Attitude, Series, One Young Man Only, One Man Only, Portrait, Photography, Adults Only, Arrogance. I wondered what the jacket designer had been searching for when she found this image? Arrogance? Attitude? How had she discovered it?

Such questions are now easy to answer. I googled the jacket designer, Gabrielle Bordwin, and found a way to send her an e-mail. Within a few hours I had her reply. Had she read *A Hero of Our Time* before she did the cover? How had she found this striking photograph that so well expressed in modern form the themes of the book? She wrote ("Hello Phyllis . . . Regards Gaby") that she usually read the books she did covers for, but in the case of the series of which this volume was part, Modern Library Classics, a huge project, she sometimes got eight to twelve titles a season and could not read them all. She had not read *A Hero of Our Time*, but had turned to online sources, "Sparknotes, Amazon and the like," for her sense of what the book was about. Some information also came from the editorial director, who encouraged her to "apply a playful contemporary view" to the classics and to "underscore that these works remain vibrant and relevant literature." She could not remember how she found the Roger Wright photo, though this cover was one of her all-time favorites. Perhaps it was just by searching for young Russian men on photography sites. But when she saw it, she was taken with it because "it conveys the egotism of the character, in particular that he appears to be quite the hero in his own mind. To me, he is attractive and charismatic and at the same time repulsive and flawed, and that makes him a very interesting subject."

Somehow Gaby had understood the book and gotten more out of it than I had, and I had read it three times and she had not read it at all.

When, for the fourth time, I began *A Hero of Our Time*, I again chose the old translation on my beloved pane of glass. I was determined to keep reading *Hero* until it meant something to me. I read "Bela" again, and then I skipped to "Princess Mary" and "The Fatalist," which Nabokov said was the best story in the book and Shteyngart said lifted the whole work to coherence and magnificence with its existential questions. To me, it seemed like the kind of story you tell around a campfire to give your friends shivers. But Pechorin was becoming a more resonant figure the longer he stayed in my mind and the more real-life associations accumulated around him.

Most important to my reading experience was that my son came to visit with his wife and baby just as I finished *Hero* for the fourth time. My son had always been a wonderful person, kind and thoughtful, but now, as a father, he was raised to a higher level of selflessness. Any youthful egotism had disappeared in the face of the needs and charm of this little creature, his son. Suddenly I understood Pechorin as an embodiment of masculine ego at a certain stage of life, the stage we usually call adolescence but which can easily last into the forties. He is the person who thinks that doing the opposite of what everyone else does is depth. He laughs at a funeral and is grumpy around kids, who get more attention than he does. In a crowded subway car, he will feel he is the only rider and the car is a stage for his shenanigans, all the other passengers merely his audience. He has feelings, but no one else does, so he is cold to old friends and seduces people he has no intention of loving just to prove he can do it. He is easily hurt but frequently hurtful. He seeks new adventures constantly and is constantly bored. He wants always to seem to be ready to throw away his life and prides himself greatly on this.

This Pechorin is a young man ready to be a father, I thought. That is what this novel is about.

When next I stopped by the library to check on my shelf, I had a big shock. The shelf had changed. William Le Queux had disappeared. Two books by him that I had read were now on the shelf above. There were several more volumes of John Lescroart. Worse, *Gil Blas* was missing. So was one of the Gaston Leroux books and both Margaret Leroys. It took me a second or two to recover from my shock and to realize that the books were missing because I had checked them out. The William Le Queuxs had probably been reshelved after I returned them. I was affecting my material in the process of observing it. I had discovered the Heisenberg principle! But there was worse still. The Nabokov *A Hero of Our Time* was back on the shelf, but next to it was a sibling, a translation of Lermontov that had not been there when I began my project—yet another translation, newer even than Marian Schwartz's.

Would I read *A Hero of Our Time* yet again?

Not right now.

*Three*

# LITERARY EVOLUTION: *THE PHANTOM OF THE OPERA*

CERTAIN WORKS OF FICTION LIVE FOREVER WITHOUT actually being read. Darwinian victors, they survive through their descendants. For each person who has read Gaston Leroux's 1910 novel *The Phantom of the Opera*, thousands have seen the silent film starring Lon Chaney or Andrew Lloyd Webber's musical. In fact, more than 130 million people have attended a production of *The Phantom of the Opera*. More than 130 million people have acquired tickets, journeyed to theaters, and sat for two hours while the masked Phantom haunts the Paris Opera House and pursues the young singer, Christine Daaé. More than 130 million people have seen the chandelier fall. The total box office sales for *The Phantom of the Opera* were, as of 2013, more than five and a half billion dollars worldwide, making it, according to the *Phantom* Study Guide, the most successful "entertainment venture" of all time.

I had seen *The Phantom of the Opera* performed on Broadway, but I had never read the novel. I looked forward to exploring the work that had spawned such powerful offspring, but I had to decide whether to start with *Phantom* or with the Gaston Leroux novels in which I was less interested. Such a choice touches on one's basic orientation toward pain and pleasure. Some people go for the less pleasant of two options, assuming it has more moral weight. Others, stoic sensualists, begin with pain because they want to get it over with and leave the taste of pleasure lingering on their palates. Some impulsive people are unable to postpone pleasure, and still others, deeply pessimistic, start with the pleasure because they may die at any moment, and at least they will have had the pleasure before dying. My usual instinct is to seize the good things when I can, on the deeply pessimistic grounds that I may die at any moment, but I also have a lot of stoic sensualist in me and like to leave the taste of pleasure lingering on my palate. In this case, I chose to postpone what I was most looking forward to. Wanting to leave the taste of *Phantom*, which I assumed would be delicious, lingering on my palate like dessert, I decided to read the Leroux books on my shelf chronologically, with *Phantom* third.

I began with *The Mystery of the Yellow Room*, published in Paris in 1908 by a house that specialized in detective stories. My English translation was published the same year in New York, showing an eager American audience for Leroux's work. To a consumer of literary fiction, the opening reads promisingly like a story by Borges. The writer creates an improbable reality by alluding to it as though it were something well-known, that "famous case" from fifteen years ago. "The entire world hung for months over this obscure problem." But the Borgesian illusion soon fades. This is a detective story: There is an attack and a mystery. The characters are located in such and such a place at such and such a time and have little more depth than Miss Scarlett, Colonel Mustard, and Professor Plum. The victim, Mlle. Stangerson, daughter of the famous chemist Professor Stangerson, is found half strangled in her locked bedroom. No access or escape was possible. The door is intact. The window is barred. Leroux provides elaborate descriptions and even floor plans to prove how impossible it was that anyone should get in or out. So how did this happen?

I do not underestimate the value of any fiction that focuses someone's attention, however momentarily, away from their own unsolvable problems, and I do not want to discount anybody's pleasures. This book has a full five-star rating on Amazon, and I respect that. But to me it seemed a shell game. Leroux directs our attention to the physical layout, but the explanation depends on relationships between the characters in the past, and the solution requires our having information the author does not allow us to have. As more of the facts of the case become known, there is indeed no mystery at all. And here, for those of you who intend to read *The Mystery of the Yellow Room*, is a warning: SPOILERS AHEAD. SKIP FOUR PARAGRAPHS.

To explain the mystery of the locked room simply: Mlle. Stangerson unlocked the bedroom door for her attacker and let him in. She was married to him, had married him many years before when she was traveling in America, but hoped and believed he was dead. The notorious criminal Ballmeyer had passed himself off as a gentleman named Roussel to woo her. Imagine her horror when she discovered that the man she had married was really a notorious criminal. She tried to get far away from him and returned to live with her father in France— but not before she had had a child with Ballmeyer/Roussel, a child who was eventually sent to boarding school in Normandy and there died. Working closely with her father on his revolutionary chemical experiments, Mlle. Stangerson naturally did not want him bothered by this unsavory personal business of hers, and so she kept him completely in the dark. At the time of the attack, she is engaged to M. Darzac, and it is to save him from unjust suspicions of having been himself the attacker that the detective Rouletabille appears on the scene with his side-kick, Sainclair.

One of the peculiarities of this book is that Ballmeyer is constantly referred to as the murderer and the event as a ghastly murder, but Mlle. Stangerson remains alive and fairly well. I wonder if this is a question of translation. It does not make these books any easier to follow that the English translator has the Stangersons one moment in Paris and the next at the rail-road station in Lyon, when evidently what was meant was that they were at the Gare de Lyon in Paris; or that they head off one moment to what's called "the Orient," when they never seem to intend to go farther than the eastern part of France. Perhaps this is Nabokovian subtlety, and the sloppiness of the translation is intended to convey the sloppiness of the original. In fact, I welcomed these French-English translation puzzles because they were puzzles I could solve, whereas the inanities of the plot, which I was expected to believe, and the puzzles it posed, which seemed like no puzzles at all, left me deeply frustrated, unsure of my own intelligence.

The young detective in this book, Joseph Rouletabille, is an ace reporter who is also a master of investigation. He is brilliant, but modest and likable. His friend Sainclair often serves as narrator, as Watson does for Holmes. This case is so important and so puzzling that two detectives are working on it. In addition to young Rouletabille, a famous detective from the French police takes up residence at the Stangerson house in the country to solve the mystery of the yellow room. This detective, who suspects Mlle. Stangerson's fiancé, M. Darzac, of being the one who tried to kill her, is named Frédéric Larsan, and—how did I not see this coming?—Larsan is one and the same as Ballmeyer/Roussel, the murderous evil genius. Unless Leroux is pulling our legs, mocking the early detective novel convention by which all disguises are impenetrable (and I think not), he expects us to believe that Ballmeyer/Roussel/Larsan can disguise himself so well that even his own wife does not recognize him.

I mean it kindly when I suggest that Leroux shows signs of intoxication: he is intoxicated by the possibilities of fiction, in which anything can be anything else. He is high on connections, manic on them! Relatively new at writing novels, savoring its difference from journalism, he hasn't yet learned to keep the ability to make it all up and tie it all together under control. Another sign of the beginner: as he feels his way toward characterization, he begins by supplying masses of backstory, characterization's most primitive form. When Roulctabille meets Mlle. Stangerson, he notices the scent she wears and then becomes haunted by it. It is the same perfume that was worn by the mysterious lady in black who used to visit him when he was a child. MAJOR SPOILER: Rouletabille is the long-lost child of Mlle. Stangerson and the evil genius Ballmeyer/Roussel/Larsan. He did not die at all. He ran away from the school in Normandy, and they were afraid to say so. In the next volume of the series, *The Perfume of the Lady in Black*, he is reunited with his mother, and it falls to him to track down his own father, who continues to persecute his mother out of some twisted passion for her, if I understand correctly, and she continues not to recognize him, even when, in the sequel, he disguises himself as her current husband.

These two novels, *The Mystery of the Yellow Room* and *The Perfume of the Lady in Black*, are the first of seven Rouletabille novels Leroux wrote, all of them popular in their time in France. There was another on my shelf, *The Phantom Clue*, but my rules (no more than three books by one author required) allowed me to ignore it. After slogging through *Perfume*, another Clue-board mystery of no interest to me apart from its setting in a fortress/house on the Riviera, I could finally get to *The Phantom of the Opera*. But did I? No. I found that I was just as interested in the descendants of the novel as in the text itself. I watched a DVD of the Lon Chaney silent film. I watched the DVD of the terrific twenty-fifth anniversary performance of *Phantom of the Opera* at Royal Albert Hall. I watched a DVD of the Joel Schumacher 2004 film version. I saw another performance on Broadway, twenty-five years after I'd seen it before. It was just as powerful, and the production had gotten better and better with time. Without reading the text, I bathed in its atmosphere. I never got tired of the story.

Nor could I resist the centrifugal pull of the Web. Fans of *Phantom* are legion (some of them must call themselves "phans"), and there are many *Phantom* websites, on some of which a high level of intelligence and imagination is displayed. People share their *Phantom* experiences and compare their opinions of performances. They can also indulge in advanced role play and get to "be" the Phantom, Christine, or Raoul. On one of these sites someone sketched out the role of Baron de Castelot-Barbazac, whose existence is merely implied by Leroux. First name: Jérémie. Age: 34. Job: Baron. Sexual orientation: Hetero. "He can come off as a bit of an idiot but he isn't as stupid as he seems. But one thing he really is is a pacifist; he truly does believe that any problem or disagreement can be solved without violence. This makes some think of him as very naïve. Which he may well be."

Whose imagination gave birth to a story with so much enduring appeal, and how did he come up with it?

According to gaston-leroux.net, Leroux, who was born in 1868 and lived into the 1920s, came from a solidly bourgeois background. His father was a wealthy contractor, and he got a good education at a boarding school in Normandy. He studied law in Paris and practiced for a few years, but he did not like the work and abandoned it. Blowing quickly through an inheritance and having to earn a living, he got a job as a reporter and feature writer for the daily paper *L'Écho de Paris*, specializing, because of his background in law, in trials.

He was born into the period in France's complicated history called the Second Empire, when Napoleon Bonaparte's nephew, Louis-Napoleon, having been elected president of the Second Republic, seized power, restored the monarchy, and made himself the emperor Napoleon III. When France under Napoleon III lost the Franco-Prussian War, a popular uprising took place and in 1871 replaced the monarchy, very briefly, with a socialist government called the Commune, which was replaced in turn by the Third Republic. These were violent times. From Russia to America, anarchists, who believed that all government was bad and should be destroyed by any means, were terrorists as feared as any group since 9/11. Between 1881 and 1901 a Russian tsar, a French president, two American presidents (Garfield and McKinley), an Austrian empress, a Spanish prime minister, and an Italian king were assassinated. Not all these leaders were killed by anarchists—Garfield was shot, as all American schoolchildren used to be taught, by a disappointed office seeker. But it gives you some idea of the level of political violence in a period we think of as complacent. Even Queen Victoria was the object of seven attempted assassinations.

Anarchists in Paris were throwing bombs into theaters, cafés, and railroad stations in an effort to injure as many people as possible. In 1893 an anarchist threw a bomb into the Chamber of Deputies, injuring several people. Gaston Leroux covered the man's trial and execution, and he did it so well that he was offered a job on Paris's leading daily, *Le Matin*. He covered the trials of two more anarchists sentenced to death, one for the bombing of the Café Terminus, the other for the assassination of the president of the Republic, Sadi Carnot. In 1899 Leroux covered the second Dreyfus trial, a touchstone in the history of French anti-Semitism.

By 1901 Leroux was making the enormous salary of fifteen hundred francs a month from *Le Matin* and had already published a collection of his pieces written for that newspaper and *L'Écho*. In the next few years he was made a chevalier of the Légion d'honneur and spent a year in Russia covering the revolution, accompanied by the woman he could not marry, because his wife, from whom he was separated, would not give him a divorce. He was reporting on everything, seemed to be everywhere. He did an interview with survivors of the Russo-Japanese War and another with explorers returning from the Antarctic. He used the latest technologies—cable and telephone—to file his stories. He was not quite forty, immensely successful, and had not yet written a single one of the novels by which he would be remembered and which ended up on my shelf. It took a fight with his boss to make him a full-time novelist. The owner of *Le Matin*, Maurice Bunau-Varilla, by all accounts a difficult character, once angered Gaston to such an extent that he decided to quit the newspaper and devote himself to writing novels. Although later Bunau-Varilla begged him to return to *Le Matin*, he never went back to reporting.

I liked this man. He lived his life with abandon. He inherited money, blew through it, got a job. He trained in law, didn't like it, became a reporter. He got pissed off at his boss, quit, and set up as a novelist. He felt like writing plays? Making films? He did that too. His wife wouldn't divorce him? He lived with the woman he loved, had a family with her, and waited for the wife to die or change her mind. He bypassed Paris and lived on the Riviera. He was a novelist in the same way that he was a reporter or a lawyer. He was not born to do it. It was not a calling or a ministry—merely an amusing way of making a living, less strenuous and more independent than reporting for a newspaper, better suited to a portly gentleman over forty with a lively mind. High-energy, competent, savvy, he is a guy you imagine being successful at anything he put his attention to. He might have been a theater producer, a chaired professor, or a hedge fund manager if that had been the direction in which life had taken him.

Given his background as a court reporter, Leroux's turning first to detective fiction makes sense. In general, detective fiction offers a useful formula for a beginning novelist: invent a crime; invent a solution; invent a detective to connect the two. Edgar Allan Poe and Arthur Conan Doyle had provided models. Poe had been translated into French by Baudelaire in the 1860s, and the Sherlock Holmes stories had begun trickling across the Channel in the 1890s. By 1909, Holmes stories in translation were flooding into France and were immensely popular, inspiring both Leroux and Maurice Leblanc, who created the detective Arsène Lupin. To set his work off from Conan Doyle's, Leroux needed a distinctive detective, and he created one based on himself—Joseph Rouletabille, ace reporter, precocious, brilliant, strangely alone in life, educated at a boarding school in Normandy. Compared to Conan Doyle's cocaine-sniffing, half-crazy/half-rational Sherlock Holmes, little Rouletabille is pallid. He is also pallid compared to Arsène Lupin, the gentleman thief who helps catch criminals more seriously evil than himself. Yet he served Leroux well enough. Before the Lon Chaney film version of *Phantom* appeared in 1925, there had already been four movies with Rouletabille as hero.

*The Phantom of the Opera* also begins as a detective story, but it morphs, if only fitfully, into something else—a wonderfully strange half-horror, half-love story in which you are never sure whether the world you are inhabiting is intended to be realistic or not. In a preface that read to me as appealingly postmodern, like the opening of *Yellow Room*, Gaston Leroux, speaking in his real-life persona of investigative crime reporter, presents a mystery—what happened to the great singer Christine Daaé and the Vicomte de Chagny and who killed the Vicomte's brother, Count Philippe—as though it had really taken place in Paris some thirty years before. Leroux claims that papers put into his hands by a mysterious man called "the Persian" allowed him to solve the mystery by connecting it with the old legend of an opera ghost. The opera ghost, Leroux informs us, really existed, and his existence explains the whole tragedy. Leroux thanks all the people who helped him with his research—the police commissioner, M. Mifroid; the acting manager of the opera; the present management; the examining magistrate in the Chagny case, M. Faure; and of course Mme. la Baronne de Castelot-Barbezac. It is all so convincing that I went to Google to check if these people had really existed. I googled "Chagny and Faure" and was sent back to the text of *Phantom of the Opera*. From the grave, Leroux must have been saying

"Gotcha!" This is fiction, and part of the fun is that the author endows it with a convincingly factual status it should not have. It is as though a famous American journalist began a novel by saying that he was sitting in his office at *The Washington Post* when someone came in with papers proving that a disaster just far enough in the past that we might not have heard of it was the work of the Phantom of the White House.

As a detective story, it is primitive—the mystery is solved, as in *The Mystery of the Yellow Room,* by discovering new information about the past. The Persian, a shadowy creature of the international secret police, who will disappear in subsequent adaptations, is able to detail the ghost's history to M. Leroux and supply proof of his existence. "With my bundle of papers in hand, I once more went over the ghost's vast domain, the huge building which he had made his kingdom. All that my eyes saw, all that my mind perceived, corroborated the Persian's documents precisely." And miraculously, shortly after the receipt of these documents by Leroux, a corpse is found buried in the lowest depths of the opera house, and this corpse had to be, because of its location, that of the opera ghost himself. In another delicious touch of boundary blurring, Leroux tells us that the corpse was found when they dug in the cellar of the Paris Opera to "bury the phonograph records," and this is something that actually took place: on December 24, 1907, a cache of phonograph records was buried in lead containers in the basement of the opera house so that future generations could hear what opera singing and sound reproduction were like in the early twentieth century.

The narrative proper begins after the preface, with a traditional third-person narrator recounting what happened at the retirement party of Messieurs Debienne and Poligny, managers

of the Paris Opera. Later adaptations begin more or less at the
same place because it allows the idea of the opera ghost to be
mooted by one generation of managers and pooh-poohed by
the next. The girls of the corps de ballet are all aflutter because
someone had just seen the ghost: a gentleman in dress clothes
but underneath, a skeleton. The narrator is skeptical. "You meet
so many men in dress-clothes at the Opera who are not ghosts."
The testimony of Joseph Buquet, a stagehand who has seen
him, supports the ghost's existence, however. His skin is yellow and stretched across the bones of his face. His eyes are two
black holes. "His nose is so little worth talking about that you
can't see it sideways; and the absence of that nose is a horrible
thing to look at." The text has a verve and a sophistication be-
fitting the most renowned writer for the leading Paris daily.
"The retiring managers looked cheerful, as is the Paris way.
None will ever be a true Parisian who has not learned to wear
a mask of gaiety over his sorrows and one of sadness, boredom,
and indifference over his inward joy." Frankly, I did not expect
so much worldliness in the text of *Phantom*. It is as Parisian as
an Hermès scarf.

The story is probably familiar. The magnificent Paris Opera House is terrorized by someone who is glimpsed occasionally but more often makes his presence felt without showing
himself. He is known as the Opera Ghost (often called O.G.).
The old management paid him a monthly stipend and saved
him Box Five. The new management invites disaster by refusing
to keep up these traditions. Meanwhile, a young singer, Christine Daaé, has become the protégée of a shadowy personage
she thinks of as the Angel of Music, who sings like an angel
himself and has given her the power to sing angelically, too. Her
father, a violinist and her first musical mentor, now dead, had

told her he would send someone from heaven to stand by her, so she is not surprised at the emergence in her life of the Angel, whom she can hear but never sees. She certainly does not put together that her Angel of Music is the same creature as the Phantom. The Phantom, who has fallen in love with his protégée, demands that she be allowed to replace the diva Carlotta as Marguerite in *Faust*. To encourage this cast change, he causes Carlotta to fall sick. Christine triumphs.

In the audience is Raoul, the Vicomte de Chagny, a childhood friend of Christine's, who goes backstage and renews their friendship. They fall in love. But Christine is not free. She is tied to the Angel of Music and under orders to care about nothing but her singing. She even wears a kind of wedding ring the Angel has given her. At one point the young lovers steal up to the roof of the opera house, but even there, the Phantom is watching them and overhears their plans to elope. He has been threatening that terrible things will happen if Christine does not continue to sing Marguerite. Carlotta and the management ignore the threats, but the next performance of *Faust* is a disaster: when Carlotta starts to sing, she sounds like a frog, and the immense chandelier in the center of the dome crashes to the floor. In the confusion, a terrifying masked figure scoops Christine up and carries her down to his hidden chambers in the lowest level of the opera house, by the shore of an underground lake. There, he promises not to hurt her so long as she does not touch his mask, and as he speaks, she is horrified to recognize the voice of her Angel of Music. He begs her to stay with him. He sings to her magnificently. Christine, half horrified, half fascinated, cannot resist ripping off the mask. He is unspeakably hideous. She is repelled. But she is also ambivalent, tied to him somehow, impressed by his enormous love for her, and she ends by kissing him. With this kiss she wins her freedom. He allows her to leave him and marry her vicomte. Brokenhearted, he feels himself dying and begs her to come back and bury him when she hears of his death—which she does. She and Raoul go off and lead a hidden life together.

As I have related it, the plot does not differ drastically from the action of Andrew Lloyd Webber's musical, but the experience of reading the original text is quite different. The prose is competent, intelligent, and even occasionally witty. The genius of the book—achieved almost inadvertently—is to establish the ghost as a reality without explaining exactly what kind of reality it is. You are allowed to believe in magic or not. You can imagine that the ghost is a supernatural being who walks through walls and occupies an opera box without being seen, or you can think that there are doors to underground cellars made invisible by mirrors, and hollow columns in which a person may hide to watch a performance. Whatever suits you. This is a significant accomplishment, the key to the enjoyment of the novel, but Leroux will throw it away before he is finished.

The actual narrative is clumsy, passing from one character to another. Retrospective and filled with remembered dialogue, it seems constantly to be doubling back on a few actions with a great many words. A lot of the exposition falls to Christine, explaining to Raoul, on the roof of the opera house, why she has been so elusive. She describes her vocal training and her first success: "The hours during which the voice taught me were spent in a divine frenzy, until, at last, the voice said to me, 'You can now, Christine Daaé, give to men a little of the music of Heaven.' I don't know how it was that Carlotta did not come to the theater that night nor why I was called upon to sing in her stead; but I sang with a rapture I had never known before and I felt for a moment as if my soul were leaving my body!" As for the Phantom: "Think of him at my feet, in the house on the lake, underground. He accuses himself, he curses himself, he implores my forgiveness! He confesses his cheat! He loves me! He lays at my feet an immense and tragic love! He has carried me off for love! He has imprisoned me with him, underground, for love."

The scene in which the chandelier falls takes place a third of the way through the book. Christine Daaé disappears from the book halfway through, never to reappear. The second half largely follows the insipid Raoul through the cellars of the opera house, both alone and with the Persian, as he looks for her. Many irrelevant pages concern the disappearance of forty thousand francs from the pocket of one of the managers of the opera, a plot wrinkle that appears in no other version, so extraneous is it to the impact of the narrative. When we lurch even further backward and learn the ghost's prehistory, it is disappointing. The possibility of believing he is a ghost is stripped away. His name is Erik. He is a man. Too ugly to be loved by his own parents, who forced him to wear a mask, he became a traveling showman and con man, then a trapdoor expert for Eastern potentates, and finally a contractor for the opera house, leading him to build his own hidden sanctuary in the basement.

Toward the end, the narrator changes again, and the Persian relates how, years earlier, he had pursued the Phantom through the Far and Middle East. There are many digressions—on the Punjab lasso technique for strangulation, on tortures in Persian seraglios, on the Indonesian pirate's technique for breathing underwater by using a reed (how the Phantom sneaks up on Count Philippe to drown him). Pages are taken up with the intricate torture of Raoul and the Persian in a chamber fitted with mirrors and a heating system designed to drive its victims mad with equatorial heat so they will hang themselves from an artificial tree, thoughtfully provided, by a rope also thoughtfully provided. *Phantom* was published serially, and it reads as though Leroux finished his story long before he expected to and had to pad it out. Hence the Punjab lasso, the Indonesian reed trick, the forty thousand francs, the gunpowder stored in the basement waiting to blow up the opera house. (I haven't even mentioned that, have I?)

Despite its flaws, I found the novel riveting. I read it as though separated from my own body, part of me in a chair reading the words, part of me far off in fantasyland, reading a female Faust story about a girl who sells her soul to the devil in exchange for artistic greatness, about a devil in torment, wanting to be loved, gifted but hideous. I was with Beauty and the Beast, Hannibal Lecter and Clarice Starling. The man is a creature of the underworld, a figure of the subconscious, a power associated with the dark and the hidden. The woman must conquer fear and join him in darkness to keep from a life of mere convention and domesticity. She must embrace her demon lover. She must descend to hell and, symbolically at least, mate with the devil. Fortunately for Christine in the novel, all she has to do in fact is kiss the Phantom on the forehead, whereas in the musical she has to give him a real smackeroo on the lips, and if it were being filmed now, a blow job would be the least she could get away with. Of the two of them, he is the less kinky. He just wants to be loved. She wants to be loved by both her suitors, the attractive young man of the upper classes and the terrifying madman of the underworld.

A bad book can tell a great story, however inefficiently.

Posterity can do an *auteur*'s work of polishing a narrative, and it did so in the case of *Phantom*, getting rid of useless plot complexity and slimming down the story to its archetypal core. The process of improvement by posterity in this case began quickly. Although the novel did not do well, something in it drew the attention of filmmakers. Setting, I think, was crucial to the book's appeal.

The Paris Opera House, now known as the Palais Garnier after the architect who designed it, was ordered up, the way one might order a birthday cake, by Napoleon III. He and his wife arrived at the old opera house one night in 1858, and a group of protesters bombed the imperial procession as it pulled up to the front entrance. The explosion did no harm to Napoleon and his wife or to the building, but it killed eighty bystanders, frightening the emperor. As part of the grand reconstruction of Paris then being planned by Baron Haussmann, Napoleon ordered a new opera house to be built, with a side entrance where the imperial family and other high-value targets might arrive discreetly.

The building site was huge, more than three acres, and exceptionally deep, to bear the weight of the massive sets and to be able to store them. The whole structure contained seventeen stories, seven of them underground. At some point in digging the foundation the construction crews hit water from the Paris aquifer. Steam-operated pumps were installed to drain the site, a process that took eight months. Then concrete cofferdams were constructed and water allowed back in to keep the rest of the cellars dry. So there is in fact a giant water tank under the opera house, if not an underground lake.

Construction started in 1861 but was suspended because of the war with Prussia. Then came the brief and brutally suppressed Commune. Various myths have the underground spaces in the opera house used as a prison in which government forces kept, tortured, and executed Communards or as a munitions storage area. In any event, in 1875, five years after the Third Republic was born, the elaborate and spectacular gilded space opened as an opera house and immediately epitomized all the glory of the Belle Époque.

The building still takes your breath away. The seven-ton chandelier, which did actually drop a counterweight and kill someone in 1907, now hangs from a dome painted with a vibrant fresco in the 1960s by Marc Chagall. But the gilded tiers rise one above the other, the red plush seats provide seating for two thousand, just as they did when the building was new. The overwhelming impression throughout is of marble, gold, sculpture, and grandeur. Few experiences reinforce the glamour of high art as successfully as attending a performance at the Palais Garnier—approaching the majestic façade, entering, confronting the immense curved staircase, and walking up that staircase, through the foyers, and taking your seat in an ocean of red and gold. Even before the curtain rises, you feel exhilarated.

Short of going to Paris, the best way to get a feel for this building is to watch the 1925 *Phantom* with Lon Chaney. The camera accompanies the audience into the opera house and rests at the bottom of the grand staircase as the people sweep upward. There are spectacular scenes on the staircase and in the stalls, as well as in the underground spaces. Piranesian arches and staircases, low-ceilinged tunnels—littered with props from old operas—suggest a hellish underworld. This glorious visual spectacle was one of the reasons producers did not think that a film of *Phantom* could be made. It seemed insurmountably expensive to reproduce the Palais Garnier on a Hollywood lot. Yet that is what they eventually did. Everything you see in the film—and I, for one, assumed it had been filmed in Paris—was shot on the Universal Studios stage 28 in California.

Leroux, whose father was a builder, had a real feel for physical space. In *The Mystery of the Yellow Room* and *The Perfume of the Lady in Black* he went into tedious detail about how rooms were laid out, even including floor plans so we could check the placement of exits and entrances and the location of windows. In *Phantom* he took this feel for layout and flipped it from horizontal to vertical. The setting of *Phantom* is, quite literally, deep, it being Leroux's inspiration to seize on the metaphoric resonance of this building, its glamour and its mystery, its brightness and its shadowy depths. Above, the palace of culture. Below, the dark lake and tunnels, hidden desires, aggression, violence, and inspiration. Every subsequent version has capitalized on this resonance. The Lon Chaney silent film, which is more straightforwardly a horror story than the novel, opens with an image of a man carrying a lantern in a pitch-black cavern. "Sanctuary of song lovers," reads the first title, "the Paris Opera House rising nobly over medieval torture chambers." As beautiful as are the opera house scenes, the masked ball scene (hand tinted), and the scenes of the corps de ballet onstage dancing, the medieval torture chambers were assumed to be the real draw.

In many ways, the silent film is a perfect telling of the story of the Phantom and Christine. The long, slow shots, the pantomimed acting, the choreographed action all heighten the dramatic impact. The fall of the chandelier is terrifying. (They lowered the chandelier to a few inches above the audience, then filmed it as it was slowly hauled back up. The film was then run in reverse, speeded up to simulate the crash.) The fairy-tale element is strongly rendered by the dramatic black-and-white images. The scenes of Christine being carried off to the underworld are particularly powerful. The masked Phantom leads her down a stone staircase, their shadows cast on the stone-block walls. The chiffon train of her costume spreads behind her, her body arched back in reluctance. He puts her on a white horse, and they descend farther, down many levels of ramps as in some nightmare parking garage, to the lake. He places her in a gondola and poles them across the lake as her chiffon train floats on the water. It is ravishing.

The film reaches its high point after the Phantom has in-stalled Christine in his hideaway; he sits at an organ wearing his rather silly, pudgy mask (nothing like the elegant white half mask of the stage production) and·madly plays the music from his opera, *Don Juan Triumphant*. Christine takes advantage of his total absorption to rip off his mask. He turns his hideous face directly to the camera. When the film opened in New York in 1925, the *Times* reviewer reported that a woman be-hind him in the theater started to scream. Some middle-aged and elderly people still remember how scared they were by this shot. A British film critic in 1975 wrote of his horror at seeing Lon Chaney's "fanged, corroded, skull-like" face. "That tin-gling hair-on-end experience has stayed with me for over fifty years." It has become a classic image of the silent screen. The film scholar Jeanine Basinger finds that "the sight of his death's-head skull with its hot-coal eyes is as unsettling today as it ever was."

There is one huge drawback, however, to the silent film. It is silent. In a story about singing and the power of music, that's a problem. Scenes in which the characters are supposed to be singing—Carlotta and Christine both have long musical sequences—seem especially perverse to modern audiences. The camera holds on the faces, the mouths open and shape notes, but no sounds come out. We must remind ourselves that when they made this film, no one knew that *The Jazz Singer* would hit the screens two years later and the era of the silent film would be over in little more than a decade.

When I consider the creative process, I end up thinking more often than I would care to admit about Woody Allen's life of the Earl of Sandwich, from his early collection, *Getting Even*. The Earl of Sandwich holes up in his laboratory and works for years, emerging to present his creation, a slice of bread, with a slice of bread on top and a slice of turkey on top of that. His work is met by laughter and scorn. He goes back to work, works for years, emerges with his second effort, two slices of turkey with a slice of bread in between. More scorn. More derision. Back to work. Years go by. Finally he emerges and presents to the world two pieces of bread with a slice of turkey between. Success at last! There are so many ways to get things wrong. A ghost, a girl, the Paris Opera. It seems so simple, but it never is.

Obvious in retrospect that what was missing was music. Also obvious that Andrew Lloyd Webber was the person to write the music, expressing both the spookiness and the eroticism of the story, but only because he did. In the early 1980s the actor-director Geoffrey Holder bought the rights to musicalize *Phantom* in the United States and got the playwright Arthur Kopit and the composer Maury Yeston to work on the project. Andrew Lloyd Webber's version has obliterated almost all traces of this *Phantom*. Some people find the music bombastic, but I am with those who regard this composer as the Puccini of our time. As I thought about *Phantom*, Lloyd Webber's variously yearning and sinister scales tumbled through my mind, with words attached like colored ribbons. Apropos of no one, just savoring the words and tune, I sang, " 'Insolent boy, this slave of fashion, basking in your glory.' "

I had not explained to my own satisfaction where the idea for *Phantom* might have come from, how a clever but uninspired writer of detective stories produced this gothic masterpiece. We know Leroux's quick mind picked up scraps of current events: the fall of the counterweight from the chandelier of the opera house, the burying of the phonograph records in the cellar, the prevalence of terrorism. (The Phantom has packed the cellars with barrels of gunpowder, and he threatens to blow up the whole opera house if Christine spurns him.) These, plus his actual enjoyment of the building, put the Palais Garnier in Leroux's mind as a setting. But what about the narrative core—the pursuit, the man, the girl, the ugliness, the mask?

Gothic fiction was having a resurgence at the end of the century. Fanged creatures sucking the blood of beautiful maidens, a man showing no signs of his debauchery while his portrait in the attic gets more and more hideous, women in the power of mad geniuses—these were à la mode. It wasn't all egret plumes, champagne, and Maxim's. There was *The Picture of Dorian Gray*, *The Turn of the Screw*, and *Dracula*. George Du Maurier's novel *Trilby*, from 1894, featured a hypnotist named Svengali and a young woman who, without him, is tone-deaf, but hypnotized, performing in a trance, becomes a great singer. If detective stories appeal to the part of us that wants life to be reasonable and make sense, gothic fiction appeals to the part of us that wants it to be inexplicable and astonishing. It was Gaston Leroux's luck, and even more ours, that in pursuing his detective formula, his imagination bubbled up a horror story.

In the two Rouletabille novels that preceded *Phantom*, *The Mystery of the Yellow Room* and *The Perfume of the Lady in Black*, the villain, Larsan, pursues the terrified heroine, Mlle. Stangerson. Larsan attacks her—in the locked room—hoping to separate her from her new lover and even to blame the crime on him. Thanks to Rouletabille, he fails. But he continues pursuing her in the next novel, wanting this time, it seems, not to kill her, but to ravish her. Buried somewhere in this mess is the idea of a twisted man of significant powers pursuing a woman who finds him repugnant but is tied to him by a hidden bond.

To explain why the pursuer so horrifies the pursued, Leroux would not have had to reinvent the narrative wheel to seize on the story of "Beauty and the Beast." A man can appall a woman because he is evil, because he is cruel, or just because he is really ugly. He is so ugly that he has to wear a mask to cover his ugliness, so ugly he has been an outcast from birth, and it has turned him bitter and mean. Add to that a perverse but pervasive psychological truth: the monster has something the beauty wants. The two are tied together in some unseemly but deeply sexy way, their relationship far more erotic than Christine's relationship with the vapid vicomte and more akin to her relationship with her dead father, the violin player who taught her to sing. There may be some of Professor and Mlle. Stangerson in the Phantom and Christine, and there was certainly a counter-rational essence inside the detective story Leroux thought he was writing.

It seems to have been part of Gaston Leroux's imaginative need to render the familiar uncanny. His mind responded to the gothic possibilities of the city he lived in. A later book, *The Haunted Chair*, would take the French Academy as the locus of horror. Every time a new "immortal" was elected, he would die as soon as he made the required speech in honor of his predecessor, and the chair would be vacant again.

There was another novel by Gaston Leroux on my shelf—*The Man with the Black Feather*—which I decided to read, intrigued by the title. Nothing like *L'Homme avec la plume noire* appeared on the authoritative French list of Leroux's works, so I assumed it was a late or posthumous work. When I started it, however, I realized that it was in the bibliography as *La Double Vie de Théophraste Longuet* (*The Double Life of Theophrastus Longuet*), a novel written in 1903—before *Phantom* and even before the two Rouletabille mysteries I had read.

It is a born-into-another-body story. Theophrastus Longuet, a good bourgeois, recently retired, celebrates his new freedom with some sightseeing in Paris. At the Conciergerie, the eighteenth-century prison, he inexplicably knows his way around and begins shouting eighteenth-century criminal slang. Yes, he has lived before! His previous incarnation, Cartouche, the king of Parisian thieves in 1721, a man who would slice off another man's ear without a second's hesitation, takes over more and more of Monsieur Longuet until, in a fit of pique, he slices off his neighbor's ear. An exorcism by a spiritualist—delicate "astral surgery"—is unsuccessful. Cartouche gets stronger all the time. It is witty and stylish, ridiculous but fun, and part of the fun is that these strange things happen in a real city. Here, what mobilizes Leroux's imagination is the tunnel system underlying much of Paris. Beginning in the late eighteenth century, former quarries were used as an ossuary, the bones of six million corpses being stored there to this day. Called the catacombs, they are open for visits from an entrance at Place Denfert-Rochereau. In the novel, Longuet and the police commissioner, Mifroid, fall into a hole in the street and are sealed in the catacombs. They wander for days, discussing problems in logic, including the most rational way to find the exit. They know the exit is near the ossuary, so they rejoice when they start seeing bones. They hear people and music and, in a truly weird touch, enter a cavern where a full orchestra is playing Saint-Saëns's *Danse Macabre* to a large audience. They return to the surface, where Theophrastus/Cartouche assumes he will be arrested, but the commissioner declines to do so, saying in effect that the world is more interesting with him in it.

Two other novels by Gaston Leroux remained unread on my shelf, *The Phantom Clue*, the other Rouletabille mystery, which an intelligent review on a mystery website says is "worth reading," and *The New Idol: Further Adventures of Cheri Bibi*, featuring another of Leroux's detectives. But I had more than fulfilled my pact with Leroux and was not tempted to go further.

Whereas, to talk with people about the other books I'd read, I had to get on the Internet, with *Phantom of the Opera* a good conversation was as close as the next encounter. Almost everyone I spoke to had seen the show or had an opinion about it. One friend, interested in opera and in the history of the Broadway musical, told me this: when opera lovers argue that opera is the goal toward which all art aspires, they often say that music and drama work together in opera to reinforce each other. But that happens less than it should, said my friend. Opera singers are sometimes not physically convincing in their roles, or they aren't good actors, or the director overwhelms the music with a pretentious production. Broadway musicals never make those mistakes. They do not tolerate conflicts of interest between the musical and the dramatic elements. You would never have to accept a Monserrat Caballé, with a body as big as her voice, as Christine. So a good Broadway musical reliably combines dramatic power and the power of the music, the way opera is supposed to and occasionally does.

I explained to my friend that I was interested in literary evolution. Sequential collaboration. *Phantom* is one example. But there are others. *La Dame aux camélias*, the novel by Alexandre Dumas, became a stage play, which became *Traviata*. *La Bohème* started with stories of artists in Paris by Henri Murger. They inspired a stage play which was so successful that Murger reshaped his stories into a novel, and that novel inspired Puccini's opera.

He threw back at me Christopher Isherwood's *Goodbye to Berlin*, which led to the play *I Am a Camera*, which produced a film, which produced the musical stage play *Cabaret* by Kander and Ebb, which produced the musical film with Liza Minnelli as Sally Bowles.

We agreed that for both of us the buck stops there. From "*Willkommen, bienvenue*, welcome" to "When I go, I'm going like Elsie," neither of us can imagine anything better than *Cabaret* with Joel Grey and Liza Minnelli. In voices resembling Carlotta's when she turns into a frog, we sang a few verses about the uselessness of sitting alone in your room.

"You know, there were two *Bohème*s, the one by Puccini and another by Leoncavallo," he said.

"Literary evolution," I replied. "The natural selection of culture. The fittest survive."

Another time, I asked my well-read daughter-in-law if she had heard of Gaston Leroux.

"Yes," she said. "French cooking."

I said, "Close. That's *Larousse Gastronomique*. This is Gaston Leroux. You'll know a book he wrote, but I bet you won't have read it, *Phantom of the Opera*."

She immediately produced a *Phantom* story. A friend of hers attended a high school where the drama teacher was a megalomaniac control freak. Although everyone knows that musicals for amateur performance should be chosen to provide the maximum number of easy singing roles, he chose to do *Phantom of the Opera*, which has relatively few parts and difficult music. The drama teacher himself played the Phantom, and the best singer in the school played Christine. All the other kids played candlesticks in the chandelier.

*Phantom of the Opera* has burrowed so deeply into our culture because something in the story appeals to people no matter what form it takes. The megalomaniac high school drama teacher is not the only man who sees himself in the Phantom, yearning for a beautiful woman he can't have, and his star student not the only woman who will kiss a frog to get the leading part. Nor are these roles necessarily tied to gender. Between power and talent or beauty the negotiations are endlessly fascinating. That *Phantom*'s impact is in the narrative archetype rather than in the text explains why it can figure so largely in the popular imagination and yet be so little read.

The house of art has many bedrooms, some on the Riviera, some cork-lined. Gaston Leroux lived and worked in France more or less at the same time as Marcel Proust, who was three years younger and died five years before him. They had little in common aside from their life spans and their upper-middle-class backgrounds. Both hit their stride as novelists relatively late, and when they did, both secluded themselves—Leroux on the Côte d'Azur, Proust in his cork-lined room in Paris—but Proust devoted himself to one immense project, which he had, in a sense, been preparing for all his life, and Leroux moved quickly from one thing to the next, publishing more than forty novels in twenty years. For Proust, writing was a strenuous activity in which sensations, fragments of memory, and inchoate thoughts were dragged up from internal depths and painfully put into the words that would allow his deepest experiences, which were profoundly nonverbal, to be communicated to others. For Leroux, a writer was a producer of entertainments. He chose a genre and manipulated it as cleverly as he could, in sentences of as much wit and elegance as he could manage. *In Search of Lost Time*, Proust's masterpiece, can be viewed as in many ways the polar opposite of *The Phantom of the Opera*, and I don't just mean according to some notion of quality. Proust's is a novel with a minimum of archetypal afterlife. It exists— despite the madeleines, insomnia, and Madame Verdurin— almost entirely in the exact sequence of its words, coming alive only as it is read. I wonder whether either of these men would have considered the other a writer. But as for me, I say, *"Vive la différence!"*

*Four*

# THE UNIVERSE PROVIDES:
# RHODA LERMAN

I DID NOT WANT TO REPORT ON NOVELS I FOUND MERELY interesting. Yes, my disappointment could be made amusing up to a point, but what was in it for either of us, me or you? I wanted to address the life-enhancing possibilities of literature. I needed someone to love. And the universe provides.

I knew nothing about Rhoda Lerman. Her name, although it sounded familiar, was merely an American name, a Jewish name, the name of somebody one might know, not something hard-edged, unforgettable, alien, inherently literary, like William Shakespeare or Geoffrey Chaucer.

Her first novel, *Call Me Ishtar*, begins with a job application.

NAME: Ishtar
OCCUPATION: Mother Goddess
MARITAL STATUS: Mother/Harlot/Maiden/Wife
PRESENT ADDRESS: In transit. (Temporary address: Syracuse, New York)

The Queen of Heaven's employment record dates back to 4,800,000,000 B.C., when her major responsibilities included the fashioning of stars and worlds. Later she was in charge of "birth, love, death, disease, seasons, etc.," but "the company failed to maintain initial commitment." Another good stretch as Queen of Heaven was ended by "personality differences (Moses and monotheism)," and she is currently unemployed, living in the wilderness of upstate New York, married to a manufacturer of carpet fibers.

I was taken with the idea of an ancient goddess incarnated in a contemporary housewife. And the first-person narrator proved to be appealingly equable and raunchy.

On Sundays, Ishtar and her husband, Robert, drive across the Niagara gap via the Robert Moses Power Access Highway to his factory in Canada. "Sometimes, if my child, who is seven years old now, hasn't come with us, on the way home Robert will touch me into orgasm with one hand while he drives. I try to arrange my climax for the moment we cross the dam. The customs officers, trained to watch for suspicious nervous twitches, are forever suspecting us of contraband."

Ishtar's secret name for her husband is Robert Moses, the great city planner of the 1960s who built highways and parks all over New York State, the power broker described by Robert Caro in a monumental biography. But he is also the biblical lawgiver Moses, the power of reason and civilization to Ishtar's life force, logic to her imagination. When she writes in his checkbook in red ink, he gets angry. His rules for checkbooks call for blue ink. She is Niagara Falls, and he is the Power Access Highway.

Ishtar is a good-natured, life-loving person. In addition to running her suburban household, she manages a band, which involves her in lots of drugs, sex, and rock and roll. The author's own enthusiasm infuses the text. Ishtar is goddess and housewife both, and a woman who responds to this novel may feel temporarily that she too is Ishtar, goddess and human, the divine principles of life and fertility inhabiting all of us. I can think of no writer who melds the mythic and the realistic as successfully as Rhoda Lerman does in this novel, except perhaps Joyce himself.

Reading *Call Me Ishtar* reminded me of the fun of reading novels in the 1960s when they became overtly sexy: *Portnoy's Complaint*, whose hero masturbates with a piece of liver, a novel soaked in youthful horniness; Erica Jong's *Fear of Flying*, with its enthusiasm for "the zipless fuck," its revelation of women's sexual urges. Those were heady days. Henry Miller made an extraordinary prediction about *Fear of Flying*: "This book will make literary history. Because of it women are going to find their own voice and give us great sagas of sex, life, joy, and adventure." Some of us felt that no generation had been allowed to live as fully, as joyously, as ours. We responded excitedly to writers like Roth and Jong, who expressed that newness. Novel after novel by women opened fresh territory, addressed issues that had never been addressed. Of our generation, but writing for those behind us, was Judy Blume; then there were Judith Rossner's *Looking for Mr. Goodbar*, Lois Gould's *Such Good Friends*, Marilyn French's *The Women's Room*, and Susan Brownmiller's *Against Our Will*, among other books. There were films, not just feminist films but films with stories that defied conventions—such as the convention of marriage being the end of the story—as in *The Graduate*. Other films showed women emerging from the imprisonment of triviality or coping—even thriving—after having been rejected by men: Jill Clayburgh in *An Unmarried Woman*, Goldie Hawn in *Private Benjamin*. Women could handle, perhaps needed, two men at once. Women could have ambitions. Women were vamps and devourers. Women, at the very least, had a whole lot to say, book after book of comment on their daily life, which turned out to be a richer field than anyone suspected. The diary was a powerful and inclusive form, and perhaps a naturally female one.

*Call Me Ishtar* reaches a broad comic climax at a bar mitzvah, where the protagonist rises up in all her immortal power and reminds the congregation that the bar mitzvah boy, to be a man, has to come to terms with his mother and other women and not just inherit power from his father. Then and there, on the altar, she initiates him sexually. Pandemonium ensues. People rush for the doors. As Ishtar herself slips away, another boy stops her to ask, "Will you come to my bar mitzvah?"

The book got the kind of reviews that writers dream about. Harriet Rosenstein for *The New York Times Book Review* said, "The book has two stars: Ishtar, once the Sumerian deity of love and war . . . and Rhoda Lerman, American first-novelist of formidable gifts." Lerman is compared to Philip Roth, who, it is said, she equals at his own best game, "the Jewish absurd." "Her eye for the give-away detail, her ear for the mad half-phrase, her ability to sustain the cadences of a comic scene, all have that peculiar mix of energy, lucidity, and hysteria at which Roth excels." The review makes the book sound like the fun it is. Piquant details are mentioned, a seduction in a bathtub colored Aegean blue by three drops of Durkee food coloring, a Joycean novocaine trip under the drill of the "Tooth Pharaoh," a late-night raid, in the throes of sexual passion, on a Hostess cupcake factory. The reviewer is unequivocal. "Rhoda Lerman is a find. Go out and find her."

But people did not. It's hard to know why. Perhaps the Jewishness of the book, though that did not stop readers of

Philip Roth. Perhaps the competition with *Fear of Flying*, which came out the same year and swept the market for erotic, outrageous feminist fiction, a slightly more realistic and therefore more accessible novel that men embraced as well as women. I remember taking a ship from Naples to Istanbul in the summer of 1974 and seeing a man reading *Fear of Flying* in Spanish, laughing out loud. I never saw such universal appeal again until a Samburu warrior in Kenya asked me to send him tapes of the Harry Potter movies.

In the *Times* review of *Ishtar*, there was one statement that, the more I thought about it, the more amazing it seemed. "An enterprise like this," Ms. Rosenstein said, referring to Lerman's novel, "would have been unthinkable five or six years ago." She meant, I believe, that in 1966 or 1967 a serious literary book about a sexy woman could not have been written—or could not have been published. We forget, and the generations behind us have no idea of, what a revolution in our culture took place in the late 1960s and early 1970s. A book that showcased a woman's sexuality in a way that male fiction always had showcased a man's felt revolutionary. Until the late 1960s, we were still living with assumptions about women and sex that dated back to the Victorians.

It took an actual movement, called "women's liberation" (a term as unattractive and un-American as "homeland security"), which sought to tie the women's movement to the civil rights battles of other minorities, especially African-Americans. These movements were so successful that it's as hard to imagine a time when they didn't exist as it's hard to remember how we made long-distance calls or mailed letters before area codes and zip codes, cell phones and e-mail. But if you gather some older women in a group and start them talking about the past, the odds are they will arrive sooner rather than later at stories of discrimination. A woman who was hired as an editorial assistant at a major publisher in New York in the early 1960s recalls how, on the first day of work, the twelve new assistants were separated into male and female groups, the men set to reading manuscripts, the women to typing. Another woman recalls learning that she had scored the highest on a chemistry final at college, asking if that meant she was getting an A, and being told that only one A could be given and a boy needed it more than she did. Others recall days when Yale, Harvard, Princeton, and Dartmouth didn't admit women, to say nothing of the Century Association in New York and Mory's in New Haven. Someone else reminds us that in France, women could not vote until after World War II.

From 1963, when *The Feminine Mystique* was published, to 1970, when Kate Millett's *Sexual Politics* appeared, the idea that women had minds as hungry as men's was secret news. To those of us with an interest in this hidden knowledge, each book that came out was a life-changing revelation and confirmation. The first volume of Anaïs Nin's diary was published in 1966. Each succeeding volume was awaited in the way that American crowds in the 1840s awaited ships from England bearing the next installment of *The Old Curiosity Shop*. I remember an argument with a friend about whether or not Anaïs Nin represented "female nature." My friend, a psychologist, said yes. I myself held out for a more rational model. My friend accused me of being co-opted by male paradigms.

Those ancient battles! So much energy spent arguing over small distinctions while the big changes took place unheralded. What was feminist and what was not was constantly monitored. Women were accused of adapting male styles. Were women emotional and men rational? Was the more important fight about child care or sexual freedom? How much housework should men be expected to do? Was it right even to admit any difference between male style and female style? For example, the 1973 *Times* reviewer opined that *Call Me Ishtar*, however unthinkable without the women's movement, was not, nonetheless, feminist. First of all, Earth Mothers, however potent, were not what the times demanded. What the times demanded, presumably, were senators, secretaries of state, and presidents. Second, dominance was still the issue, even if Woman was on top instead of Man; matriarchy was no better than patriarchy. At this lovely moment, equality between the sexes was taken so seriously that a reviewer could disapprove of a novel she very much enjoyed because its image of sexual power was overbalanced in favor of women.

Do I like this book so much because it reminds me of the joy of reading feminist fiction when I was young? Am I like the elderly Russian critic reading Lermontov and recalling the excitements of his youth? Perhaps.

But the second book of Lerman's I read could have been written yesterday, so deep is its cynicism. *The Girl That He Marries* is a smart story of a New York woman, a curator at the Cloisters, who wants to get married but realizes that the guy she's set her heart on won't want her unless she treats him badly. She sees that in transforming herself, suppressing her natural kindness in order to get him, she will have permanently altered her soul and the nature of their relationship, but that is what must be done, and that is what happens. By the time she lands him, she no longer loves him—and yet they live happily ever after. The tone is both hard-edged and good-natured, an unusual mix. Cynicism is usually said to be "corrosive," but this cynicism actually comes across as bracing. Truths are being told about the politics of the mating game and of marriage that had not been told before—truths women needed to hear at a time when the mythology of love was so strongly enforced that a person was considered low-minded for mentioning that there was any power issue in marriage at all, or that sadomasochism played a part in many relationships.

*Eleanor*, the novel Lerman wrote next, follows naturally from the concern with marriage as an institution and the politics of marriage that was at the heart of *The Girl That He Marries*. It is a fictionalized account of Eleanor Roosevelt's life with Franklin, and there's nothing funny about it. It's heartbreaking. Lerman creates a completely convincing picture of a marriage in which the man holds all the cards. Franklin betrays Eleanor constantly. And she feels it deeply. This is a fine, serious book, and I loved it when I eventually read it, but as I had no interest in a fictionalized account of Eleanor Roosevelt's life, and as I could see it was serious, and as the funny Rhoda Lerman was the one I craved, I did not read it next. If I had read it next, I might have formed a different sense of Rhoda Lerman's career from the one I did form. Instead I chose to read next the one that looked funniest, *God's Ear*, putting off also *Animal Acts*, in which a woman leaves both husband and lover and runs away with a gorilla. All I knew about Rhoda Lerman was that she was currently raising dogs in upstate New York and had not published in years, and the story about running off to live with a gorilla sounded too autobiographical. I was in love with the writer I was assembling in my mind, and I didn't want to learn just yet who she really was, if she was different from my imagined love object.

So I read *God's Ear* and was completely blown away. It mixes Lerman's comic, generous spirit with her feeling for mysticism, her grounding in Judaism, and her concern with relations between men and women.

This is the story. Yussel Fetner, a young Hasid from a renowned religious family, rejects the family tradition of prophecy and rabbinic service to devote himself instead to his own little family. He is happy and successful as an insurance salesman living in Far Rockaway. His father, a revered charismatic leader, begs him to take over his congregation in—of all places—Kansas City (HaShem leads where he leads) and, finally, on the verge of death, extracts the son's reluctant agreement. Even after death, the sainted and hilarious rabbi continues to be his son's closest companion, nagging him, guilt-tripping him (he cannot get into heaven unless his son accomplishes his mission) into taking his congregation of schmegeggies (his word) to a new promised land in America's Wild West, farther west even than Kansas City, a part of desert Colorado somewhere near the actual New Age mecca of Crestone. Here the Hasids in their beaver hats set up their improbable community, buying land from a Native American who foresees that the Jews will be good guardians for the patch of desert the Indian promises will someday be a sacred lake. Soon enough, the lake appears—the rabbi's first miracle. So does a beautiful neighbor named Lillywhite, with whom the rabbi falls desperately and agonizingly in love. He is shocked by his passion. He fights his desires. This is a man, after all, who is not even supposed to shake hands with a woman. His father had always accused him of being cold and unfeeling. He needed to "circumcise his heart," to learn to feel pain. His passion for Lillywhite accomplishes this. My fervent wish for them to go to bed together, as well as my delight in every sentence, drove me at a gallop through the narrative. Will Yussel betray his principles? Will he obey his heart? The conclusion could only have been imagined by a feminist of Lerman's era. Lillywhite herself is the destined inheritor of the line of the Fetners. She is the one who will have the following. Reb Fetner himself can return to selling insurance. There is much more: the young, zaftig second wife and widow of the father; Yussel's enemy Chaim; Chaim's devastating secret; the father's humiliating companion in purgatory, a horse thief from the shtetl. It's a deeply Yiddish book, suffused with Chagall-like joy and invention, embracing zaniness as a kind of sacred unworldliness. I felt more alive for having read it, more immersed in the pleasures and responsibilities of being human. Yussel's job as rabbi is to lead his self-involved, earthbound schmegeggies up the ladder to heaven. Lerman seems to be doing the same for me. For the time I spent reading the book, I felt moved, enlarged, on the ladder to heaven.

Again the rave reviews. ("Lerman effortlessly works an immense amount of Jewish learning and Hasidic lore into a novel that's moving, wise, and very, very funny. Irresistible storytelling." Kirkus) Again, although *Eleanor* had sold well, few readers.

After *God's Ear*, Lerman wrote one more novel, *Animal Acts*, which was also on my shelf, and then a nonfiction book about her work with dogs, called *In the Company of Newfies*, and then, nothing. After 1996, no more publication. She became, as far as I could tell, a full-time dog breeder, someone who showed dogs and sold them, who lived with a pack of them, who got more out of her relationships with her animals than her relationships with people.

This interested me—and pleased me—because I myself had entered the zone of silence at about the same time as Rhoda Lerman, my last book having appeared in 1997. I had respect for people who wrote when they had something to say and stopped when they didn't. I had respect for people who changed direction when a given path either led them to where they wanted to go or didn't. I had respect for people whose interests were too different and too demanding to be filled in one life-time. I had no idea which was the case with Rhoda Lerman. I barely knew which was the case for myself.

Actually to see what is in front of you is very, very difficult. They say you can only know what you are prepared to know, what you already know, or what you hope to be true. I wanted to have found another Grace Paley, another funny feminist humane earth-mother Jewish writer. I thought Grace Paley was one of the best and most important American writers of the twentieth century. I wanted to write in praise of that rue-ful, Slavic, urban, smart, deep, balanced, tragicomic sensibility, and of writers who put women at the center of their work without writing "domestic fiction." Lerman's truncated out-put, like Grace Paley's, enhanced her credibility. I hoped it was for the same reason: "There's a lot more to life than just writing."

Setting myself to explain Rhoda Lerman's career, I devel-oped a hypothesis. Here was a funny feminist writer, the au-thor of *Call Me Ishtar, The Girl That He Marries,* and *God's Ear,* who is derailed by Eleanor Roosevelt. She surrenders to a stronger personality and never recovers her own voice and vision. Morally and practically, Eleanor Roosevelt overwhelmed her. Morally, because she was so serious a person that she made Lerman want to eliminate some of the wickeder and funnier parts of her personality. Practically, she was overwhelmed because *Eleanor* led her to a new role as an expert on the great First Lady and into writing for stage and film. Jean Stapleton, the actress, had met Rhoda at the Hyde Park library when she was doing research there. She asked Lerman to write a one-woman show in which she'd portray Eleanor. Lerman did. The play was successfully produced, and Stapleton traveled with it, often taking Lerman with her. And so she was swept away (my hypothesis went) from her novelistic path and into the world of the Roosevelts and Jean Stapleton. But *God's Ear*, to my mind her most perfect novel and the most Lerman-esque in its mixture of wisdom, humor, and inventiveness, was written after *Eleanor*. So she hadn't been completely derailed by that venture, or shoved into the world of film and theater, or driven into the permanent glooms by Eleanor Roosevelt's plight.

What I didn't want to admit was that Lerman was not, in fact, a funny feminist writer.

When I got around to reading *Animal Acts*, the last book of Lerman's I "had" to read because it was on The Shelf, it was exactly as I had feared: it seemed to be the work of a woman who was going to leave ordinary social life behind in favor of more intimacy with animals. In its smartness about marriage and its freshness of expression, its quick rhythms and syncopated prose, it was recognizably the work of the author I loved, but it seemed to have something else on its mind, something on a different wavelength from me, something rather somber.

Linda Morris, the protagonist, is fed up with her husband and almost as fed up with her lover—an Englishman, perhaps a spy, perhaps a killer—whom she spends time with at a hideaway in Britain. She decides to run away from home, but the only functional vehicle in the driveway contains a gorilla rented from a company in Coney Island that supplies living props for parties and performances. When she tries to return the gorilla, the place has gone out of business. Its owner is dead. Stuck with the gorilla, forced to drive down the Eastern Seaboard sharing her SUV with him, worried about his health, she tries to transcend her own consciousness in order to understand him. This exercise proves more satisfying than life with either husband or lover, with whom she conducts imaginary conversations as she heads to Florida. Whether she actually fucks the gorilla (her husband poses the question) remains unclear.

What disturbed me in the novel was a didactic strain. Women come from the sea and think in watery terms. Men are harder, more linear than women. Men's cruelty is as innate to them as maternal sensitivity is to women. These and other theories about the origin of the sexes, evolution, and the beginnings of life lurk below the text, surfacing occasionally. Nothing brings narrative momentum to a dead stop faster than ideas, whether they take the form of the sermons on Christian virtue with which Dickens and Dostoyevsky laced their novels or discourses on the evolution of sexual difference and our relationship to animals, as in Rhoda Lerman's work. Christian or New Age, these didactic moments seem like the commercial in a television program, and naturally at such moments we feel the urge to fast-forward.

There was no copy of *The Book of the Night* on my shelf, so my rules did not require me to read it, but I liked Rhoda

Lerman's work so much and was so caught up in the mystery, as it seemed to me, of her career, that I wanted to read it. Chronologically, this is her fourth novel, written after *Call Me Ishtar*, *The Girl That He Marries*, and *Eleanor* but before my favorite, *God's Ear*, and before *Animal Acts*. That it wasn't my kind of novel I guessed from the cover, whose typography was Celtic and which featured a map of an island, Iona, with place names like "White Strand of the Martyrs" and "Hill of the Angels." It was set in a monastery in 900 A.D.

**It is soon told. I, Generous, chronicler, Saxon, write of the vast woman.** August fifteenth. Dawn is far away and the night large and I small and my brothers are together and I alone on the strand in a cup of sand at the lip of the high and treacherous sea and the crescent blade of a new moon cuts at my throat . . . Stars fall and die and a vastness is out there pulling at the sea waves and my faith. Injured that vastness. Moaning it is in the shower of stars, in pain, and I wish mightily for the light and the end of the night.

More than "not my cup of tea," alas, this is a book I cannot read. Self-consciously poetic prose in novels afflicts me viscerally. My stomach clenches at the word "dawn" and draws tighter at "the night large and I small." "The crescent blade of a new moon cuts at my throat" signals to me that a writer is trying too hard. Whatever benefits this prose might have for someone with a different sensibility, it does nothing for me.

I flipped through the rest to make sure that the opening was not anomalous, but it was not. In the first chapter, Generous, the chronicler, witnesses the hauling in of nets as ordered by his abbot, because one part of every catch goes to the monks, one to the crofters, seven to the finder, and one is tossed back to the sea, "into the crack of the Dark Gods, into the knots of the nets of Naught." The wordplay leaves me cold. A dead soldier from World War I washes up in the nets of 900 A.D. and after him a "vast woman," who is staked through the eye and cooked to feed the people of the island but comes back a millenium later as a tourist. The transcendence of time leaves me cold. Generous turns into a cow but goes on narrating. The transcendence of species leaves me cold. The tourist who may be a reincarnation of the vast woman talks to the narrator: "Listen, cow, listen. Kore, kowrie, cow, wealth, wheel, vache, vaca, vache en roulette, baca, vacant. Think of these things." The narrator himself starts speaking in etymologies. "Does Guinevere mean Whenever? A sexual joke? Like Lance a lot? Que? Quo? Quando? Qui? Cow? How?"

Where was the editor on this book? Shouldn't someone have said, "Rhoda, darling, no. Even *Finnegans Wake* is unreadable."

It is not Rhoda Lerman's fault that when one reads the words "Dark Gods" today, it is almost impossible not to think of Voldemort, Sauron, and Darth Vader. It's not her fault that when we read "injured that vastness" and "moaning it is" we may think of Yoda, who holds the patent on vatic inversions. ("Named must your fear be before banish it you can.") We now have a rich culture of fantasy and Manichean battles between good and evil. Many people around the globe, of all ages, like Lerman, want to live in a world that never was, where the underlying ideas are rich and resonant and magic is everywhere. Even I, with my bias toward realism, want this. I have read every Harry Potter novel and seen every film. I love *A*

*Game of Thrones.* I am not a complete slave to *Mimesis.* But for me, questions of tone and authorial stance are central. The Harry Potter books display a commanding effortlessness: they assume we will like them; we are not asked to worship. But more and more I was picking up in Rhoda Lerman's work something that wanted to convince me, convert me, something beating me over the head and demanding my attention if not my assent. "Night, Nike, Victory, victim, victual, vici, vice, Sin." She wanted to teach me. She was no longer Ishtar, but Lillywhite.

When I had read all the Rhoda Lerman novels on my shelf (before, as it happens, I read *The Book of the Night*), I felt it was okay to contact Rhoda Lerman. It wasn't hard to find her. Blue Heaven Kennels, the business she runs with her husband, Bob, is a major breeder of champion Newfoundlands. Their website is filled with pictures of the soulful giants they've bred and raised and Rhoda's vivid accounts of their characters. I wrote to her saying how much I liked her books and that I intended to write about them and about her, if she was willing. Her first answer was dry and cautious: "Flattering to say the least. We can certainly talk about it." She gave me her phone number.

When I called, I felt an instant rapport. She had spent the first seven years of her life in Far Rockaway, New York, where I had lived the first three years of mine. We both came from second- or third-generation eastern European Jewish families, where the men went into business—insurance, law, accountancy—and the women savored the arts. She understood the suburban shtetl culture in which I grew up, which worshipped respectability and whose Golden Calf was footwear. Some of her cousins lived in the same place I did, the "Five Towns" of Long Island, and had gone to my high school. I had known her favorite cousin. "We drank out of the same pools," as she later wrote me. "Probably the salt in the Atlantic."

Rhoda Lerman could have been my sister or my cousin. If she were my cousin, I would have adored her for her free-spiritedness and brilliance. My parents would have told me of her every exploit, encouraging me to match her achievements. "Cousin Rhoda is on the dean's list." "Cousin Rhoda has gotten engaged." They were always coaxing us into being the people they wanted us to be. If they boasted to their friends about us, to us they were often dismissive. "This is the best thing you've ever written," my mother said to me about an anthology I put together of other people's work. Rhoda's mother asked her why she spent so much time trying to write. Weren't there enough books in the library? After the critical success of *Call Me Ishtar*, her mother had said, "Well, I better read it again." Those Jewish mothers were out of a mold that's been broken. Criticism was their business, nudging us along through life, shaping us up, like lionesses picking up cubs with their mouths and plopping them down where they wanted them, not like mothers of today, in the business of boosting self-esteem.

Rhoda had wanted to write from the time she was in second grade. There was a story we all read as children about a little boy in India who was threatened by tigers, but the tigers started fighting with each other instead of the boy, and they chased each other around a tree faster and faster until they turned into butter and melted away. It was in that sequence, Rhoda told me, in that image, tigers racing so fast around a tree that they blur and look like butter, then *are* butter, then melt like butter, that she first felt the power of language. Language could refer to something real and not real simultaneously, and that made her want to write.

Our e-mail exchanges became intense, daily. Rhoda, it emerged, had not stopped writing even though she had not published in a long time. She had an unpublished manuscript she wanted me to read. I did read it and wrote her what I thought about it in some detail. I loved reading the book, set in the Amazon, but thought there were problems with it, notably the attribution to characters of ideas that Rhoda herself held about historical evolution, about language, about the colonization of the New World by Jews. The strain I had faintly detected in *Animal Acts* and that ruined *The Book of the Night* for me was there. I told her that I wished the book were funny and suggested ways in which, improbable as that might be, this novel about Nazis in South America could be made comic. I held my breath until I heard back from her. I feared she would be angry. But, large soul that she is, she was not. She was grateful. She could not, she said, make the book comic. That was out of the question. But a lot of what I said was helpful, and she particularly took my point about using characters as mouthpieces for her own beliefs. She said she was going to take one whole character out of the novel—herself.

This was not what I had imagined when I started my adventure in the library. I never thought that I would influence the work of a writer on my shelf. Rhoda herself was less surprised. That I had picked the LEQ–LES shelf of fiction in the New York Society Library and come upon her work and introduced myself into her life and proved useful as an editor did not upset her applecart of expectations. "I believe that the universe provides," she said.

When she was a young wife in Syracuse, dutifully going to

the country club, wishing she were a writer but with nothing to write about, her hairdresser one day asked her if she knew someone who would be interested in managing a rock band. Rhoda said she thought her husband might be interested in doing it as a lark, and he was. Both of them got involved in the local rock scene, and out of their ensuing raucous experience came *Call Me Ishtar*. The universe provides.

"Of course," said Rhoda, "the universe also provides cancer."

She was visiting New York City from her home upstate. We met twice, at my place, for hours and hours of wonderful talk, and then at her friend Carol's apartment on the Upper West Side, for more. She wore white pants and a loose white shirt with a silky gray scarf around her shoulders. Her white-gray hair was up and pierced by Japanese-style ornaments with glass beads at the tip. I had expected Ishtar to be small and golden, but of course she was big and silvery, like the moon. She had brought her own lunch because she was on a low iodine diet of her own devising, hoping to improve the chances of the radiation therapy working, and she told me I should be taking organic sulfur to improve my health.

Rhoda's phone rings constantly. It's her husband, one of her children, the dog handler back in Binghamton, her agent, her editor, an Episcopal priest who has turned to her as a spiritual adviser, other woman friends. ("Heavy-duty women, not dreamers like us.") People who buy her dogs call her every day and put her up when she comes to Manhattan. Soon after we became friends, Rhoda sent me a card she thought I'd like, with a photograph of four women standing in water around a game board on a raft. Floating mah-jongg. And so we are, all of Rhoda's friends—a floating mah-jongg game.

She was happy to talk about herself. "On my mother's side, the Europeans were descendants of a big Hasid, Nachman of Horodenka. On my husband's side they were out of the Vilna Gaon." The Gaon of Vilna was a brilliant eighteenth-century rabbi who emphasized the study of Torah and eschewed the more ecstatic Hasidic movement. "And we, Bob and I, reflect the whole mystical versus logical biases of our bloodlines. I surf, and he concentrates." This difference showed up, she said, even in the way they played poker. "I just played and ate the bridge mix. He had everybody's card in his head, knew where everything was. And I won as often as he won." She claims to get information "sideways," without working for it, hears entire symphonies in her head, "has ears." "I most often feel that the universe provides, which drives Bob crazy because in fact it is he who actually provides."

She had grown up in Florida, where her family relocated after her father died when she was thirteen. She went to the University of Miami on a scholarship, majoring in geology. What made the biggest impression on her was that she wasn't allowed to go on field trips because she was a woman. It was one of those routine obstacles that men didn't notice and that turned a generation of women into feminists. When she went back years later to speak at her alma mater as a successful novelist, she said she had to be grateful to the geology department for excluding her, because it helped her become a writer.

Married to Bob Lerman, living in Cazenovia, New York, east of Syracuse, she wrote *Call Me Ishtar*, and the splash it made opened some doors but closed others. The door that closed was at Syracuse University, where she had gone to study writing in the graduate program because she wanted literary mentorship. But when *Ishtar* came out, she was in an odd situation. Students in M.F.A. programs don't usually publish books that get great reviews in *The New York Times*. The head of the writing program, a novelist named George P. Elliott, called her into his office. He didn't congratulate her. He said she may have gotten a good review, but no man would like her book. She quit the program. Arguably, she had never needed it. Later she herself would teach writing courses at Syracuse and at the University of Colorado at Boulder, among other places.

The door that opened was to a group of people she called futurists. When I asked for a name to associate with this group, she gave me that of William Irwin Thompson. *Wikipedia* revealed that Thompson was a professor of humanities at MIT who left the academy in the early 1970s to pursue, with other scientists and artists, his interest in a new planetary consciousness, founding the Lindisfarne Association, a New Age think tank in Crestone, Colorado. Some of the other members of the Lindisfarne Association were Gregory Bateson, the anthropologist; his daughter Mary Catherine Bateson; Stewart Brand, the author of the *Whole Earth Catalogue*; Robert Lawlor, the author of *Sacred Geometry*; Elaine Pagels, the scholar of religion; and Gary Snyder, the poet. Lindisfarne was named in honor of the group of early Christian monks on a North Sea island who had, according to Thompson, effected a change from one system of consciousness to another, as well as holding on to ancient knowledge in violent times. Among Thompson's other beliefs were that all religions had begun with the worship of a universal Mother Goddess and that *Finnegans Wake* was the greatest book ever written. He believed in something he called "Wissenkunst" or "knowledge-art," a coinage based on the German word for science, "*Wissenschaft*." Wissenkunst is "the play of knowledge in a world of serious data processors." In Thompson's view of literary evolution, the epic was the genre of the agricultural-warrior society, the novel was the genre of industrial-bourgeois society, and Wissenkunst, examples of which were the scholarly fictions of Borges and Stanislaw Lem, is the literary form of our own apocalyptic moment, when the universe is breaking through to some new form of consciousness. "At the edge of consciousness, there are no explanations," he wrote. "There are only invocations of myth." It is easy to see why the Lindisfarne people were interested in the author of *Call Me Ishtar* and how they in turn had an impact on some of her later novels, especially *The Book of the Night.*

Much of this I did not know as I talked to Rhoda. Some, she touched on. She told me that although she was a person with her feet very much on the ground, she employed a psychic to talk to her dogs, alive and dead. When the psychic ("animal communicator") first spoke to Ishtar, one of Rhoda's matriarch Newfies, she said, "It's a privilege to communicate with such a wise being." Rhoda assured me, "This woman is for real. She only does dogs. Well, once she told me about a cat. This cat was sick and couldn't wait to die so she could go to Heaven and have a cigarette. You can't make up stuff like that."

This was all fascinating. It was fascinating to learn, too, that through the futurists she had met Curtis Roosevelt, the son of Eleanor and Franklin's daughter, Anna, and it was Curtis who convinced her to write about Eleanor. One thing leads in ways we can never imagine to another.

But what I really wanted to talk to Rhoda Lerman about was Grace Paley. I knew she would be a fan, as devoted as I am. I asked her who her favorite fiction writer was, certain it would be Grace Paley. It was Norman Mailer. I was stunned. "What do you like about Norman Mailer? I mean, not that he isn't terrific. But you? Norman Mailer? Okay, you like Norman Mailer. The voice. The testimony. The authenticity. The pugnacity. I get that. But you do like Grace Paley, right?"

She hadn't read Grace Paley.

She did not, she told me, read much fiction.

She mentioned *The Singing Neanderthals* as the kind of book she enjoyed. Subtitled *The Origins of Music, Language, Mind, and Body*, it posits that the ability to generate rhythmic sounds is connected to the evolution of our body and that music preceded language as our species evolved.

John Anthony West was another person whose work she admired. He and another archaeologist had discovered signs of rain erosion at the base of the Sphinx and the Pyramids, which suggested that they predated the dessication of the Sahara and hence were much older than anyone thought.

Another favorite was Laird Scranton, a software designer who has studied the beliefs and symbolism of the Dogon of Africa. The Dogon, Rhoda explained, have advanced cosmological and astronomical knowledge, including knowledge of an invisible star next to Sirius. "The Dogon—I don't want to say myths—explanations of the origins of the universe and Stephen Hawking's are the same, and Laird Scranton put them together.

"In the ancient language, before 4000 B.C., the letters *P* and *R* indicated 'river.' 'Para' meant 'river.' Paris, Paraguay. The original name for the Amazon was Para. 'Paradise' is simply 'two rivers.' Cross-Atlantic sailors in those ancient days named the rivers for their gods, the river of Is, the river of Og, the river of Mus. Paramus. Mus was a reptile god, muse, music, messiah, moses. Mus was ugly. Think of the Yiddish word *miskeit*. This comes from Cyrus Gordon's work. He discovered that Jewish and Phoenician sailors followed ocean currents to the New World in biblical times, some of them sent by King Solomon. The Amazon was a Spanish name, a later name, but part of the river is still called Solimeno, for Solomon."

Rhoda loves learning. To prepare to write *God's Ear*, she studied mysticism with a Hasidic rabbi. For *Animal Acts* she studied gorilla behavior and interviewed gorilla experts all over the country. For *The Book of the Night* she studied Irish monasticism and became close to a Benedictine community near her home in Binghamton. Learning and teaching are connected in her mind with her father, whom she lost too soon. "Distant father, search for knowledge. Father equals knowledge," she explains.

When I first talked to Rhoda on the phone, she had alluded to her ten-year withdrawal from publishing. She was discouraged by the response to her books. She said, "I couldn't do any better." I understood perfectly. I agreed that she couldn't do any better than *God's Ear*, and if people did not want to read that novel, what was the point of writing more? But now, as we talked at her friend's West Side apartment, she said again, "I couldn't do better," and I thought to ask, "Better than what?" "Better than *The Book of the Night*. That's my best book. And *In the Company of Newfies*. Dog people love that book. It's their bible. They ask about *Call Me Ishtar*, 'Is it about dogs?' When they find out it isn't, they're not interested."

Leaving the Newfies aside, how could she think that her worst book was her best? Here, I said to myself, was a first-rate novelist hijacked by weirdos to sing loony tunes. We drank from different pools after all. I was on Bob's side of the mystical/rational split. My grandfather came from Vilna and studied at the Kovno yeshiva. I wouldn't be surprised if we were descended from the Vilna Gaon. I believe in narrative. Rhoda believes in theories. She is a visionary *Wissenkunstler.* I am a bourgeois-industrial critic. She is open to the universe. I am not.

But I wanted to be. For Rhoda's sake. Because I really like her. And perhaps she's right. Perhaps I have approached everything with the wrong side of my brain. Rhoda had said to me in an e-mail, "My sense is that you are about to truly open yourself to the universe . . . let the other brain take over." What would it be like if I did open myself to the universe? If I let the other brain take over? How exactly would I do that? If you are purpose-driven and led by reason, how do you surrender to the Force? When I just play cards and eat the bridge mix, I lose. When I think sideways, I get hit by a delivery boy on a bike.

I thought the Newfy book might help me. Among nonhuman consciousnesses, my preferred consciousness is that of dogs, so I read *In the Company of Newfies*, and it did help. Along with John Muir's *Stickeen* and J. R. Ackerley's *My Dog Tulip*, it's about the best dog book I know, and dogs are the best cure there is for the human condition.

It begins with an absorbing account of the whelping of a litter and the subsequent months of care until the puppies' time of extreme vulnerability is passed. Other chapters are about individual dogs—Ben, the patriarch; Ishtar, who looked unpromising but turned into a champion; Molly, mother of the new brood of puppies; Pippa, the maiden aunt who helped

Molly with child care until she became a mother herself just when we were beginning to despair for her; and my favorite, Toby, the bad boy. It reads like a collection of short stories.

Sadly, the other dogs never accepted Toby. They knew he was a newcomer, not really part of the pack, and the hostility between him and the others made Rhoda and Bob decide that they would have to place him somewhere else. With infinite delicacy, they kept bringing Toby back to their house from his new one so he would not feel abruptly displaced, but every visit was made shorter and shorter. When Toby left for the last time, Rhoda cried, and so did I reading about it.

Newfoundlands are remarkable animals, known for their gentleness and loyalty. They were bred for ocean rescue work. Their huge bones and muscles give them the power to swim against waves, and they have webbed feet and water-shedding coats. J. M. Barrie immortalized his Newfy as Nana, the child-caring dog in *Peter Pan*. They are in fact good with children, if they don't happen to fall on them. They are huge, almost like bears. A large dog, one you could see in Central Park and wonder how he'd fit into a New York apartment, might weigh eighty pounds. Rhoda's dogs routinely weigh between 130 and 170.

Until I read *In the Company of Newfies*, I did not fully realize how immersed in dogginess Rhoda was. It is one thing to know that someone breeds dogs. It's another to realize they are feeding a half dozen puppies every two hours round the clock for the first weeks of the puppies' life, to realize that they have to keep the mother from inadvertently hurting her offspring and from intentionally harming any other dog that comes too near them. Imagine the work of dealing with an infant, the constant tension, the physical exhaustion, and multiply that by the size of a litter of dogs. And Rhoda is not a breeder who gives up on any life. If a puppy is deformed, like her dog Celeste, whose front legs didn't develop well, Rhoda stops at nothing—orthopedics, acupuncture, medicine, or surgery—to rehabilitate her. She is fiercely on the side of life.

It is hard to accept that my Rhoda Lerman, the writer, is a person who calls a female dog a bitch and a male a dog, who discusses bloodlines, who is friends with people with portraits of their dogs on the walls instead of portraits of their ancestors, who goes in "Newfy caravans" to distant dog shows, with playpens and grooming paraphernalia on the roof of the van, the dogs in crates inside, who walks them, washes them, trains them, exercises them, disciplines them, encourages them, feeds them, studies them, communicates with them, sleeps with them, who talks of champion canines with the reverence I reserve for Alice Munro and takes the Westminster Kennel Club Show as seriously as I do the Guggenheim fellowships. But this is the case. She has a full other life with her dogs and the many people devoted to them. She belongs to a whole other ecosystem. "There is more to life," as Grace Paley said, "than just writing."

Okay, okay, I promise to stop with Grace Paley. I will try to open myself up to who and what Rhoda is, a person with a way-out imagination, a magnificent writer, a person with mystical leanings who likes things to connect, a person who's gotten kinder and perhaps less inclined to laugh as time goes on, a person who spends her days and nights with her pack. I will try not to dismiss the time-bending antics and wordplay out of hand. Or the evolutionary theories. Or the ones about King Solomon and South America. All that is Rhoda—Rhoda who is part dog, part dolphin, part Lillywhite, part

Ishtar, part talking cow, and wholly wonderful. Whatever it means, I will try to be more open. I feel lighter and larger already. I can't wait to get in touch with Vinny, my beloved Yorkie who passed to the other world a year ago. Belief has its privileges.

*Five*

# WOMEN AND FICTION:
# A QUESTION OF PRIVILEGE

SOMETHING WAS BOTHERING ME. BESIDES RHODA Lerman, there were two other women on the shelf. Only two? Yes, only two. Three out of eleven writers, 27 percent. Eight books by women out of thirty books on the shelf—the same percentage, 27. You might think that the number of women authors on a somewhat randomly chosen shelf of books has no significance. But that turns out not to be true. In 2010 the literary organization VIDA began surveying the number of books by women as opposed to the number of books by men reviewed in major American publications. In *The Atlantic*, ten books by women were reviewed as opposed to forty-three books by men (23 percent); in *The New Yorker*, nine books by women as opposed to forty-five books by men (20 percent). *The New York Times Book Review* did best, with 283 books by women to 807 books by men (35 percent). *The New Republic* and *The New York Review of Books* did the worst, with percentages respectively of 14 and 16. The average for the group of six publications, which also included *Harper's Magazine*, was 23 percent. The survey was repeated the following year, and the results were up, but only slightly. So the 27 percent representation of women on my shelf is not out of line. How can it be that half the population—the half that does most of the novel reading and book buying—produces only 27 percent of the novels in a random sample? I began my experiment in reading to avoid the gatekeepers—the reviewers, the prize committees, the college curriculum designers—yet, fee fi fo fum, I sniff gatekeeping.

Let's ignore for the moment how women might still be being filtered out of prestige locations, and let's go back to the fundamental question of women and literary achievement, the question Virginia Woolf raised in *A Room of One's Own*. What conditions are necessary for women to produce great literary work? Woolf's answer was, to begin with, down-to-earth, practical, material. Women need an income and time and space to themselves in order to write—metaphorically, five hundred pounds a year income and rooms of their own. When Woolf was writing, in 1927, married women had only had the right to own property since the year of her birth. So women, as a class, were poor, and Woolf believed that their poverty affected their creative power in subtle as well as obvious ways. For one thing, they were not educated as well as men. If they were lucky, they might attend the women's college at Oxford or one of the two women's colleges at Cambridge that existed at that time. But even there they would see, from the austerity of their own surroundings and the splendor of the men's colleges, what relative value their society put on their minds and the minds of their brothers. This, in turn, would affect their self-confidence, and more than anything else except talent, self-confidence is what an artist requires, a belief that what you have to say, or the vision of the world that you feel it in yourself to convey, is important.

Here the argument shifts from the economic to the psychological underpinnings of creativity. The sense of self and entitlement to speak were very tenuous in Virginia Woolf herself, and of course she was writing autobiographically. Although her father was a learned man and something of a philosopher, he was a classic Victorian patriarch who did not believe that his daughters should be educated. Their brother went to Cambridge, but Vanessa and Virginia Stephen were made to stay at home and run their father's household, until he died and they were freed to live their own lives. Virginia never quite recovered from the unfairness of her domestic servitude, the sacrifice of her potential, as she saw it, to that of the male side of her family, and this psychic wound was the source of a sustaining combativeness, just as Dickens's childhood trauma of being made to work in a blacking factory instead of going to school shaped his life in its sympathies and resentments.

In an unforgettable section of *A Room of One's Own*, Woolf imagines a sister for Shakespeare, an equally gifted sister, named Judith. Will is sent to school. Judith stays at home and is uneducated. He becomes a playwright in London. She, Cinderella-like, becomes the household servant. When her father produces a husband for her, she runs away to London to be a playwright like her brother, or an actress. But she is laughed at: women can't write; women can't act. A playwright named Nick Greene takes pity on her, which means he sleeps with her and gets her pregnant. In despair, Shakespeare's sister ends her own life. What presents itself in some part as melodramatic spoof is an autobiographical, compensating fantasy: Why am I, Virginia, not as great as Shakespeare? Because I have been hounded, confounded, and driven to stifle my own talent. I am not Shakespeare because I'm his sister.

The sustaining combativeness I referred to was Woolf's

feminism, which gave her a way of understanding the world and justifying to herself the role she played in it. She was what she was because she was a woman. She hadn't been allowed to have the wide experience of a Tolstoy. But even more important than experience was the ability to transcend anger. She called this state "the androgynous mind" and saw it as a state of consciousness in which all of the artist's sense of his or her own individuality was burned away. For Woolf, even Charlotte Brontë and George Eliot seemed too aware of being women, too angry, to be writing at the highest level.

Woolf was writing in the 1920s and 1930s. Now we are in the twenty-first century. Women write at that masterly level, transcending gender, which Woolf could only envy. Alice Munro, Annie Proulx, Hilary Mantel come to my mind, and there are dozens more. So if incandescence is the criterion, I think we've made some headway. And yet women novelists are still not where they should be.

V. S. Naipaul, winner of the Nobel Prize in Literature, should be able to explain the mystery. Why are women writers not more respected? The question was put to him by a member of the press, and he replied forthrightly. There are no great women writers because all women suffer from "sentimentality, the narrow view of the world." And yes, he is more than willing to include Jane Austen, whose "sentimental ambitions" and "sentimental sense of the world" he could not possibly share. As another example of female triviality, he offered up his former editor, who wrote an astonishing memoir about her old age, wholly unsentimental in most people's usage of the word, though not, I suspect, Naipaul's. He seems to use the word "sentimental" in the eighteenth-century sense, to refer to any discussion of feelings or any display of sensitivity. She was a great editor, said Naipaul, but when she started to publish her own writing, "Lo and behold, it was all this feminine tosh. I don't mean this in any unkind way."

Naipaul, whom I think of as Sir Grumpus Maximus, belongs to a dying breed, at least in the literary world. More representative of the present moment is Really Good Guy, who lives in New York and works as an editor at a really good publishing house. Guy blogs and tells this story about a road-to-Damascus moment he had one day when lunching with a woman editor friend. "I was going on about some novel I was reading and loving and she cut me off and asked, when was the last time you read fiction by a woman? And I honestly couldn't come up with anything for a few minutes. It was a pretty shameful moment . . . because I've spent a lot of time advocating the reading of books outside of the reader's direct experience as a way of understanding the world . . . and apparently I've been ignoring the literary output of half the human population." We know Guy hasn't been ignoring half the population, but that is his way of reminding us he is a Really Good Guy who knows he shouldn't ignore half the population. I can't hold anything against Guy, even this sneaky rhetorical trick, because I like him so much. I don't see his picture on the blog, but I bet he is good-looking.

Guy knows from observation that "women are willing to buy books by male writers, but men seem much more reluctant to buy books by women. And while I've never seen it quantified in any way, there's definitely a feeling out there that men—even when writing about frivolous subjects—are taken more seriously as literary writers and are more likely to be presented to serious readers by the various literary gatekeepers." With characteristic optimism and readiness to roll with the zeitgeist, Guy welcomes the coming "bookquake" in the publishing industry as a chance to "disintermediate" some of those gatekeepers and their incredibly enduring biases. But I don't know. As much as I would like to disintermediate the gatekeepers, I don't think the cure is that easy. Guy's personal solution was to make himself read a book by a woman for every one he read by a man. He is embarrassed about the idea ("This sounds stupid, I know"), but as I suspect he knows I would, I find his solution lovable and, could it be legislated, highly effective, solving all kinds of problems, including, probably, the one of respect for women writers.

In 2001 Jonathan Franzen published *The Corrections*, a great novel—great in every sense of the word, big and capacious—and, in what has become a notorious sequence of events, Oprah Winfrey, who was still doing her immensely powerful daily TV talk show, chose it for her book club. Selection by Oprah's Book Club, with its coveted *O* logo on the cover of a jacket, meant an extra print run and possible sale of a half million copies. It offered, too, an appearance on her show and the chance to be interviewed by her gracious and intelligent self, a massive bookselling opportunity. Oprah was at that time the heroine of the publishing industry, its savior, some said, who used her own media time to sell books. How could you not love what she was doing? But she was selling literature to an audience almost exclusively of women. And that made Franzen nervous. He did not want to be identified as a writer of domestic fiction, a women's writer. Although his novel concerned an American family and the tensions between the old-fashioned midwestern parents and their sophisticated yuppie children, classic matter for domestic fiction, he worried about being penned into the lesser category rather than vaulted into the greater one of serious literary fiction. First in an interview with an Oregon magazine and then on NPR, he expressed discomfort with the Oprah association.

> So much of reading is sustained in this country, I think, by the fact that women read while men are off golfing or watching football on TV or playing with their flight simulator or whatever. I worry—I'm sorry that it's, uh—I had some hope of actually reaching a male audience and I've heard more than one reader in signing lines now at bookstores say "If I hadn't heard you, I would have been put off by the fact that it is an Oprah pick. I figure those books are for women. I would never touch it." Those are male readers speaking.

Understandably, Franzen didn't want his book narrowed in its appeal. Women routinely anguish over the same thing, but there is little they can do about it. Every woman who writes, as Joyce Carol Oates has said, thinks of herself as a writer but is thought of by others as a woman writer.

Offended by Franzen's comments, Oprah Winfrey canceled his appearance on her show. Most people in the publishing industry sided with Oprah. Franzen was not only unmannerly and ungrateful, he was naïve, saying what more prudent writers would not allow themselves to say: men don't read women's books, and if you seek admission to the exclusive circle of Great American Novelists, it is the kiss of death to be loved by women.

At the same time, it is the kiss of death not to be loved by women, who buy most books. This makes the current male contenders for the Great Novelist title a little mealymouthed compared with the boisterous, woman-disrespecting Great American Novelists of yesteryear, Updike, Roth, and Mailer. I included the "uh" and hesitations and apologies in quoting Franzen to show that he and Guy have learned their style in the same self-deprecating, apologetic school of masculinity, far different from the previous generation's chest-thumping. But the difference is largely one of style. The Really Good Guys know they should respect women writers, but it doesn't come naturally.

For Joe Pubgoer it's different. He doesn't even try. In England, four hundred women and four hundred men were questioned about which novels had seen them through life crises—the researchers called them "watershed" moments. They discovered large differences between the reading habits of men and women. Women use fiction as a way of understanding life, and they read metaphorically, seeing, for example, that the specific problems of a governess in Victorian England may not be their problems, but that *Jane Eyre* nonetheless may have personal meaning for them. Joe considers reading itself a female activity, and he wants little to do with it. He watches sports on TV for narrative excitement. He doesn't like to admit that he has had any watershed moments, but if he has, he certainly hasn't turned to fiction to help him through them. If he reads at all, he goes for action and adventure stories. He likes stories with a theme of overcoming obstacles. But more and more, as he ages, he reads only nonfiction. If he ever were to use a novel as a guide to life, he would do so quite literally, as though the novel were a handbook. "Between [the ages of] 20 and 40, many men we talked to openly showed an almost complete lack of interest in reading which drew them into personal introspection, or asked them to engage with the family and the domestic sphere."

Maybe Joe's sense of his own masculinity is as tied up with not reading as it is with loving soccer. Even worse, there may be something in his biological programming that works against his reading. Imagine him, Cro-Magnon, spear in hand, defending his family. He has to ward off the aggressor. He has to go chase down an antelope for dinner. Does he have time to read *Jane Eyre*? Of course not! Does it help him in his evolutionary quest to think of the antelope's feelings? No! A good, rousing adventure story might work him up to confront the foe—or give him some tips on tricky trapping techniques. Pornography might help too. A good sex scene might get him worked up enough to father a new generation, ward off the neighbor, and kill an antelope, all in one day. But a story about feelings? The family? What evolutionary purpose could that possibly serve?

I love this kind of explanation as much as anyone. We are all, Americans particularly, in love with evolutionary biology, which has settled the question of differences between male and female nature so vexing to the 1960s generation of feminists. Does a difference exist between male nature and female nature? Does it matter? Evolutionary biology has taught us that of course there's a difference, for all kinds of good reasons. "Researchers have discovered that female chacma baboons with strong sororal bonds have lower levels of stress hormones, live significantly longer and rear a greater number of offspring to independence than do their less socialized peers." And the like. But does this mean that women writers cannot be respected? Does it mean that men can never be brought to enjoy domestic fiction?

Poor Jonathan Franzen. Ten years after he walked into his first flap about women and fiction, he walked into another. He published another excellent novel, about a midwestern family, a woman who feels she hasn't lived fully enough, a man who takes up with a younger woman, children who follow the usual unusual bumpy paths through life. Again, this was the turf of domestic fiction, traditionally the realm of women, and this time some women writers (and I mean women writers, not writers who are women) got offended because Franzen was being praised for dealing with material for which they were routinely scorned. That he received two great reviews in one week from *The New York Times* particularly bothered Jodi Picoult, who tweeted, wouldn't it be nice if the *Times* paid attention occasionally to someone other than its "white male darlings." Another popular writer of books about women, Jennifer Weiner, caught the pass and ran with it. "I think it's a very old and deep-seated double standard that holds that when a man writes about family and feelings, it's literature with a capital L, but when a woman considers the same topics, it's romance, or a beach book—in short, it's something unworthy of a serious critic's attention." Picoult and Weiner outsell Franzen by millions (there are fourteen million copies of Picoult's books in print). But the point is respect. They want to be respected as writers. And respect decreases as sales increase. It is one strike against them that they're women and another strike that they sell lots of books. Their irritation makes no sense and yet is perfectly understandable. Of course they are writers. Did those books spew themselves into being from some gooey feminine core? No, they were constructed sentence by sentence, day after dedicated day, and their authors want people to recognize that. They aren't playing jacks. And probably if they were, men would want to do that too, and call it jacks for the women but war games for the men.

Decades ago, the ways in which writing by women could be dismissed were wittily chronicled by Joanna Russ. Denial of agency: *She didn't write it.* (Her husband or lover did, or her own "masculine side.") Pollution of agency: *She wrote it, but she shouldn't have.* (It's unwomanly—coarse, shrill, and limited.) Double standard of content: *She wrote it, but look what she wrote about.* (Women, family, kitchen, children.) False categorizing: *She wrote it, but it isn't really art.* (It's a thriller or a romance, chick lit or young adult, sci-fi or children's literature.) Isolation: *She wrote it, but she wrote only one of it.* (What has she written besides *Wuthering Heights? Frankenstein?*) Anomalousness: *She wrote it, but she is a special case.*

Joanna Russ's book was built on and was part of a wave of work in the late 1960s and 1970s by such literary critics as Ellen Moers (*Literary Women*), Mary Ellmann (*Thinking About Women*), Patricia Meyer Spacks (*The Female Imagination*), Elaine Showalter (*A Literature of Their Own*), Kate Millett (*Sexual Politics*), and Gilbert and Gubar (*The Madwoman in the Attic*) who paid new attention both to the context of women writers of the nineteenth century and to their reception over time. Partly thanks to their work, some forms of suppression in literary criticism are hard to maintain, for example claiming that a woman didn't really write the work she wrote. This lasted well into the 1980s. When Beryl Markham's *West with the Night*, about her experiences as a pilot in Africa in the Hemingway era, was reissued and made the bestseller list, word spread that she couldn't possibly have written the book and that her husband did. I haven't heard this one recently, and the charge of unwomanliness has lapsed entirely. But the double standard of content is still with us. If *The Corrections* risked diminishment just by being championed by a woman, think how much less important it would have seemed if it had been written by a woman. We think we have come far in surmounting gender bias, from the nineteenth-century world in which Mary Ann Evans called herself George Eliot and Charlotte Brontë called herself Currer Bell to hide their sex, but J. K. Rowling's publisher may have been right to take no chances. Who knows if the Harry Potter books would have been as successful with Joanne's feminine name on the title page.

False categorizing, too, is still with us. False categorizing is what made Jodi Picoult so angry. It's perhaps the most potent continuing form of suppression of women's writing. Such and such is popular—or women's fiction (I can't bring myself again to use the term chick lit, which exists only to dismiss). It doesn't count as literature. False categorizing is especially insidious if we include false dichotomies. Feelings are feminine, thoughts are masculine. Detail is feminine, abstraction is masculine. Concern with the individual, especially the individual woman, is feminine. Concern with the world and with history is masculine. Family is feminine, war masculine.

When V. S. Naipaul trumpeted his superiority at the Royal Geographical Society (for that's where it happened!), he included the boast that within a paragraph or two he could tell whether something had been written by a man or a woman. *The Guardian* obligingly produced a ten-passage test in which one could match one's gender-sniffing abilities against Naipaul's. Naturally, I took the test. I've always done well on tests and thought I could do well on this one. I had my own theory of what was male prose and what was female, involving greater specificity, more detail, in women's prose. This served me well. An appreciation of hard-boiled eggs led me to identify Margaret Atwood as a woman. Irony about American foreign policy identified John Irving as a man. The words "Love, thick and dark as Alaga syrup," with their poetic construction and specificity of reference, helped me nail Toni Morrison's gender. When I was wrong, it was usually on passages that seemed too obviously female. I had to back-engineer my answer and often guessed wrong. A discussion of virginity seemed so female that it had to be male, I thought. But it was by a woman, Zadie Smith, writing about a man. A soupy passage about a woman, all relationships and concern with appearance, was by Nicholas Sparks.

By sending this test around to some friends, I learned what good, close readers most of them are, picking up nuances of style, whether they thought those nuances suggested male or female authorship. More than that, it showed how competitive my friends are, male and female. All wanted to do well on the test. Only one person refused to take it, saying it didn't interest her. The rest of us were sucked into Naipaul's false categories. My own score was 70 percent. Not very good, the test taker in me said, but not bad enough, said the feminist. I had proven Naipaul's point. It was possible to tell women's prose from men's. It took me much ruminating about this before I could come up with the right answer: So what? False dichotomy plus double standard of values. Screw Sir Grumpus. I don't mean this in any unkind way, but if some women are missing an abstraction gene that prevents them from writing "like men," some men are missing a relationship gene that prevents them from living like mensches. No more extreme example of this than Sir Grumpus, who lived in a bubble of disdain for others, as self-absorbed as Gertrude Stein but without her affability.

Gertrude Stein. The very name brings me back to the theme of false categorizing. Note, for one thing, that Stein disobeyed a primary restriction against women and loudly tooted her own horn. Note that she did nothing but benefit from this. By saying over and over (or putting the words into the mouth of Alice B. Toklas) that she was a genius, she came to be taken seriously more quickly than if she had not spoken up. In fact she created the category "genius" and put herself into it. ("Only three times in my life have I met a genius," she has Alice B. Toklas say, referring to Picasso, Alfred North Whitehead, and Stein.) Most women tend to be modest about their achievements and do themselves no good thereby.

Note, too, that Stein has always been considered a special case. Just as Willa Cather has been a special case. Courses on modernism routinely include James Joyce and T. S. Eliot and have started to include Woolf as well. But much more often Woolf was put into the false category, the socially defined and therefore minor category, of "Bloomsbury," if not the socially defined and therefore minor category of "woman novelist." When major aesthetic movements were being charted by cultural historians, these women were left out. To me they are all modernists, and had they gained respect as modernists instead of as anomalous women, they would have been respected sooner and more robustly. I would add to the group Colette, who is always treated as a woman more than a writer, but who, in her blurring of boundaries between fiction and memoir, her offbeat narrative rhythms, is as much a modernist as the other three— Woolf, Cather, and Stein.

There's a way of suppressing respect for women writers that Joanna Russ didn't mention, unless I have not understood her categories and this is somehow included. It is pointing to the woman writer and accusing her of privilege. What shall we call this? False populism? It's bait-and-switch class warfare in

which women, who might well be considered a class in themselves, are attacked for belonging to the middle class—or, heaven
save us, the upper class—by male critics who are themselves
usually middle-class but speak as though they were working a
twelve-hour shift in a steel mill. The woman writer enjoys a
privilege that offends them. Her focus on family and relationships seems trivial. Her way of getting at truth seems indirect
and banal. Her feel for the specific detail verges on an obsession
with brands.

I hate to keep picking on Jonathan Franzen, whose work I
love, but a piece he wrote on Edith Wharton provides a good
example. Her wealth is off-putting to him. It constitutes a
problem in sympathy. "No major American novelist has led a
more privileged life than Wharton did. Although she was sel-
dom free of money worries, she always lived as if she were."
Like a husband whose wife doesn't appreciate how hard he
works to make a living for her, Franzen is upset that Wharton
lived *as if* she had no money worries, although she did have
them. "Privilege like hers isn't easy to like; it puts her at a
moral disadvantage." Privilege, however, is in the eyes of the
beholder. Many of us see a male writer like Hemingway as
privileged, in his freedom to live as he chooses, to experience
what he wants, to fish, to fuck, to fight, to write, whatever,
while Hadley or Pauline or Martha or Mary takes care of getting dinner on the table, the laundry done, and the children
put to bed. So far as I know, no one has ever raised the issue of
privilege as an obstacle to appreciating Hemingway, Henry
James, John Cheever, or Gore Vidal. Privilege was exactly the
issue Virginia Woolf was getting at in *A Room of One's Own*
and later *Three Guineas*—male privilege.

The biggest obstacle, however, to respect for women's

writing results from the way many of us were trained, in reading, to see women as specialized and different but men as universal. As a young woman, I identified with Dorothea Brooke, Isabel Archer, and Elizabeth Bennet, but not Lord Jim, not Gatsby, not Nick Adams. Yet I was continually asked by teachers and professors to read books about men as though their gender were unimportant. Thus many of us—male and female—learned to read men's novels as though they were larger and deeper than novels by women. If a woman were to say *"Moby-Dick* has no women in it, so I won't read it," a whole academic enterprise exists to convince her that she should read it. Ahab's quest for the white whale or Gatsby's quest for Daisy become types of human desire with social and spiritual resonance. The same can be done for books by women, but it takes time and dedication.

I remember exactly when I was told that Jane Austen's novels were not about marriage, but about money. I sat in a large lecture hall with hundreds of other undergraduates at Harvard in a course called The Nineteenth-Century English Novel. The lecturer was Edgar Rosenberg, who later went on to teach at Cornell. He was funneling to us a new view of Austen that began with attention to her irony as a mechanism of moral and social criticism and a new recognition of her stature. Most of the critics who helped build Austen's reputation as a major English writer were men, but Edgar Rosenberg leaned heavily on the insights of one American critic, a woman named Dorothy Van Ghent:

> "It is a truth universally acknowledged, that a single man in possession of a good fortune must be in want of a wife." This is the first sentence of the book. What we

read in it is its opposite—a single woman must be in
want of a man with a good fortune—and at once we are
inducted into the Austen language, the ironical Austen
attack, and the energy, peculiar to an Austen novel, that
arises from the compression between a barbaric subsur-
face marital warfare and a surface of polite manners and
civilized conventions. Marriage—that adult initiatory
rite that is centrally important in most societies whether
barbarous or advanced—is the upper-most concern . . .
It is as primitively powerful an urgency as is sex in a
novel by D. H. Lawrence.

This was the most powerful cultural criticism I had ever encountered. "Falling in love" was a palliative cover-up for a
ruthless manhunt, with economic desperation at its heart? It
was the magic I'd come to college hoping to learn how to perform! Its insight came not from ideology or applying a gender
perspective—this was a decade before the women's movement—
but from a close reading of text, scrupulous attention to tone
and distance, purely literary techniques. Dorothy Van Ghent
had nowhere near the reputation of F. R. Leavis or Ian Watt.
She had no overarching theory. Her major book is merely a
series of magnificent readings of individual novels, and to develop a following in this line of work, you have to have a theory and a vocabulary. But I'm convinced that her influence is
felt in the way we respond to Jane Austen to this day.

These things happen in discussions of culture. Dickens was
a sentimental purveyor of family entertainment until literary
critics started praising his later novels over his earlier ones, em-
phasizing his darkness. Trollope was considered shallow, a
mere observer of manners, but he got larger the more he was

read and discussed. Horror movies, once brain-rotting junk, are now a formative experience for all sorts of speculation and fantasy, which are themselves more serious business than they used to be. Fluffy entertainments morph into weighty artifacts. If we've learned one thing, it's that cultural objects are malleable and change in time. Critics read them in the light of current needs and preoccupations. This is a normal process. It's part of what Shelley meant when he called artists "the unacknowledged legislators of the world." Changes in consciousness begin with art and take shape through discussion of art. But the process takes a long time and involves a lot of people working in many small ways.

If I were writing an update of *A Room of One's Own* today, I would try to create a character to match Shakespeare's sister. I would create a more entitled woman, someone with even more advantages than Virginia Woolf could imagine when she was writing in 1927. I would call her Prospero's Daughter.

My Prospero's Daughter lives in England—for me, an imaginary kingdom where everyone is articulate and witty, where women can have titles, where literature is the national sport. Exiled to this island by evil usurpers in his native land, Prospero brought with him his family traditions of respect for knowledge, love of art and music, and philosophical skepticism. He was a powerful wizard with the great gift of being able to explain his wizardry on television. He and his wife had four daughters. Miranda was the oldest. With no boys in the family, Prospero treated her as though she were his son. From the time she could talk, he took her education in hand. He started playing chess with her when she was four years old. A gifted mathematician, Miranda was treated as special, her father's heir, until she went to the university. This was the early 1960s, and for the first time she encountered remnants of the world Virginia Woolf had written about, including women instructors who had been trained to believe in their own inferiority. Miranda studied math with a woman who told her she would try to have her reassigned to a man because women weren't as good at math as men. Horrified, Miranda ran to a pay phone and called her father. "Is it true," she asked, "that women can't do math?" "That's rubbish," he said. But the damage had been done. Her relationship to math now became tentative. She moved into another field, history. The years of her education passed, and she started to teach and write. She wrote an original work and got an excellent teaching position. She fell in love with another historian and they married, but competing at the same job was hard, and they divorced. She raised their child alone, married again, and had two more children.

Now, although life was pleasant, it got very hard for her. She was teaching and writing. She was bringing up three children. When they were babies and toddlers, she was always exhausted. She had to get up in the night when they did. She didn't get enough sleep but still had to go to work the next day. Yes, she had child care, but it was always failing for one reason or another. Yes, she had help in the house, but it was never enough, and also, the help needed supervision and instruction. The children got sick. New arrangements had to be made. And always, there was laundry to be done, food to buy, food to cook, a messy household to live in, pathetic efforts to tidy up, classes to prepare, meetings to attend, newspapers and magazines to keep up with. Then the demands of the children became less physical: there wasn't diapering or so much laundry, but there were lessons to take the children to, performances at school to attend, teachers to talk to, doctors to be seen, and, as always, food to be bought and prepared, clothes to be shopped for. Most important, there were the relationships with the children, listening to them, answering them, directing, reassuring, and understanding them, containing one's anger at them sometimes, advising, encouraging, and guiding them—in short, bringing them up, hoping and trying at the same time to keep a living relationship with her husband.

Twenty-five years go by, endless and laden as they are being lived but seeming like a moment in retrospect. The children are gone. Now Miranda finds herself with lots of time, and she knows how to use it, accustomed as she is to squeezing the most out of every minute. She sets to work and writes brilliant books that no one but she could produce. She is seventy, but still in full swing. Her marriage is good. Her children are thriving. She is Dame Miranda. The only discrimination she has encountered in her life has been because of her gender, but she has lived a full life despite it. Her biggest problem has been balancing the demands of family and work. But this, although she doesn't complain about it—she would never have given up the joy of having children, the satisfaction of family life—is a big problem, the problem that a new version of *A Room of One's Own* would address. The main burden of family life still falls on women. Prospero's Daughter solved the problem by superhuman energy and by readjusting the life cycle, putting some of her creative work toward the end rather than the middle of her life, using productively the later years we often think of as leftovers. If you look at her life from the outside, you would say she was privileged, but she doesn't feel privileged. She feels overworked—until suddenly she has acres of time. It's far from being the gross servitude of Shakespeare's sister, but the burden of family is now the central issue of women and creativity, whether the creativity is expressed in novels or interior design schemes, litigation or business plans, cupcakes or algorithms.

Motherhood and their personal lives affect the professional lives of women who are writers as much as they do the professional lives of women who are bankers or lawyers, and it goes beyond balancing the time demands of family and career. Such women as Jodi Picoult may write novels that flow naturally from family life, and they may be very successful in some ways but wish for more respect. Another writer, Grace Paley, might feel the claims of family and community so strongly that she writes much less than her fans would want her to. Another Daughter of Prospero might foreswear children, find a nurturing husband, and write prolifically. Joyce Carol Oates took that path. Toni Morrison had race to contend with as well as gender as a factor in keeping her from getting the respect she deserved. It took a public demonstration on her behalf and a protest against her failure to be given prizes before the prizes were prised loose and started to come to her as regularly as she deserved.

Respect may come. We will become more accustomed to authority in women and the forms it takes—greatness not being incompatible, for example, with wanting to have one's hair done twice a week. I can imagine a culture in which self-deprecating men make tiny distinctions while women make connections between matters large and small and ponder the big questions that affect societies, even if they address these issues in a style incompatible with older ideas of dignity and seriousness. The one thing I suspect will not change is that men are not likely to start reading women's books. Fortunately, this is matter for the unacknowledged legislators and not for the elected ones.

Reading is almost always subversive. From the time you read the next night's fairy tale under the covers by flashlight when you have already had your bedtime story from Daddy and are supposed to be asleep to the time you are an adult reading junk, hoping no one catches you at it, reading is private; that's the most seductive thing about it. It's you and the book. Women's reading will respond to women's needs. Men's will respond to men's. And if men never begin to read fiction by women, well, as my mother always said to comfort me when I didn't get something I wanted (and it never failed to work), "It's their loss." We're all better off for enmeshing ourselves with what we are not, and that may best be done in love, but fiction works, too.

*Six*

# DOMESTICITIES: MARGARET LEROY AND LISA LERNER

I THINK THAT MARGARET LEROY IS JUST THE KIND OF novelist a man would not read. He might have trouble merely getting past the title of *Yes, My Darling Daughter.* I had some trouble myself. It comes from a nursery rhyme:

> *Mother, may I go out to swim?*
> *Yes, my darling daughter.*
> *Hang your clothes on a hickory limb,*
> *And don't go near the water.*

As the title of a Dinah Shore song of 1941, it was a familiar phrase in my childhood, and my mother used to quote it, her voice dripping with irony, when I made a demand on her she considered excessive.

Grace, the protagonist of this novel set in London, has an impossible child, a child so bad that she gets kicked out of nursery school. "We don't have the resources to deal with children as needy as Sylvie," Grace is told. Sylvie wakes up sobbing in the middle of the night, insisting that she wants to go home. When her mother assures her that she is home, she says again that she is not. She thinks that a coastal town in Ireland is her real home. She refuses to call Grace "Mum," calling her "Grace" to everyone's discomfort. She has an irrational fear of water, shrieking when she's splashed with soda. Dunking for apples at a children's party upsets her so disastrously that the party is ruined. When Grace comes home with a boyfriend, the four-year-old throws up on her mother's pretty new blouse. Eventually, she causes Grace to lose her job.

Isn't this a mother's fundamental fear? That her child's life will end her own? If your child turns out badly, if something goes wrong, how will you cope? You cannot turn your back. On the border between consuming love for one's children and consuming fear lies a rich ground for fiction to explore, and Margaret Leroy has found it.

The explanation of Sylvie's weirdness requires, however, a massive suspension of disbelief. Grace begins to suspect that Sylvie was traumatized in a previous life. Traumatized? She was murdered, drowned. Everything, water especially, reminds her of this. She obsessively draws pictures of the house she used to live in, in a town in the west of Ireland she recognizes from a photograph. In despair, Grace seeks out an academic who has researched the phenomenon of children who've lived before. (He holds an academic position but stands on shaky ground, as his colleagues in the psychology department do not respect his field of research.) He suggests that a trip to the town in Ireland that Sylvie remembers may bring about a cure. This man, Adam Winter, is handsome. All the men in this novel are handsome: Grace's married lover who is Sylvie's father, the one guy she dates, the guy who will try to burn her alive—they are all physically attractive. No paunches, no saggy eyes, no pitted cheeks. Will the visit to Ireland cure Sylvie, as the parapsychologist suggests? Yes it will. Will everything, in the English phrase, get "sorted"? Will Sylvie then start calling Grace "Mum"? Of course. The horrible story once told, Sylvie is free to live her own life. Silly as I found much of this novel, I couldn't put it down.

Other readers understood something that I did not—the book fits into a recognized genre, the gothic romance, like the novels of Victoria Holt. People who read gothics, says the reviewer for the *Library Journal* guardedly, may like getting to know Grace and Sylvie. Another reviewer says it may be enjoyed by "literary readers who like a touch of *Rebecca* in their reading." Note the precision of these recommendations. They resemble Web endorsements of recipes: if you like the taste of oregano, you will like this dish.

*Rebecca* is a distant if fond memory for me, but I am a fan of maternity horror stories. *Rosemary's Baby,* in which a woman is offered by her husband to the Devil and forced to give birth to the Devil's child, is perhaps the greatest of these, and note, for whatever the significance, that it was written by a man, Ira Levin. More realistically, without the gothic elements, Sue Miller's *The Good Mother* tops my list of favorites, in which a moment of innocent sexuality leads a mother to the brink of losing her child. Again a deep fear is mobilized—that if a woman maintains her sexual identity, she impairs her functioning as a mother. Losing a child one way or another is the ultimate maternal nightmare, and the movie that dramatized these fears in my own youth was *Kramer vs. Kramer.* I watched it with my fingers over my eyes, as though I were watching a horror film.

*Yes, My Darling Daughter* evoked a lower but still real level of horror—not the existential question of did the Devil father my child or the legal nightmare of deciding custody of a child in court, but the administrative horror of getting through a day with a child problem—or problem child:

> Sleep is a door I can't get through. I lie in my bed with open eyes, staring into the sepia dark of my room, at the clotted black that gathers in the corners and the delicate stippling of apricot light where the glow from the streetlight seeps in. Questions jostle in my mind. Can I find another nursery to take her at such short notice? And even if I manage it, will the same thing happen again? Will it just go on happening? What kind of life is now unfolding before us? I go through these questions again and again. I can't find any answers.

*Yes, My Darling Daughter* is not a great book—its premise is preposterous, the paranormal elements clumsily handled. Nonetheless, I could wish it were assigned reading for men. Let more men experience the terror of wondering where child care will come from next. It would be as useful a moral exercise as trying to imagine whether, like Lord Jim, we would abandon a sinking boat filled with strangers we are nominally responsible for. By and large, women don't have the choice of abandoning the ship.

An earlier novel of Leroy's on my shelf, *Postcards from Berlin*, is more satisfying. Again, it turns on a single mother with a child problem. In this novel the eight-year-old daughter is sick, but no one can figure out what's wrong with her. Eventually the doctors begin to suspect that the girl is not sick at all and that the mother is the problem—that she has MSBP, Munchausen's syndrome by proxy, in which a caregiver claims or causes illness in a child in order to satisfy psychological needs of her own. Another maternal horror story, and for me, another one that resonates. When my son was six weeks old, he began throwing up whatever he was fed. He lost so much weight that he was back to his birth weight. I took him to a pediatrician who diagnosed me as the problem. I was trying to work and be a mother at the same time. That was unnatural. He suggested I take a vacation. A second pediatrician diagnosed my son with pyloric stenosis, and an emergency operation fixed him right up.

As sympathetic as I was to the plight of the mother, Catriona, in *Postcards from Berlin*, she was so self-defeating in dealing with the doctors (why no second opinion?) and so weak in dealing with her daughter that I began to wonder if the doctors weren't right and this was a clever example of an untrustworthy narrator, with the mother suffering indeed from MSBP and creating her daughter's illness. She fit the profile. Abandoned by her own mother, she was raised in an orphanage, married young a man who controlled her completely, and devoted herself to their child, Daisy, and his child from a first marriage. The postcards of the title are from her mother, whom she has not seen or cared to see since childhood but who re-emerges just at the right moment, begging Catriona to contact her because she is dying. When, as a last resort, before Daisy is taken away from her, Catriona scoops her up and flees to her mother's home in Berlin, the mother reveals that Cat's father had celiac disease, a gastrointestinal problem that caused him to die young. That's the diagnosis. Not MSBP, but celiac disease, aggravated by allergies. The cure is a gluten-free diet.

A little strained—it takes a lot of plot device to keep Catriona from knowing sooner about celiac disease—a little rushed toward the end, but gripping. Many readers on Amazon testify that they find this a convincing and moving portrait of a mother's attachment to her child. That these readers were 85 percent women, by my count, didn't surprise me at all. Who would want to live in this world, the dreary world of post–World War II National Health Service bureaucratic Britain, who would want to spend imaginative time with these horrendous problems of maternity if one didn't, in some sense, have to?

It's no accident that Margaret Leroy writes the kind of books she does. She has spent the past twenty years raising two daughters, one of them with a serious illness. Raising children has been at the center of her life, yet as she complained in an interview on her publisher's website, it's rarely the focus of novels. The novel, she says, quoting David Lodge, is all about sex and hardly at all about parenting, whereas life is generally the other way around. She likes both to read and to write fiction that reflects her own concerns, her own experience. Who can blame her?

"The idea for *Postcards from Berlin* came from a difficult encounter with a pediatrician when our younger daughter was ill. And I also drew on the experience of my daughter's illness in *Yes, My Darling Daughter*, in writing about the loneliness of a woman who has a troubled child—though in that story the mother comes to suspect that her daughter's troubles may have a supernatural origin."

If her background as a mother shows in her novels, so does her training and employment, before she became a novelist, as a psychiatric social worker. Her first job required her to interview people being admitted to a hospital after attempting suicide. "As a social worker, you learn how people behave in extreme situations, under extreme pressure . . . You meet so many people who live lives of quiet heroism against terrible odds. But you also see a lot of cruelty, especially the cruelty of parents to children and men to women." Every case history is a story someone tells you, and the experience of listening to all those life histories, Leroy reports, helped shape her writing.

Before writing novels, she wrote a couple of nonfiction books related to her work in psychology and therapy. One in particular beckoned to me—*Pleasure: The Truth About Female Sexuality.* I certainly wanted to know the truth about female sexuality, so I ordered a copy from the online used-books market.

It arrived from England at an awkward moment. We had weekend visitors who were book mad and eager to see what book I had sent all the way to England to acquire. Not realizing it was *Pleasure: The Truth About Female Sexuality,* I opened the package in their presence—and started babbling an explanation. But whatever embarrassment I suffered was worth it. Because what Leroy reveals in this book is remarkable, especially to Americans who are used to pep talks about everything concerning sex.

In the early 1990s Leroy talked to fifty women of all ages about their personal experiences of sex at all stages of the life cycle, interested in how libido comes and goes, motherhood's effect, aging's effect. There is, at least in Britain, a whole lot less pleasure involved in sex as actually practiced by women than a man would want to think, and a whole lot more sensual pleasure in child care than is often acknowledged. Sex is organized for the most part around a man's pleasure and a man's fantasies, according to Leroy, and for many women, "fake it and forget it" is the order of the day. What she discovered was the extent to which women have been trained to adapt their sexuality—their image of themselves, the things they present themselves as enjoying—to suit the pleasure of men.

If I had planned it, I could not have chosen a better book to read as preparation for *Just Like Beauty* by Lisa Lerner, a novel, published in 2002, portraying a world in the near future where women are systematically trained to give men pleasure. I can't remember the last time I was shocked by something I read, but I was shocked by the opening of this novel. A girl is being trained by her mother, in preparation for a beauty pageant, to give a man a blow job, with particular attention to the use of the tongue. The girl, Edie, practices on a "polystroob" dummy, complete with facial and pubic hair (to accustom her to being scratched) and genitals. In this world of the future, where everything is artificial and the Just Like That Conglomerate produces most food and consumer goods, girls become pageant contestants at fourteen and have to participate in such events as Freestyle Walking, Poise and Cookery, Electric Polyrubber Man, and, hardest of all, Sacrificial Rabbit. Each girl must train a rabbit to do tricks: Edie's rabbit can bake a mini pie and then balance it on her nose. The rabbits display their skills at the pageant, and then their owners, who have come to love them deeply, must kill them, skin them, and turn their fur into muffs on sewing machines wheeled onstage for the purpose.

Most of this novel is pretty scary, especially the way teenage boys are permitted to terrorize girls. They are armed with blowtorches, and if you are "torcher-ed" you are out of the competition. The only people protesting this culture are a group who advocate "Happy Endings"—that is, suicide. Nature has completely disappeared. Only a few immigrant leftovers such as Edie's grandmother and the Italian family of Lana Grimaldi, Edie's beloved, value anything real, symbolized by their love of real food. *Just Like Beauty* is funny in the way people who tell an unpleasant truth are funny. You smile because just what you thought was true is true, and there's nothing funny about it. I think Electric Polyrubber Man, waiting to be pleasured, and the Sacrificial Rabbit—the enforced surrendering of what one loves in order to make a cute accessory—will haunt my dreams. But I could hardly blame a man if he didn't want to read this.

It was never part of my plan to contact the writers on my shelf, but I wanted to know something about Lisa Lerner I couldn't find out any other way. I was developing an interest in the shape of writers' lives, especially those of women. Why had she not written another novel in the ten years since *Just Like Beauty* was published in 2002? Like Rhoda Lerman, she seemed to have fallen silent. Why?

I had a strangely hard time finding her, considering that I believed she lived right across the East River in Brooklyn. She had a website for *Just Like Beauty*, but when I used the contact link and sent her an e-mail, I didn't get an answer. I noticed that the novelist Roxana Robinson had blurbed the book, and I know Roxana, so I e-mailed her and asked about Lisa. She replied that she had known her at MacDowell, the writers' colony, when Lisa was writing *Just Like Beauty*, but had lost touch. She thought that Lisa had adopted a daughter and more or less dropped off the face of the earth.

In the acknowledgments of her novel, Lisa thanked her editor, Becky Saletan, so I tracked down Becky, hoping she could give me current contact information. Becky had changed jobs two times since 2002, from Farrar, Straus and Giroux to Harcourt to Riverhead/Penguin, but someone who works in an office is not hard to find. Within minutes we were talking on the phone, and the story she told me was saddening.

She had loved that book. Everyone at FSG was excited about it. The sales director, Spenser Lee, was excited about it. The art director, Susan Mitchell, who worked on the cover, was excited about it. The graphic designer, Claire Williams, was excited about it. The editing had taken a long time. Becky couldn't reconstruct the process without her files, which were either back at the FSG offices or lost in cyberspace. But with work on the text and the designing and printing and working up the sales campaign, it had been about two years. Then it was reviewed in the daily *Times* by Richard Eder. She remembered the morning the review came out. When she woke up, her husband had already read the paper and said, "Becky, bad news. Your book got ripped apart." And after that, the book withered. It sold in French translation. It was optioned for the movies. But it never sold as well as the publisher and the author had a right to expect.

"I think she has to make a living. I don't think she could afford to write another novel. She has a child to support. Fortunately, there's another string to her bow, I forget what it is. Textbooks, maybe."

Every writer has one review they cannot forget and cannot forgive. For one of my friends it's Brad Leithauser's review, for another John Updike's. Mention the cursed name, and you'll hear a shriek or a gasp, and the story of the unforgivable assault is retold. "She said my characters do not have to work." Or "He used the word 'hysterical.'" Or "She said those things in *The Boston Globe*. The *Globe!*" My own nemesis review was one I never read. It was faxed to me, and my husband read it as it came in on the fax machine. His face turned white. I had never seen a face do that. It made an impression. He said, "Do not read this," and I never did. Perhaps that's why Becky Saletan's story of her husband breaking the bad news to her means a lot to me. Behind every book, behind every author, there's the friend or partner, lover or spouse, children and parents, brothers and sisters, agent, editor, the editor's or agent's friend or partner, lover or spouse, the sales director and the art director and their lovers and spouses perhaps as well, and brothers and sisters and children and parents, and all of them know that there has been a death in the family, the death of the book baby.

I had not read the Richard Eder review of *Just Like Beauty*, but now I looked it up. As shocked as I had been by *Just Like Beauty* itself, with its opening scene of the mother tutoring her daughter in oral sex, that's how shocked I was by Richard Eder's review. Because, discussing this novel, which for me concerned women bent out of shape to satisfy men's sexual desires, he didn't mention sex at all. For him the book is a satire of corporate capitalism. Its specific target is the Just Like That Conglomerate. It is "futuristic fiction" for which he has certain rules. Futuristic fiction must be grounded in the present, for example. But Lerner's grounding is "sketchy" and the satire gets out of hand.

Satire, like salt, wants using with some sense of the flesh it works upon. *Just Like Beauty* gets eclipsed at times in a salt-shaking whiteout. At Deansville's school, the teachers use thumbscrews and leg racks for discipline. A roving gang of teenage boys pursue Pageant's competitors with blowtorches and other implements of disfigurement.

Such excess might work, or at least pass, if the characters in Ms. Lerner's novel, her first, were able to achieve a hold on us. It is the plaintive present-day humanity of George [*sic*] Smith, and the deflected horse-humanity of Boxer, that connect us to the grotesque futures of Orwell's *Nineteen Eighty-four* and *Animal Farm*. It is the autumnal refusal of Bernard Knox that makes *Brave New World* more than abstractly credible. Jonathan Swift's mini-worlds allow us the plodding perplexity of Lemuel Gulliver.

Lerner is shoving Eder's nose in a polyrubber dummy's pubic hair, and he comes up spouting History of English Literature, Part 1. What I saw in this review was a man so threatened by a novel's subject that he cast about for ways to attack it without ever acknowledging what it was about. Few tasks are more thankless than trying to rebut a negative review, and there may be some truth in what he says, but the vicious overall dismissal needs explaining, and the explanation, I think, relates to gender. A fourteen-year-old girl being trained to please men was not able to "achieve a hold," evidently, on this seventy-year-old male reviewer. None of the women in this novel—Edie, her appalling mother, her spunky girlfriend Lana—registered on him at all.

I wanted more than ever to contact Lisa Lerner to find out how she had felt about this review, and as a last resort, I tried Facebook. There she was. I sent a friend request. She almost instantly confirmed me as a friend. I sent her a message, explaining my project and my desire to talk to her, and soon we had made a date to talk by phone the next day. Satisfied, I went to the gym for a workout. I have a trainer to whom I recount every detail of my day. I told her about looking for Lisa Lerner and finally finding her through Facebook. She stopped counting and looked at me, bewildered. "Why didn't you start with Facebook?"

There is, I now understand, a generational difference between people who use e-mail and people who use Facebook, Twitter, and text messaging. Plugged-in people like my trainer and Lisa Lerner rarely look at their e-mail, the Pony Express of communications. A friend who is a college professor says he has to tell students at the start of a semester that any changes in class schedule will be communicated by e-mail, so they must check their e-mail. Otherwise, they wouldn't.

Nevertheless, I had found her, and like Rhoda Lerman, she recognized the weirdness of the universe in the fact of my having come to her by randomly choosing the LEQ–LES shelf in the library.

"I never intended to write a novel," she told me. "I was a performance artist. I fall into everything I do through the back door. I came to New York to be involved in theater. My original idea for *Just Like Beauty* was a one-woman show. It grew into a novel. I wrote a whole draft of it and when I finished it, I hated it. I was absolutely bored by it. Literally, I threw it into the fire. I realized it left out the best part of me, my sense of humor. So I started again, and I wrote the first eight pages in a frenzy, what's now the prologue of the book. Then I started to have a great time. I'm glad I sacrificed the first draft. I was trying too hard to be taken seriously. I think a lot of people writing first novels are telling stories that they need to tell. It's a personal, cathartic, therapeutic endeavor that they're embarked on, making sense of the chaos inside them by organizing it on these pages. But that's not what a novel is. You have to be somewhat removed."

When the manuscript was finished for the second time, she sent a letter and the prologue to a dozen agents who had been recommended by other writers. The submission was so strong that many of them wanted to read the book, and from them, she chose Jane Gelfman, who in turn sold the book to Farrar, Straus and Giroux in June 2000. Then Becky entered the picture and worked with Lisa to edit the book, taking out a hundred pages. Lisa was easy to work with because she understood that she couldn't retain total control of her writing and didn't really want to. She thought she still had things to learn.

"The longest part was waiting to be published. It was two years from the time the book was bought until the time it appeared. I was really grateful to everyone who had anything to do with getting it published. Everything about that book was a joy to me and a gift. I wasn't upset at all by the Eder review. There had been a fabulous review in *The Sunday Times Book Review* a few days before, and I was still floating from that. I didn't expect to be reviewed in the daily, and I didn't care if it was bad. Everyone said Eder was an old curmudgeon. He was so befuddled, so violently opposed. Why did he bother to review it? He got so much wrong, he made so many errors of fact, the thing self-destructed. The *Times* had to print retractions and corrections for the next three days. But what do reviews amount to anyway? The great one boosted my Amazon rating for a couple of days, but that was it. My neighbor said, 'I saw you were reviewed in the *Times*. I didn't read it, but your picture looked great next to the crossword puzzle.'

"After that I dropped off the map. I decided to adopt a child as a single parent. I went to India and brought a toddler home from an orphanage in the south. Then it became a very crazy life. I wrote a couple of personal essays, but that was all

I could manage. I was a freelance writer and I was the bread-winner. I was both parents rolled into one. I was taking care of a child and I was trying to make a living. It was so precarious. Every day began with my breath held—would I get through it? I couldn't afford much child care. My mother died some years ago. My father is eighty-nine and lives on the Upper West Side. He helps me. It's so hard to be a single parent and a writer in New York. I know five people like that who've left the city."

One day Lisa was at the playground with her daughter and saw a woman with twins. She was well dressed and seemed to have everything in control. Lisa developed a fantasy about her, envying her the loving husband who supported her and helped with the kids. The two women started talking, and Lisa blurted out her fantasy. It turned out that the other woman was also a single mom who had decided to have a baby and had gone to a sperm bank. Now she has twins.

"She had a nanny and some help, and her children are the joy of her life, but she's like, 'I'm so fucking overwhelmed.' We became really good friends. I have a group of good friends like that, single moms. Everybody makes it work somehow."

At one point Lisa wrote a short story and sent it to her film agent in Los Angeles who suggested that she would be great writing for television. A lightbulb went on.

"I couldn't keep getting up every day not knowing if I could get to the end of it. I started writing screenplays, and now I'm transitioning from novel writing to scriptwriting, which is much more lucrative. Every literary writer I know is writing pilots for television. It's the marketplace." (Aha! The other string Becky mentioned, I thought.)

Mostly what she has written until now is alternative world and sci-fi, but currently she is working on straight comedy.

Writing is a pleasure for her, and she's excited by the possibilities of all the different kinds of things she can write. Maybe a graphic novel next. What she wants is to make something that gets out into the world and that people like, and if that means scripts rather than novels, it's fine with Lisa. Then too, she says that scriptwriting fits better than novel writing into the odd minutes of the day that you have when you're raising a kid.

"When my daughter was a baby, every day seemed like a year, but now it's flying by. I know she'll be off to college before I can blink, and I don't look forward to that at all. I work in the morning, then I pick her up at school and spend time with her, then make dinner. I like that life. People who are married, in a way they have even less time. These men need attention. I've had some serious relationships, but it's hard. I can't be a writer *and* a mother *and* take care of a guy. The guy I'm seeing now is an artist, and he's different. He's more understanding."

I told Lisa how shocked I had been by the opening of *Just Like Beauty*, and she said she's shocked herself—or more shocked—now that she has a daughter. She asked me to tell her about my project, and I did, about how I chose the shelf, what I was finding in the books, the stories I was being led to tell, the people I was meeting.

"That's so like today," she said.

I didn't know exactly what she meant, but I took it as a compliment and thanked her, inviting her to come by and visit with her daughter, her father, and her father's new wife next time she found herself in Manhattan.

When Margaret Leroy talked about parenting as the central concern of life but not of the novel, she mentioned two notable exceptions, that is, two writers who did write good books about parenting. One was Joanna Trollope and the other, Jodi Picoult. Jodi Picoult keeps coming up! I had begun my project specifically saying I was not going to read Jodi Picoult, but I was beginning to think I had to. And, now that I thought of it, why did I not want to? Because she was a women's writer? I was exhibiting the very bias I had been writing against. So it was decided. I must read Jodi Picoult.

But first I found her on YouTube being interviewed by Ellen DeGeneres. In her mid-forties, she wears her long reddish hair unstyled, in loose curls. She has a pretty face and makes a lovely impression although (or perhaps because) she is slightly overweight and not especially well dressed. She seems like your next-door neighbor. She is totally comfortable on television and speaks in contemporary uptalk.

She had always wanted to write and went to college at Princeton because they had a good creative writing program. She studied with wonderful people. She did not start writing novels immediately after college.

"I worked on Wall Street? But the stock market crashed? That was probably a good thing for me?"

Her first son and her first book came at the same time. Since then, it's been a baby or a book every year, three babies and eighteen books.

"A book takes me nine months? It's a little embarrassing."

At first it was hard for her to find time to write. She wrote when Barney was on TV or when the kids stopped hitting each other with sippy cups for a few minutes. Sometimes she wrote sitting in the car with her laptop on the steering wheel, waiting in a parking lot. Then, miraculously, the kids went to school, and she had eight free hours a day to write. She went into her office at 7:30 and stayed there until the kids came home at 3:30. Sometimes, when her husband came home later on, she would throw the kids at him.

Ellen wants to know how she gets ideas for her books. She seems genuinely impressed by Jodi's fecundity, as am I. "Usually it starts with a what-if question I can't answer. It's like a splinter in my brain. Gradually the characters grow. They start talking in my head, and I write them down. I love diving into really tough issues."

The tough issue of the current book has to do with gay family life. Jodi says she'd been wanting to write about gay rights for some time, as they were the last civil rights to be granted in America. But it took a more personal turn when her oldest son, Kyle, applying to college, came out to them. She and her husband were very accepting. She says she'd known Kyle was gay from the time he was three. But now the book changed. "It was me having a mission as a mom." She didn't want Kyle, when he came to marry and have children, to have the same problems gay people were having now.

Ellen reveals, in a guarded way, that she hadn't really wanted the audience to know that the book was about gay issues. She wanted to emphasize that it starts with a marriage and then surprises you and surprises you again. Its demands are on your moral imagination, though those aren't her words. "It makes you think, 'What would I do in this situation? What is the right thing to do?'" It's about family, not gay rights. Clearly Ellen, too, knows the power of false categories.


Did I read it? Yes, I did. And liked it. And respected it. And understand Jodi's frustration. What indeed makes Franzen's

*Freedom* a better, more serious book than *Sing You Home?* Daily book reviewers can't be expected to answer questions like that. It's a question for literary critics, taking time to answer. It involves connoisseurship, an art that hasn't been taught for two generations. For me, spontaneity, inclusiveness, and uniqueness are marks of great fiction, as they are of a satisfying life, but that is a personal choice. I make no claim for the universality of my standards. "Large" is one of my personal praise words. *Freedom* seems larger to me than Picoult's *Sing You Home*, an extremely well-written and well-constructed novel but finally a novel tied to one issue. I hope I can inspire someone to explore these standards—how *do* we make aesthetic judgments?—but I have to move along with the reading of my shelf. My men are waiting to be led across the ice floe. I must rescue them.

And so my mission rescues me.

# Seven

# SMALL WORLDS:
# THE NIGHTINGALE
# AND THE LARK

I WANTED A CHANGE FROM WOMEN, AND THAT WAS NOT hard to arrange because there were no more books by women on my shelf. I gave myself a choice between two writers: the twentieth-century Austrian Alexander Lernet-Holenia, who wrote about war and ghosts, or Alain Le Sage, the seventeenth-century Frenchman who produced one of the earliest novels ever written. The French book was almost eight hundred pages, the Austrian two hundred and fifty. I went with the Hapsburgs, Vienna, waltzes, ghosts, frantic gaiety, red uniforms, large families with governesses, doomed cavalry charges, hunting chamois in the Alps, bayonets, Mannlichers, drunken evenings in the barracks.

The volume on my shelf by Lernet-Holenia is called *Count Luna: Two Tales of the Real and the Unreal*. It consists of two short novels or long short stories, and the first I turned to, *Baron Bagge*, suited my needs perfectly. After sick children, suspicious physicians, and maternal angst, guys flying off the handle and challenging each other to duels were just the ticket: "At a recent reception given by the Minister of Agriculture, a certain Baron Bagge became involved in a dispute with an immature and hot-tempered young man named von Farago." The objectivity! The distance! The magisterial all-knowingness of "a certain Baron Bagge" and "an immature and hot-tempered young man named von Farago." The clarity, the worldliness of "a recent reception given by the Minister of Agriculture." Even if I didn't know that this was published in 1936 and was set decades earlier, I would know that I had entered a distant and different world, one in which duels are fought and characters can be described in two peremptory adjectives. Von Farago forbids Bagge to speak with his sister, and Bagge replies by challenging him to a duel. The duel is averted with an apology, but Bagge feels he owes it to his seconds to explain why the young man distrusted him.

It is true, he admits, that two women have already killed themselves for his sake, although he clearly warned them he was not available. In fact, he is already married, although he has no wife. "When the war started so unexpectedly," Bagge relates, starting the story over again in the fashion of the oldest tales, the preceding narrative being no more than the frame, "I was traveling in Central America," hoping to attend the opening of the Panama Canal. He succeeded in returning to Europe and took part in the beginning of the campaign against Russia, serving in the Count Gondola Dragoons. He is so brisk, so masculine. The world is his. He tells you firmly about all the officers in his regiment—Maltitz, young and uncertain; Hamilton, the rich American, treating everyone to whiskey; the commanding officer, Semler, a bit unstable. And he tells you straight off, pulling no punches, that there is a time after life and before death. Souls wander for nine days. That's all there is to it. An afterlife exists, brief, confusing, misty, but real.

Lernet-Holenia's descriptive writing, in the translation of

Richard and Clara Winston, is as precise as his descriptions of character. "Wisps of mist tracked across the frozen marshes and Bodrog River. Then the clouds deepened to a woolly, blue black color. We took it for granted that it would snow." Bagge's cavalry squadron pursues the Russians into a remote part of Hungary at the foot of the Carpathians. A scout warns them not to cross a certain bridge, but his warning infuriates Semler and makes him do exactly what the scout tells him not to do. He orders a charge on the bridge, on the other side of which the enemy lies in force. Amazingly, the attack is a success. Bagge himself is hit painfully by a pebble dislodged by his horse, but he suffers no greater injury. After that, everything becomes strange. Semler becomes noble in victory, Maltitz and Hamilton unaccountably sullen.

They make their way to the town of Nagy Mihaly, whose inhabitants are overjoyed to see them and insist that there are no Russians anywhere. The town is thronged, "as though nobody ever died there." A beautiful girl named Charlotte Szent-Király throws herself at Bagge, and they fall immediately and madly in love. They sleep together that night and marry the next, just before Semler forces his troops off yet again in an increasingly desperate search for Russians. Everything is hallucinatory yet perfectly clear. They come to a bridge covered with gold, which most of the squadron rides over. Bagge does not. He wakes up. The whole squadron, excepting himself and a few others, had been destroyed in the assault on the bridge. Bagge was grazed by a bullet that he thought was a pebble. Charlotte had been dead for many years when Bagge dreamed he had met and married her. When the dead souls were wandering, they could see only the dead, which is why there were no Russians and why Semler was so desperate to find them.

Bagge forever after considers himself married to Charlotte and unavailable to other women.

The creation of a world not quite real, unfamiliar yet believable, the melancholy, the code of behavior, the mesmerizing storytelling—the only thing I've read remotely like *Baron Bagge* is Isak Dinesen's *Seven Gothic Tales*, of about the same period. I don't know why the story isn't better known, except perhaps because there has been little interest in Old Guard writing in German from the period between and including the two world wars. We want our German-language writers to be more left wing, more incendiary, more openly critical of the establishment and especially of what took place under the Nazis, more engaged with the world as it is and as it should be, than the backward-looking Lernet-Holenia.

*Count Luna*, published in 1955, describes a very different world from that of *Baron Bagge*. Set during the Second World War, after the Germans have taken over Austria, it focuses on a wealthy businessman—Alexander Jessiersky, scion of an immoral and disreputable line of men who have always married well—and his relationship with the shadowy Count Luna, whom, by inaction rather than malice, he inadvertently sends to a concentration camp. Jessiersky's company needs to take over some land owned by Luna, which Luna doesn't want to sell. Jessiersky's board of directors mobilizes so much government pressure against Luna that he is arrested for being anti-German, thus losing not just the land but everything he owned and his freedom, too. Jessiersky, although not directly responsible, feels guilty for Luna's fate and sends him food packages, but eventually, when the war ends, Luna is lost and presumed dead.

Now comes the unreal part. Jessiersky becomes obsessed with Count Luna, spends hours researching the count's genealogy, his family's background in Spain, their history in Austria. He is convinced that Luna is alive and pursuing him in order to get revenge. Luna is the gentleman in the park who has given candy to his children. When his daughter gets ill, Jessiersky believes that Luna gave her a poisoned candy. He hears Luna walking in his very own house, on the floor above him. He chases him out into the street. He thinks that Luna's influence waxes and wanes like the moon. He makes charts. He predicts his next appearance. He takes his family to the high Alps to escape him, but even there he knows or imagines that Luna has followed him.

It's a splendid narrative of guilt and punishment, obsession and lunacy, whose concern with mutability and eternity is typical of Lernet-Holenia. His way of seeing life as a brief moment between possibility and nonexistence shows up in even seemingly irrelevant passages, as in this description of insects in the countryside.

Every August . . . they were, so to speak, on the threshold of existence; but then so many bad Septembers came along, they were never able to achieve it. For years they would lie in wait for the opportunity to come into being, confident that the year would come that was bound to give them life. At last such a year would come, and they existed. But then it was as though their existence already belonged to the past, so strangely, so much like ghosts, did they stagger through time.

With people, as with insects, Lernet-Holenia takes the long view. We are all staggering through time. Although he began by being determined not to resemble his ancestors, Alexander

Jessiersky is the current occupant of his family's role of hapless destroyer. His very diffidence did him in, his failure to fight. Hard not to compare the passivity of Austrians before the Nazis and to read this novella as an urbane, indirect indictment. Lernet-Holenia served in the Austrian army in World War I and then again—very briefly—in the German army in World War II, when he was already well-known as a poet, playwright, and novelist. Injured almost immediately, he was sent to work in the German army film bureau. He does not seem to have enjoyed the confidence of the authorities, probably because there was nothing boosterish in his aesthetic. The Nazis could tell that he was not one of them, whatever he was.

In a few months at the end of 1939 and the start of 1940, he wrote a novel, *Mars in Aries*, based on his experiences at the start of the war, and this, after having been printed in an edition of fifteen thousand, was banned just before publication by the Propaganda Ministry. It portrayed the invasion of Poland on September 1, 1939—which Hitler and his generals liked to present as a spontaneous response to Polish aggression—as long premeditated. It was overly sympathetic to the Poles. Because of this, Lernet-Holenia emerged from the war uncompromised politically. In fact, he was one of those aristocratic, monarchist throwbacks who hated the vulgar Bolsheviks as much as he hated the vulgar Fascists, and in 1972 he resigned in protest from the presidency of Austrian PEN when Heinrich Böll was awarded the Nobel Prize. For him, there was no difference between Heinrich Böll and Stalin or the Baader-Meinhof Gang. They were all thugs.

*Mars in Aries* is a remarkably cool, distanced, and unemotional addition to the literature of World War II. Wallmoden, the officer who is Lernet-Holenia's stand-in, serves in the blitzkrieg on Poland in September 1939. Unreality is the hallmark of the invasion. It can't be happening, and therefore it isn't happening. It is happening, but how could it be happening? The whole of Poland seems stunned, a red face in a distant window reminding Wallmoden of toads he used to kill for bait, "and which, while being killed, would remain without motion, as if they were the ones in the right, and somehow they remained in the right even when they were dead . . . Poland seemed to be staring at him like that face he had seen; it did nothing but stare."

His writing has the atmospheric beauty of a Turner painting superimposed on a canvas by Bosch. A prose stylist, a painter of epic battle scenes, he evokes a million people suddenly migrating from west to east. "No window panes were intact, no man was shaven, no woman combed . . . Towns were going up in flames, as if spontaneously. There was no food left, no more cigarettes, nothing to drink . . . The houses either stood empty or overflowed with refugees. No regiment was receiving rations . . . the entire land seemed as though it were decomposing alive." Then the whole mass, under the pressure of the Russian advance from the east, started moving back in the other direction. No one knew what was happening, and the disaster played out in intense heat. The Poles prayed for rain to make mud to slow the German tanks, but there was not a drop. Everything was covered and filled with dust, "sucked in by capillary action, into the tiniest parts everywhere. It filtered into watches, into the locks of weapons."

There is little gore in this war novel but much epistemological uncertainty. Wallmoden meets a beautiful woman with the unlikely name of Cuba von Pistohlkors and rushes toward a tryst with her that is prevented by the invasion. But is she or isn't she Cuba von Pistohlkors? Or is Cuba the woman

Wallmoden meets later in an empty house in Poland, whose passport has been stolen by the other one? Is Wallmoden's commanding officer dead when he last sees him? Does Wallmoden actually slide into a mortar-shell hole or does he dream it? Although it is immensely readable, the novel swishes and sloshes rather than marching straight forward. The soldierly monarchist writer shares with people otherwise so different from him as Schnitzler and Freud the Viennese fascination with dreams and in-between states, neither dream nor waking, neither life nor death, neither truth nor lie.

For me, Vienna is a portly city made of Wiener schnitzel and Sacher torte. Actually going there some years ago did nothing to disabuse me of my idea of it. Into the imagined landscape of deep-fried veal cutlets is now inserted a great museum where, between viewing masterworks, one sips *Kaffee mit Schlag* in the rotunda; an opera house, where they are always performing *Salome*; and the golden hall of the Musikverein, in which the Vienna Philharmonic is always playing Mahler. Vienna is built in rings. Follow one of the great circle avenues to the river, walk along the river and back to the circular street, and you can end up where you started without ever turning right or left. The quality of always-ness of Vienna is, I think, what Lernet-Holenia was re-creating in his fiction. Musicians come and go, but the orchestra never changes. It always performs in the Musikverein, the ghosts of players past standing behind the present occupants of their chairs whether you see them or not. Are the current musicians stable or transient? Alive or dead? A little of both, in Lernet-Holenia's view. We are always passing from one state to the other.

•

Interested now in Austria, I planned a field trip to the Neue Galerie, a museum on the Upper East Side devoted to twentieth-century Austrian art. It was founded because of the shared enthusiasms for Austrian and German art of Austrian-born art dealer Serge Sabarsky and financier and former ambassador to Austria, Ronald Lauder. I secured a companion for this field trip with the promise of Viennese pastry and *Kaffee mit Schlag* in the museum's Café Sabarsky, the closest you can come to experiencing a Viennese coffeehouse outside of Vienna. So we approached the Klimts, Kokoschkas, and Wiener Werkstätte jewelry and furniture on the upper floors sweetly, by way of the café and gift shop on the first floor.

In the gift shop I found a memoir by Marjorie Perloff called *The Vienna Paradox*. A distinguished literary critic who taught at Stanford for many years, Perloff was born Gabriele Mintz, to an upper-middle-class Jewish Viennese family. Her book includes a riveting account of the harsh awakening Austrian Jews were forced to undergo at the time of the Anschluss, the annexation of Austria by Germany. Perloff was six and a half when the Germans took over Austria on March 12, 1938. A few months later she wrote this account of that day: "My mother came into our room and said now we are no longer Austrians. Hitler has taken Austria. I cried hard but there was nothing to be done. Then when I went into my parents' room, I saw that our suitcases were packed and when my brother Walter and I asked why, my parents said maybe we will go away."

The borders to Hungary and Czechoslovakia were already closed, but they were able to escape the next day by train to Zurich. The trip was terrifying, and Perloff quotes a letter her mother wrote describing it for her sister. All Jews had to get off the train at Innsbruck. They were taken to the police station, where one after another their passports were closely examined, their money confiscated, and their luggage ransacked. "Our thought was only: will they let us travel further? Will we be arrested?" The snowy mountains, the gorgeous blue skies—nothing made Frau Mintz regret leaving their homeland, so her sister could imagine how awful it had been in Vienna, everyone wearing swastikas, the school across from their apartment turned into barracks for Hitler Youth.

Perloff points out that her mother's reaction contained no acknowledgment that their having to leave Austria was connected to their being Jews. Her words were "Now we are no longer Austrians. Hitler has taken Austria." Perloff explains that despite their nominal Jewishness, they were all brought up as Austrians first, and she makes the point vividly with photographs in which all the members of the family are dressed in the traditional Austrian outfit of lederhosen or dirndls. As late as 1937, her father, dressed in loden jacket, lederhosen, embroidered suspenders, high white socks, and mountain boots, holds the hand of his little girl dressed in a dirndl. The next year, the Nazis passed a law forbidding Jews to wear this national costume, so important was it to Austrian identity.

Perloff's grandfather, Richard Schüller, had been a distinguished diplomat, highly valued by the Austrian government, which he had represented in negotiations with many other nations. But when the Nazis came in, he became "the Jew Dr. Richard Schüller," and his bank accounts were emptied. He was able to escape to Italy by crossing over the border in the Alps and invoking his old diplomatic friendship with Mussolini, who sent a personal telegram saying "Friend Schüller is welcome."

So assimilated were upper-middle-class Jewish families in

Austria that their persecution by the Nazis was a shock. Many, especially those who had converted and been baptized for generations, did not think of themselves as Jews at all. Another relative of Perloff's had even been a Nazi official. But when the Nazis discovered that three of his four grandparents were Jewish, they sent him to his death at Auschwitz.

Other Austrian Jews were harder to pry loose from Austria than Perloff's parents. Two days after the Anschluss, Ernest Jones, head of the International Psychoanalytic Association, flew into Vienna from London to extricate the founder of psychoanalysis. Princess Marie Bonaparte came in from Paris on the same errand. Freud, however, did not see any reason to leave until, a little over a week later, the Gestapo arrested and interrogated his daughter Anna. What was this International Psychoanalytic Association she was involved with? Was it a terrorist cell? Anti-German? Freud, usually unflappable, suffered terribly while Anna was in custody, and the episode made him quickly understand the need to get out of Austria. With his deep historic perspective and his sense of psychoanalysis itself as a persecuted religion, he now took exile with equanimity. The temple was wherever the high priest resided. Aged over eighty and not far from death, Freud, too, was suddenly not an Austrian anymore, and the Nazis enforced the same abrupt identity change on people all over Europe. In a matter of days, French Jews would learn they were not French, Dutch Jews that they were less Dutch than Jewish.

The crown jewel of the Neue Galerie is Gustav Klimt's 1907 portrait of Adele Bloch-Bauer, a wealthy Jewish socialite who died of meningitis in 1925, leaving her husband, Ferdinand, in possession of this portrait, the Viennese *Mona Lisa*, as it has been called, and several other Klimts, which he used in making of their bedroom in Vienna a shrine to his wife. It is a ravishing canvas, golden, gold-leafed, painted as though it were made of gleaming mosaics, flat and hieratic, with its image of a sophisticated woman's face almost floating over and haunting the rest of her. My friend somewhat dimmed the glory of the painting for me by pointing out how the visual disconnect between face and background reads differently in the age of Photoshop than it did before: it's hard to fight off the thought that the face has been photoshopped onto the background.

The story of this painting is another story of Jewish Vienna, of Austrian identity betrayed. When the Nazis took over, Ferdinand Bloch-Bauer, like the Mintzes, escaped to Switzerland, but he had to leave behind everything he owned. The Nazis divided the spoils. A diamond necklace he had given Adele on their wedding day ended up around the neck of Emmy Göring. A summerhouse near Prague went to Reinhard Heydrich, a high-ranking Nazi who was one of the chief architects of the Holocaust. The portrait of Adele hung in the Austrian Gallery of the Belvedere Palace in Vienna until, half a century later, in a hard-fought legal battle, Adele's last living heir, a ninety-year-old woman living in Los Angeles, won the painting back and sold it to Ronald Lauder for the Neue Galerie. The battle was hard because Adele's will had expressed a wish that the Klimts go to Austria. How could she have imagined that within twenty-five years of her death, her family would be stripped of its wealth and forced from Austria with her beloved homeland's complicity? As unjust as it was, there seemed to be reason for the Austrian claim on the Klimts, until Adele's actual will was located in the 1990s and the gift to Austria was seen merely to be stated as a wish, not a legally binding bequest.

"Regionalism" is usually used as a term of dismissal, implying that a body of literature will appeal only to a reader who is interested in the language, customs, and characters of a certain geographic region. Realism, by contrast, is the honorific bestowed on literature about the region, however extensive, that is home turf to the literary establishment. In the States, where the publishing industry is based in New York, anything very far from New York is liable to seem regional: the Midwest (Willa Cather), the South (Faulkner, Flannery O'Connor, Eudora Welty, Lee Smith), distant New England (Sarah Orne Jewett)—all are regional. But the regional writer does not aspire to be regional, any more than the woman writer aspires to be a woman writer.

For Germans, Austrian literature is regional. It is written in the same language as German literature, but it is different in subject and style. According to one observer of the Austrian literary scene, "German editors have always tried to adapt their Austrian writers to the German market by weeding out 'national-linguistic idiosyncrasies' in their texts. The more they found the greats, [Thomas] Bernhard and [Elfriede] Jelinek, hard nuts to crack, the more keenly they nibbled away at the idiomatic 'problem areas' of the lesser writers . . . often begetting bilingual cross-breeds." Many Austrian writers, this observer tells us, Germanize themselves of their own accord, racing to do what the large German market wants, while others make a point of their linguistic nonconformity and limit their audiences in the process.

Regionalism is in the eyes of the beholder. If you are a German, Lernet-Holenia may be a regional writer. If you are Austrian, he is not. It's striking to me that whatever presence the work of Lernet-Holenia has obtained in the United States has been due to the partisanship of Austrians. Robert Pick, an editor at Knopf in the 1950s, Austrian by birth, championed Austrian writers, and it was probably thanks to him that Criterion, a small Europe-oriented house, published in 1956 the volume on my shelf by Lernet-Holenia with an introduction by Pick. Pick also included a story by Lernet-Holenia, "Mona Lisa," in a collection of German stories and tales he put together for Knopf in 1954. Until the 1980s, nothing else by Lernet-Holenia was translated into English. Then, because of the dedication of one professor at the University of Colorado whose background is Austrian and who has made Lernet-Holenia's cause his own, a couple of other novels, including *Mars in Aries*, became available.

My shelf has turned me into a partisan of Austrian literature. I haven't read Bernhard or Jelinek, who won the Nobel Prize in Literature in 2004. It's been years since I read any Peter Handke. I have had a nice edition of *The Man Without Qualities* sitting in my library for sixteen years unread. Now, however, I have a list of names, and every one is a good intention: Joseph Roth, Stefan Zweig, Rilke, Schnitzler, Sacher-Masoch, Bachmann, Broch. Some of these writers were citizens of the old Austro-Hungarian Empire and therefore "not really Austrian." But since I am just making a list, reading conceptually, as it were, I can be inclusive. Daniela Strigl, the observer of the contemporary Austrian scene I've been reading online, surveys eighteen novels and makes me want to read eight of them. I add to my list of good intentions Daniel Kehlmann, Michael

Köhlmaier, Arno Geiger, Olga Flor, Lilian Faschinger, Thomas Glavinic, Bettina Balaka, Anna Mitgutsch, and Peter Henisch. Strigl's account of Austrian literature is part of a series in *Eurozine*, an online literary magazine devoted to the "retransnationalism of literary criticism" in Europe. "Transnationalism" is a term referring to the transcending of national boundaries, but this series seems to savor national differences. Re-nationalism would be closer to the mark, I think. All over Europe, it seems, local literary scenes are thriving—Croatia, Lithuania, Flanders, Estonia, Slovenia, Northern Ireland, the Netherlands, Ukraine, and Hungary. In each of these enclaves, according to the reports, the same struggle is going on as in Austria—to have a distinct local literature but to appeal to a larger audience at the same time. Flemish writers work to distinguish themselves from the Dutch, as Austrians from the Germans, and yet aspire to be read by them.

If in one sense "regional" is a term by which a dominant literary culture makes it unnecessary to be interested in a body of work, in another sense a great deal of literature is regional. Many people write in an effort to fit their world together, to make it make sense, and more often than not they start with what's around them, either to distance themselves from it or to claim it. V. S. Naipaul writes the Caribbean into existence so he can leave it behind and become a British gentleman. Philip Roth creates New Jersey so he can move to New York and rural Connecticut. Lernet-Holenia creates a haunted Austria so he can resign in protest against the modern world. On the other hand, Willa Cather creates the midwestern prairies and the cliff dwellings of the Southwest so her imagination has fit spaces to wander in when she is, in fact, in New York City. Faulkner creates Yoknapatawpha County so he can still be home in Mississippi even when he's in Charlottesville or Princeton. The banal advice of writing teachers is "write what you know," but the truth is, you don't know a place until you write it. "Write what you want to know" is more like it. Great fiction makes its location so real it appears to generate the work, rather than the other way around, but it's an illusion.

Some say that the more fiction is particular and regional, the more of a chance it has to appeal globally. David Brooks, trying to explain how fifty-six thousand Spaniards at a Bruce Springsteen concert can shout "I was born in the U.S.A.!," cites the notion of "paracosms"—detailed imaginary worlds that all children invent and that help orient them in reality. We carry the need for paracosms, "structured mental communities that help us understand the wider world," into adult life, and paradoxically, "the artists who have the widest global purchase are also the ones who have created the most local and distinctive story landscapes." Thus the Harry Potter books can be seen as a triumph of regional literature, taking the English public school and universalizing it by particularizing it as Hogwarts. "If you build a passionate and highly localized moral landscape, people will come." (I would add, If you build it, they will come and you can leave.) Writers from small countries would seem to operate at a severe disadvantage reaching broad audiences. Yet this has not proved to be the case. People the world over have embraced Stieg Larsson's Sweden, with its passionate fighters for justice in the guise of a slovenly journalist and a Goth computer hacker. If a novelist reaches a certain pitch of intensity with his characters, for all their embeddedness in a real cultural and geographic context, they are no longer local.

•

Libraries make strange bedfellows. Sitting next to *Count Luna* on my shelf is a book called *The Habitant-Merchant* by James Edward LeRossignol, a collection of stories about old French Canada. This is the rarest volume on my shelf. If you wanted to check out another copy of *The Habitant-Merchant*, you would have to go to the University of Toronto Library. According to the WorldCat catalog, there isn't another copy in any library in the world, so regional is the book's audience.

We are introduced to a traveling salesman from Montreal, Edouard Marceau, who calls on customers in their own shops to show them new stock and take orders. In Quebec, his best client is Jovite Laberge, a rustic but clever habitant-merchant. "Habitant" is the name that French Canadian farmers of the St. Lawrence valley gave to themselves, and Laberge was one of them, a small farmer who, like his neighbors, sacrificed one day a week to take his meager produce to market, until he got the brilliant idea of buying his neighbors' produce and taking it all to market himself, selling it for more than he paid them for it. From this beginning, he became a merchant, eventually owning his own thriving store. But it is a point of pride with him to wear the same clothes that his farmer friends and relatives wear rather than the more elegant garb of the city.

Marceau is always trying to get Laberge to place an order, but the merchant is more interested in smoking his pipe and telling stories. They are folksy, good-natured stories of romance, courtship, family, inheritance. Interspersed are scenes of commerce in the Quebec store, of Laberge's wily responses to Marceau's attempts to get an order or customers' attempts to get a bargain. Hours go to selling a stove marked $60 for $49.25, and most of the time is spent haggling about the last quarter. In the course of the narrative, Laberge modernizes in several ways, notably by replacing the system of bargaining with a fixed price. And as he succeeds in marrying his daughters to fine and useful young men, such as the traveling salesman himself, you realize that you have been witnessing the birth of a great merchandising empire. The Laberge dynasty has not yet reached the level of the Viennese Jessierskys, the stakes are nowhere near as high as in Nazi Austria, but Lernet-Holenia and LeRossignol, in their focus on the growth of wealth over time, as in their savoring of tradition, their backward gaze, their embrace of the role of storyteller, have more in common than merely the—to me—extraordinary fact that they sit next to each other on the LEQ–LES fiction shelf of the New York Society Library.

LeRossignol was born in 1866 and raised in Quebec. His father, Peter, came from a Norman French family on the Isle of Jersey, and his mother, Mary Gillespie, was a Quebec native of Scotch and Irish ancestry. Thanks again to the Internet, which gives me access to genealogical material of immense range and depth, I know more about LeRossignol than I know about my own grandfather. He graduated from McGill in Montreal in 1888, then went to the University of Leipzig in Germany to study philosophy, obtaining a doctoral degree with a thesis on Samuel Clarke, an early-eighteenth-century British philosopher. This stay in Leipzig was as close as LeRossignol ever physically came to Lernet-Holenia, who was waiting for the opportunity to be born in Vienna five years later and begin staggering through time.

Back in the New World, LeRossignol studied psychology at Clark University in Worcester, Massachusetts, at that time psychology's red-hot American center. In 1909 Freud would deliver his Five Lectures on Psychoanalysis at Clark, his only

American speaking appearance, with Jung accompanying him. With his training in ethics and psychology, LeRossignol made himself an economist at a time when the field was just coming together. He started teaching in 1894 at the University of Denver as a professor of history and political economy, then, in 1908, moved to the University of Nebraska, where he spent the rest of his career, helping to found the College of Business Administration, which he ran for two decades. In the First World War, when Lernet-Holenia was serving in the "Count Gondola Dragoons," pursuing Russians into the Carpathian Mountains on horseback, LeRossignol was chairman of the Lancaster County Fuel Commission. In 1940, when Lernet-Holenia was writing *Mars in Aries*, about the Nazi obliteration of Poland, in which he had participated, LeRossignol was dean of the College of Business Administration and active in civic affairs in Lincoln, a member of the Chamber of Commerce, the Lincoln Association of Credit Men, the Rotary Club, the Nebraska Schoolmasters Club, and the Nebraskana Society. He spent the long summer holidays back in his native Canada, near Quebec.

According to someone who knew him, LeRossignol was "a model father, a gregarious, fun-loving man, and an ardent trout and salmon fisherman, though even on summer holidays he reserved every morning for his writing. His other activities included bridge, chess, college football, and reading. His regular diet of reading included scientific journals in English, German, and French, with the occasional foray into Western stories and detective fiction." He wrote an enormous number of articles on economics, many sketches and essays published in *Prairie Schooner*, many books on economics (*Monopolies, Past and Present*; *Taxation in Colorado*; *Orthodox Socialism*; *State Socialism in New*

*Zealand; Economics for Everyman*), and five works of fiction: one novel, and four collections of stories, *The Habitant-Merchant* being the final and most accomplished. It was published in 1939, the year that World War II started and Lernet-Holenia fought in Poland.

And there they sit, next to each other, the nightingale and the lark, the singer of night and the singer of day, cosmopolite and provincial, though which is which can change in the blink of an eye, like the black and white birds of an M. C. Escher drawing. It's a miracle they've both made it here to New York. Lernet-Holenia has Robert Pick to thank. Who knows whose enthusiasm brought LeRossignol to the library shelf? But someone loved him enough to put him here. I imagine the two of them chatting companionably in German, LeRossignol telling Lernet-Holenia nostalgic tales of old Quebec and Lernet-Holenia responding with stories of the good old days under the Hapsburgs, like two *alter kockers* sitting on a bench in Central Park, in whatever kind of eternity a library provides.

# Eight

# LIBRARIES: MAKING SPACE

E XACTLY WHAT KIND OF ETERNITY *DOES* A LIBRARY provide? How likely is it for a manuscript to become a book on a library shelf? How hard is it to stay there? Let us say the novel is written. It has taken form. It is four hundred or so typed pages or a file on a computer disc. The work of art is actualized; it exists in the world. But it exists in a fragile form. The manuscript must find a publisher. At the end of the film made from Miles Franklin's autobiographical novel, *My Brilliant Career*, the young heroine, living in the outback of Australia, gives up conventional happiness in order to write her novel, which she then finishes, wraps in a brown-paper parcel, and deposits, bearing a London address, in a remote mailbox. A friend in publishing commented acidly, "I hope she kept a copy."

What actually happened is instructive. Miles Franklin, who began writing the novel when she was just sixteen, had it rejected by several Australian publishers, only one of whom thought enough of it to offer suggestions for revision. In a Hail Mary pass, the young author then sent the manuscript to an Australian literary figure, Henry Lawson, whom she did not know. Lawson liked the work and encouraged Franklin to make some of the changes that had been suggested. About to move to London, he told her to send the revised manuscript to him there, which she did. (The manuscript was handwritten, and it's unlikely a copy existed.) In London, Lawson found Franklin an agent, and eventually the agent found an excellent publisher, William Blackwood. The author was twenty-one when the book was published—to enormous acclaim but also distressing criticism from family and friends. She never produced anything on its level again, although she went on writing.

Consider the unlikeliness of Miles Franklin's novel making its way to the New York Society Library after its unlikely publication. It appeared in 1901, a year when the library was acquiring a lot of English fiction, including everything William Le Queux wrote, but the story of a teenage Australian girl would probably not have appealed to the library's readership, and no copy entered the collection at that time or for three-quarters of a century thereafter. Then, almost simultaneously, two things happened: an Australian bought the rights to the novel with the idea of making it into a film, and Carmen Callil, the English editor, founded a publishing house, Virago Press, to specialize in reissuing literature by women. The film, directed by Gillian Armstrong and starring Judy Davis, debuted in August 1979, and the novel was published by Virago (and in New York by St. Martin's) in July of the following year. Had there not been a film version of this novel, had Carmen Callil, with her feminist agenda, not reissued it, it is very unlikely that it would occupy shelf space today in the New York Society Library. Its life was prolonged by two political currents—Australian nationalism and feminism. Literary merit had little to do with it. The book has a certain bouncy energy and addresses issues of interest to ambitious young women caged in places too small for their spirits. It has found a permanent place in the Greater Shelf we call Literature, but it could just as easily not have.

Choosing books for a library like mine in New York is a full-time job. The head of acquisitions at the Society Library, Steven McGuirl, reads *Publishers Weekly*, *Library Journal*, *The Times Literary Supplement*, *The New Yorker*, *The New York Review of Books*, the *London Review of Books*, *The London Times*, and *The New York Times* to decide which fiction should be ordered. Fiction accounts for fully a quarter of the forty-eight hundred books the library acquires each year. There are standing orders for certain novelists—Martin Amis, Zadie Smith, Toni Morrison, for example. Some popular writers merit standing orders for more than one copy. But first novels and collections of stories present a problem. McGuirl and his two assistants try to guess what the members of the library will want to read. Of course, they respond to members' requests. If a book is requested by three people, the staff orders it. There's also a committee of members that meets monthly to recommend books for purchase. The committee checks on the librarians' lists and suggests titles they've missed. The whole enterprise balances enthusiasm and skepticism. They want a full collection but don't want to be saddled with books nobody reads.

Boosted by reviews, prizes, large sales, word of mouth, or personal recommendations, a novel may make its way onto the library shelf, but even then it is not guaranteed a chance of being read by future generations. Libraries are constantly getting rid of books they have acquired. They have to, or they would run out of space. The polite word for this is "deaccession," the usual word, "weeding." I asked a friend who works for a small public library how they choose books to get rid of. Is there a formula? Who makes the decision, a person or a committee? She told me that there was a formula based on the recommendations of the industry-standard *CREW* manual.

CREW stands for Continuous Review Evaluation and Weeding, and the manual uses "crew" as a transitive verb, so one can talk about a library's "*crew*ing" its collection. It means weeding but doesn't sound so harsh. At the heart of the CREW method is a formula consisting of three factors—the number of years since the last copyright, the number of years since the book was last checked out, and a collection of six negative factors given the acronym MUSTIE, to help decide if a book has outlived its usefulness. *M.* Is it *Misleading* or inaccurate? Is its information, as so quickly happens with medical and legal texts or travel books, for example, outdated? *U.* Is it *Ugly*? Worn beyond repair? *S.* Has it been *Superseded* by a new edition or a better account of the subject? *T.* Is it *Trivial*, of no discernible literary or scientific merit? *I.* Is it *Irrelevant* to the needs and interests of the community the library serves? *E.* Can it be found *Elsewhere*, through interlibrary loan or on the Web? Obviously, not all the MUSTIE factors are relevant in evaluating fiction, notably Misleading and Superseded. Nor is the copyright date important. For nonfiction, the CREW formula might be 8/3/MUSTIE, which would mean "Consider a book for elimination if it is eight years since the copyright date and three years since it has been checked out and if one or more of the MUSTIE factors obtains." But for fiction the formula is often X/2/MUSTIE, meaning the copyright date doesn't matter, but consider a book for elimination if it hasn't been checked out in two years and if it is TUIE—Trivial, Ugly, Irrelevant, or Elsewhere.

Obviously, the CREW formula is not in the same class as $E = mc^2$. A lot of subjectivity is required to decide if a book is Trivial or Irrelevant, even if a book is irretrievably Ugly. And if Elsewhere includes the Internet, the formula raises the whole question of whether it's worth keeping paper copies of older books in your local library, as almost all of them, if Google has its way, will be available online. The writer of the *CREW* manual emphasizes that the librarian's judgment must be constantly engaged in making these decisions. The CREW formula is a guideline, she insists. "It is important to remember that guidelines are not intended to act as a substitute for professional judgment calls and common sense." Discard works no longer in demand, she recommends, especially second and third copies of past bestsellers. "Retain works of durable demand and/or high literary merit." It is not clear to me that the author of the *CREW* manual has any idea of how hard it is to determine "high literary merit" as opposed to "durable demand." My friend said they had done a recent fiction "weed" in which all the books that met the CREW requirements were then reviewed by a librarian to see if the book had a local connection or local interest and also to make sure that such classics as one of Trollope's Palliser novels wouldn't be thrown away, even if no one had checked it out in two years. That's fine for the Palliser novels, but what about, let us say, Rhoda Lerman? Etienne Leroux? Sigrid Undset, the Nobel Prize–winning novelist whose work my mother's generation of women revered, who is now largely unknown? Or even Lawrence Durrell— whose *Alexandria Quartet* I once bought at a library book sale, being discarded from the collection?

Weeding, even in the garden, has become a remarkably controversial subject. There's a powerful school of thought, more philosophical than botanical, going back to Emerson, that regards a weed as a misunderstood plant. Many people believe that all green life is holy and should not be inhibited. Weeding, to such people, is akin to eugenics and murder. Some people feel the same about books: no book should be removed from a library. They are all worth preserving. Thus, there is a tone of defensiveness whenever librarians discuss their weeding procedures. This is from the New York Society Library's 2010 *Annual Report*:

> Circulation count is never used as the sole criterion for deaccessioning a book. The Head of Acquisitions then reviews the list weighing a number of factors: other library holdings, books by the same author in the collection, price and availability via second-hand booksellers . . . age of the material, citation in bibliographies, book condition, whether subject coverage by other books in the collection renders the book in question obsolete or redundant, as well as other variables such as illustrators, binding, donor bookplates, and so forth. It is important to keep in mind that many books have research potential precisely because they are out of date and provide a window into the cultural attitudes of a previous time. It is an involved process, and it can take much longer to select a book for withdrawal than it can to select it for purchase.

The novelist Nicholson Baker is perhaps the most vocal critic of deaccessioning in libraries, first in 1996, in a much-discussed exposé of the San Francisco Public Library (SFPL) published in *The New Yorker*, and then in a book called *Double Fold.* Concerned initially about the disappearance of card catalogs and the way that enthusiasm for information technologies was damaging the traditional culture of libraries, he sued the San Francisco Public Library for access to their old card catalog, which had been replaced by an electronic one as the library moved into a new building. What he discovered went far beyond the issue of paper versus electronic cataloging. He found that there were many books noted in the card catalog that no longer existed in the library. Between the time the SFPL left its old main building and the time it moved into its high-tech, built-for-the-future, and supposedly more roomy new one with its electronic card catalog, somewhere between a hundred thousand and a quarter of a million books were removed from the collection. This was weeding on a scale—and in a time frame—that suggested reckless destruction more than considered selection. Many books that existed in no other copies, many books arguably with historic value, had been simply thrown away and buried in landfill. Partly this had been done because the new library, while boasting great architectural flourishes and lots of architectural space, did not have enough shelf space. Partly it had been done because the current librarian had a view of what books belonged in the collection that differed from that of previous librarians. He saw the library as serving the general reader, as opposed to researchers and literary professionals, arguing that with the Berkeley and Stanford university libraries nearby, there was no lack of research libraries in the San Francisco Bay Area. He conceived of the SFPL rather as a library for a current urban population and therefore saw an opportunity to pare its collections radically.

A weed is something you don't want growing in your garden—more formally, "a plant that interferes with management objectives for a given area of land at a given point in time." Every garden represents someone's "management objective," and so does every library. The definition reflects the careful relativism and systems orientation of our time. Management objectives might change, and then the weed would be very welcome. But skeptics of library weeding, like Baker, are keenly aware of the difference between gardens and libraries: once you've weeded out a book, it isn't going to grow back again.

Still, Baker may have ignored the extent to which a library must articulate and fulfill its own objectives. Viewing libraries as repositories, he overestimated their preservation function and underestimated their need to serve a specific community. I find myself sympathetic, if unequally, to both parties in this dispute, wholeheartedly to Baker's book-loving bellows of rage at the destruction of precious objects but also to the librarian's desire to create an institution that serves its community. That this battle about the form and function of libraries is not over was made clear when the New York Public Library's announcement of new construction caused protests from people (like me) who fear sweeping changes to libraries.

The New York Society Library is in the fortunate position of not having to worry as much about weeding as many other libraries. They consider the forty-eight hundred books a year they acquire a magic number. If it were three or four times greater, they would have to weed their collection much more severely. As it is, they can concentrate on finding ways to make more space while keeping the collection—at any rate the fiction collection—fairly stable. Last year, McGuirl moved the collections of O. Henry prize stories and *Best American Short*

*Stories* to closed storage in the basement while leaving the last few years' volumes on the open stacks. That freed up a lot of room. Eliminating duplicate copies of books that were popular in the past but are no longer read much frees up more room. Inch by inch, space has to be found for the new. Regarding it as a collection with a special character—to record the reading tastes of New Yorkers over the years—the NYSL librarians are reluctant to deaccession unique copies of fiction.

Elsewhere, the process is more complex and potentially contentious—for example at a university library like mine, where professors are ready at every turn to watchdog and yelp. The Wesleyan University library is engaged in a three-year project to weed out sixty thousand volumes. They are out of space, and weeding on the small scale, as the Society Library does, only frees space that is immediately filled. To achieve the goal of weeding sixty thousand volumes, the library has undertaken to consider ninety thousand, or 6 percent of all the books in the library. Lists of books that meet the initial weeding criteria are available to students and faculty, members of which can champion any volume they care to. The scale of the operation is stupefying. I looked at the list for the Library of Congress category PR—English literature—and there were nine thousand entries. This means that nine thousand books, published before 1990, had been checked out only two times or less since 1996 and not at all since 2003. To my deep sadness, I recognized titles on the list. They were works of literary criticism that had been written by friends of mine when we were young and now were considered at the end of their useful life, just like their authors. Their removal from the library was like an actual death, a kind of death I had never imagined.

People who feel strongly about retaining books in libraries

have a simple way to combat the removal of treasured volumes. Since every system of elimination is based, no matter what they say, on circulation counts, the number of years that have elapsed since a book was last checked out, or the number of times it has been checked out overall, if you feel strongly about a book, you should go to every library you have access to and check out the volume you care about. Take it home awhile. Read it or don't. Keep it beside you as you read the same book on a Kindle, Nook, or iPad. Let it breathe the air of your home, and then take it back to the library, knowing you have fought the guerrilla war for physical books. This was the spirit in which I checked out the third book in Etienne Leroux's Welgevonden trilogy with no intention of reading it.

So many factors affect a novel's chances of surviving, to say nothing of its becoming one of the immortal works we call a classic: how a book is initially reviewed, whether it sells, whether people continue to read it, whether it is taught in schools, whether it is included in college curricula, what literary critics say about it later, how it responds to various political currents as time moves on.

We like to think that merit is eventually recognized, that a great book will make its way, but we know only the success stories. *In Search of Lost Time* was rejected by three publishing houses, one of the readers being no dummy, André Gide. The first volume was published by Grasset only when Proust himself agreed to pay the costs. Then, despite all the ha-ha's about fifty pages on going to sleep, it was quickly recognized as a masterpiece. Gide wrote to Proust and apologized, saying that rejecting the manuscript had been the worst mistake of his professional life. James Joyce's *Ulysses* was published marginally and then was reviled even by readers as discriminating as Virginia Woolf. Eventually an audience educated itself to appreciate the novel, embraced it, and fought for it. But you have to be a hard-core optimist to believe that that was inevitable. In another scenario, *De Rerum Natura*, lost for fifteen hundred years, was found and its merit recognized. But how many other works of antiquity were not found? How many works from past centuries never got published or, published, were never read?

If you want to see how slippery a judgment is "literary merit" and how unlikely quality is to be recognized at first glance, nothing is more fun—or more comforting to writers— than to read rejection letters or terrible reviews of books that have gone on to prove indispensable to the culture. This, for example, is how the *New York Times* reviewer greeted *Lolita*: "*Lolita* . . . is undeniably news in the world of books. Unfortunately, it is bad news. There are two equally serious reasons why it isn't worth any adult reader's attention. The first is that it is dull, dull, dull in a pretentious, florid and archly fatuous fashion. The second is that it is repulsive."

Negative reviews are fun to write and fun to read, but the world doesn't need them, since the average work of literary fiction is, in Laura Miller's words, "invisible to the average reader." It appears and vanishes from the scene largely unnoticed and unremarked. "Even the novelists you may think of as 'hyped' are in fact relatively obscure," writes Miller. "I've got a battalion of perfectly intelligent cousins who have never heard of either Jonathan Franzen or Dave Eggers . . . They've never read a book because it was praised as a work of genius on the front page of the *New York Times Book Review*." Whether reviews are positive or negative, the attention they bring to a book is rarely sufficient, and it is becoming harder and harder for a novel to lift itself from obscurity. In the succinct and elegant words of James Gleick, "The merchandise of the information economy is not information; it is attention. These commodities have an inverse relationship. When information is cheap, attention becomes expensive." These days, besides writing, novelists must help draw attention to what they write, tweeting, friending, blogging, and generating meta tags—unacknowledged legislators to Shelley, but now more like unpaid publicists.

On the Web, everyone can be a reviewer, and a consensus about a book can be established covering a range of readers potentially as different as Laura Miller's cousins and the members of the French Academy. In this changed environment, professional reviewers may become obsolete, replaced by crowd wisdom. More than two centuries ago, Samuel Johnson invented the idea of crowd wisdom as applied to literature, calling it "the common reader." "I rejoice to concur with the common reader; for by the common sense of readers, uncorrupted by literary prejudices, after all the refinements of subtilty and the dogmatism of learning, must be finally decided all claim to poetical honours." Virginia Woolf agreed and titled her wonderful collection of essays on literature *The Common Reader*. Now the Common Reader exists slightly less notionally—the average of unsolicited responses on Amazon.

One of my pleasures this year has been getting to know the Common Reader. I go online, to see how the Common Reader has responded, for example, to *God's Ear*, my favorite Rhoda Lerman novel, and find to my delight that it has a five-star rating on Amazon. But it has only two reviewers. One, "A Customer," is so articulate and thorough that I suspect he or she is a friend of Rhoda's. The other, however, seems wholly unbiased. A retired physician, she lives in Washington State and is looking forward to a new career as a novelist. She has already published one novel. She aspires to be as great as Bernard Malamud, Thomas Hardy, Stefan Zweig, and Proust. Meanwhile, she is active in her community, skis and hikes, reads "avidly," and participates in a book club. She tends to like books with spiritual content or an adventure arc. Reviews of books alternate with reviews of shoes and muffin pans: "*I hate to say it but this shoe is dreadful* . . . I put them on and within moments there were painful pressure points on my feet. I took off the shoes and my feet had red marks where the pressure areas were literally 'killing' me . . . My feet felt as if they were encased in cement." She is as faithful to describing the experience of reading a book as she is to the experience of putting on a shoe. Of Stefan Zweig's *Chess Story*, she writes,

> The descriptions are powerful and cause a visceral reaction that is astonishing. As I was reading, I started to note a racing pulse and sweating and a sense of uncontrollable foreboding. As the story raced to its conclusion, I had the urge to shout, "Halt! Don't play again!" I wept when I set the book down. The tears were for Dr. B, all of the victims of the Nazi carnage and perhaps also a reaction to what came to pass, the suicide of the author. This gem of a small book explores and disturbs the human psyche like no other.

Twelve out of twelve people found this review helpful, so perhaps, like me, they went on to check out the reviewer's other preferences. Bob's Red Mill cereal muesli? Five stars! Aroma Land Massage and Body Oil? Five stars. Crest Glide dental floss? Five stars! She hated a book called *One God Clapping* by Alan Lew and gave it only one star, but she loved *God's Ear.* "Her character portrayals are vivid; they leap off the page and demand your attention. They grab you with a stranglehold on your heart. No matter how she describes their deficiencies, you love them even more and relish each adventure not wanting the book to end. You learn that mitzvahs, good deeds, come in all sizes and shapes." I would say that she's exactly right, and I would follow her advice for dental floss, too.

The Common Reader, however, is not one person. It is a statistical average, the mean between this reader's one star for *One God Clapping* and twenty other readers' enthusiasm for this book, the autobiography of a "Zen rabbi," producing a four-star rating. What the rating says to me is that if I were the kind of person who wanted to read the autobiography of a Zen rabbi, I'd be very likely to enjoy it. That Amazon reviewers are a self-selected group needs underlining. If you are like Laura Miller's cousins who have never heard of Jonathan Franzen, you will be unlikely to read *Freedom*, and even less likely to review it. If you read everything that John Grisham has ever written, you will probably read his latest novel and might even report on it. If you read *Lolita*, it's either because you've heard it's one of the great novels of the twentieth century or because you've heard it's a dirty book. Whatever brings you to it, you are likely to enjoy it. Four and a half stars.

The idea of the wisdom of crowds, popularized by James Surowiecki, dates to 1906, when the English statistician Francis Galton (Darwin's cousin) focused on a contest at a county fair for guessing the weight of an ox. For sixpence, a person could buy a ticket, fill in his name, and guess the weight of the animal after butchering. The person whose guess was closest to the actual weight of the ox won a prize. Galton, having the kind of mind he did, played around with the numbers he gathered from this contest and discovered that the average of all the guesses was only one pound off from the actual weight of the ox, 1,198 pounds. If you're looking for the Common Reader's response to a novel, you can't take any one review as truth but merely as a passionate assertion of one point of view, one person's guess at the weight of the ox.

"I really enjoy reading this novel it makes you think about a sex offender's mind. I'm also happy that I purchased this novel on Amazon because I was able to find it easily with a suitable price for me."

"Vladimir has a way with words. The prose in this book is simply remarkable."

"Overrated and pretentious. Overly flowery language encapsulating an uninteresting and overdone plot. Older man and pre-adolescent hypersexual woman—please let's not exaggerate the originality of that concept, it has existed for millennia now. In fact, you'll find similar stories in every chapter of the Bible."

"Like many other folk I read Lolita when it first came out. I was a normally-sexed man and I found it excitingly erotic. Now, nearing 80, I still felt the erotic thrill but was more open to the beauty of Nabokov's prose."

"Presenting the story from Humbert's self-serving viewpoint was Nabokov's peculiarly brilliant means by which a straight, non-perverted reader is taken to secret places she/he might otherwise dare not go."

"A man who was 'hip' while maintaining a bemused detachment from trendiness, what would he have made of shopping malls? Political correctness? Cable television? Alternative music? The Internet? . . . Or some of this decade's greatest scandals, near-Nabokovian events in themselves, like Joey Buttafuoco, Lorena Bobbitt, O. J. Simpson, Bill and Monica? Wherever he is (Heaven, Hell, Nirvana, Anti-Terra), I would like to thank Nabokov for providing us with a compelling and unique model of how to read, write, and perceive life."

What would the hip, bemused author of *Lolita* have made of Amazon ratings? I like to think that he would have reveled in them as evidence of the cheerful self-assurance, the lunatic democracy of his adopted culture.

"Once a populist gimmick, the reviews are vital to make sure a new product is not lost in the digital wilderness," the *Times* reports. But when crowd wisdom becomes self-conscious, aware of its own power, it becomes subject to manipulation and no longer works. Amazon's own gatekeepers have removed thousands of reviews from its site in an attempt to curb what has become widespread manipulation of its ratings. They eliminated some reviews by family members and people considered too biased to be entitled to an opinion, competing writers, for example. They did not, however, eliminate reviews by people who admit they have not read the book. "We do not require people to have experienced the product in order to review," said an Amazon spokesman.

There's an element akin to secondhand smoke in the world of literature—a general consensus about whether a book is good or not that develops apart from actual ingestion of the book, as in the case of the student who, asked by her professor if she had read *Madame Bovary*, replied, "Not me personally." I would have said it was necessary to experience the product in order to rate it, but then I have to remind myself how much more Gaby Bordwin, the designer, got out of *A Hero of Our Time* not having read it than I did having read it three times.

To achieve classic status, to have a chance at shelf space and immortality, it helps a novel to be adopted by the educational establishment, and in the United States, what is taught in schools can be fiercely fought-over ground. There are many people who distrust literature entirely and many parents on the lookout for books that might damage their children. There is no corresponding group of parents insisting that their children be offered high-quality or difficult fiction.

For an update on what is currently under attack, a good place to go is the website of the National Coalition Against Censorship. There you see that because of parents' claims of content harmful to children, Laura Esquivel's *Like Water for Chocolate* was pulled from the reading list in Nampa, Idaho; *Fight Club* by Chuck Palahniuk, *A Thousand Acres* by Jane Smiley, and Hemingway's short story "Hills Like White Elephants" were removed from AP English classes in the Katy, Texas, high school; and Sherman Alexie's *The Absolutely True Diary of a Part-Time Indian* was taken from the curriculum in Springfield, Massachusetts. The NCAC spends a lot of time writing letters to school districts like those of Katy and Springfield, diplomatically protesting the interference with the curriculum and defending the works in question, citing reviews and awards as evidence of merit, and reminding school boards that there are constitutional issues and other people's rights to be taken into account besides those of squeamish parents.

It becomes easier in some ways and harder in others for a novel to make it onto a reading list after high school. Easier in that there is less likelihood of parental interference and censorship, less pressure to avoid any sexual or controversial content; harder because now the writer has somehow to crack the canon. College professors are smart, opinionated, and skeptical people, and most of them get to compose the curricula for their own courses. To reach another generation, to start on its way to immortality, a novel has to appeal to one of these quirky people enough so that he or she will put it on a reading list. Usually this means that the novel fits into a personal agenda of the professor's, an idea he or she wants to promulgate, or at the very least reflects his or her taste. Hazel V. Carby, professor of African American studies at Yale, used to teach at my university, Wesleyan. At both schools she taught a course on the Caribbean novel, a highlight of which was Michael Thelwell's excellent novel about a reggae singer, *The Harder They Come*. Carby herself is of mixed Jamaican and British background. Hence her particular interest in the Caribbean novel. A friend of mine has two sons, one of whom went to Wesleyan, the other to Yale. Both studied with Professor Carby and so both read *The Harder They Come*. In this family *The Harder They Come* was more of a classic than *David Copperfield*. (*The Harder They Come* has a full five-star rating on Amazon, confirming my faith in the Common Reader.)

Like a search engine, a professor is an algorithm about what is important, a highly specialized formula for choice. Every college course is a statement about importance. As a visiting professor at the University of California at Berkeley, I was asked to teach one course under the rubric "major authors." To me, "major authors," in addition to being a pretentious phrase for "terrific writers," was a red flag that meant "any writer that you, Phyllis, feel a rapport with isn't major enough." By this time, 1982, I could have taught Virginia Woolf as a major author without raising eyebrows, but I decided to push even harder and offered a course on Willa Cather. My initial motivation was mischievous, but by the end of the semester I felt no irony at all in calling Cather a major author. My experiment worked, at least for me, and I hope for my students who didn't tend to know a major author from a minor one until a professor told them which was which.

When Nabokov taught at Cornell in the 1950s, before the success of *Lolita* released him from academic duties, he offered a lecture course on European novels. His goal was to teach his students to be good readers, that is, to read "not for the infantile purpose of identifying oneself with the characters, and not for the adolescent purpose of learning to live, and not for the academic purpose of indulging in generalizations," but to read novels for "their form, their vision, their art," to learn to see novels from their creators' point of view and to appreciate their artistry. He liked to compare novels to mechanical toys whose mechanism he could explain to his students. He wanted to teach them to "tingle" in response to great literary art.

The novelists who made him tingle were Flaubert, Joyce, Kafka, and Proust. He was required, however, to teach at least two English novelists as well, and he turned to his friend, the literary critic Edmund Wilson for advice. Wilson promptly chose Jane Austen and Dickens, and Nabokov just as promptly rejected Jane Austen. "I dislike Jane," he wrote back, "and am prejudiced, in fact, against all women writers." He decided to include Robert Louis Stevenson as his other English novelist. Wilson was horrified: "Stevenson is second-rate. I don't know why you admire him so much." He insisted that Nabokov give Jane Austen another try, specifically *Mansfield Park*. In the end, Nabokov took Wilson's advice and taught both *Mansfield Park* and *Dr. Jekyll and Mr. Hyde* in addition to *Bleak House*. If you were expecting to see Stendhal on a reading list of European masters, you have forgotten Nabokov's scorn for Stendhal's French, exceeded only by his scorn for Lermontov's Russian.

What professors put on their curricula is an important guide to excellence not because professors are uniquely able to define quality, but because they are serious readers and their teaching a novel means they are willing to reread it again and again. This is the test of time on an individual basis, and I recommend it as a practical guide to merit. The fiction I esteem is fiction I would reread. The test of time is beyond us as human beings with a limited life span, but the test of *times* is possible. We can prefigure the successive readings of generations, bringing to bear on literature, as we age, our own changing needs and responses.

I would locate literary merit in those qualities in a written work that would allow a good reader to read it more than once with pleasure, whether or not the reader ever gets around to it, and whatever those qualities are for that reader—good plotting, good dialogue, exact prose, slyness, bluntness, irony, elusiveness—the possibilities are many. I am fairly certain, however, that whatever qualities the reader values, they are likely to require in the writer the habit of being choosy about words. A fast-moving, action-packed book may have literary merit. A sci-fi novel, a mystery, a romance may have literary merit. The merit doesn't lie in the genre. It lies in an author's approach to the work. And because a novel is an experience in time, it will never be exactly the same experience twice.

You cannot know at a book's birth if it will become a classic. It will be a classic if it appeals to generation after generation of readers, and you would be able to know that only if you could hover in eternity and watch. Hovering over a work of fiction for merely a lifetime is the job of the literary critic, who is to a book reviewer as a pediatrician is to a midwife. The midwife is for a one-time event. The literary critic is for the life of the book. A book reviewer tells you, when a book first appears, whether he or she believes it is worth your time. The literary critic sees to your relationship with the book later. He or she tries to make sure that people continue to discuss a work as years go by. By talking about it over and over, through the years and centuries, we help to nudge it into eternal life. If we go on reading it, it is worthy to be read, proving itself to be not of an age, but for all time.


At the end of the summer, I went with Mark Bartlett, the head librarian of the New York Society Library, and Steve McGuirl, the acquisitions chief, to visit my shelf. They had asked me to show it to them, which made me happy. This shelf, this run of books, would from now on be special because I had singled it out. If any of the books on the shelf risked being deaccessioned before, certainly none of them did now. I had rescued my shipmates.

Mark picked a book out—it was *Gil Blas*—and showed me where the acquisition date was stamped in it, along the spine a few pages in, perpendicular to the type. This particular copy of *Gil Blas*, printed in 1895, entered the library's collection in 1952. It was probably in a member's personal library and donated to the New York Society Library at his death. Mark pointed out some conservation work that had recently been done. "See the Japanese paper added at the edges to keep them from crumbling more?" (I hadn't.) "The pages must have been falling apart. If they didn't print on acid-free paper, the paper turns yellow. The pages crumble as you turn them. If a book is falling apart, we have to rebind it or maybe decide that it's come to the end of its useful life. This cover was stamped with gold letters. It was pretty, but it had problems. You can see where each element, the spine, the covers, have been cut apart and glued back together." He was like a surgeon explaining a complex reconstruction. He said, "George, our restorer, must have just done this work. It looks like his. I guess someone took the book out and when it was returned, we noticed the condition." "That may have been me," I said guiltily. Every night, I threw it down on the floor next to my bed with a pen to mark my place. I had not been kind to it. I noticed when I returned it to the library that it looked worse than it had before. It astounded me that the librarians had noticed, too, and called George to the rescue.

In fact, I was amazed by how intimately Mark and Steve knew the collection and by the extent to which they wanted to discuss individual books. Someone had recommended a certain British thriller from the 1950s (John Lodwick, *Contagion to this World*), and they were happy to find that it was already in the collection. Someone mentioned a gritty 1960s novel about inner-city Newark (Nathan Heard's *Howard Street*), and they were proud that their copy could be checked out, whereas the New York Public Library's two could be read only in the library. On the other hand they were distressed that a novel by mystery writer Stanley Ellin, which had been printed on non-acid-free paper, was in such a bad state of disintegration that they had to retire it. But, said Steve, finding the bright side of things, "We gained an inch."

# Nine

# LIFE AND ADVENTURES:
## *GIL BLAS*

CONFRONTED BY THE 758-PAGE BULK OF *GIL BLAS*, I felt at the edge of a channel I didn't have the energy to swim. Everyone has his own technique for entering the water. I sneak up on it, get as little wet as possible at first, and even pretend I have no intention of swimming. I trick myself into immersion. With novels, I sometimes read the introduction or find out about the writer's life or, these days, check for interviews on YouTube. I pretend I'm not reading until, suddenly, I find myself in it up to my neck.

A lot is known about Alain Le Sage, the author of *Gil Blas*, considering that his time on earth took place over three hundred years ago. His parents died when he was young. He was raised in rural France by an uncle who neglected him, and he was helped by a Jesuit who nurtured his talents—rather like the young Gil Blas, sport of fortune, bouncing from one person who robs him to another who does him favors. At twenty-five, Le Sage went to Paris to make his fortune as a writer and came to specialize in translating plays from the Spanish. Only at forty did he have success with his own work, a farce called *Crispin* in 1707, performed at the Théâtre Français; a comic novel called *Le Diable boiteux: or the Devil upon Two Sticks*; and another play called *Turcaret*. They say that Le Sage's conversation was so delightful that when he went to his favorite coffeehouse in Paris, people would crowd around to hear his words. Tobias Smollett, the eighteenth-century novelist who translated *Gil Blas* into English, wrote of Le Sage: "His character was said to be truly amiable; he was free from ambition and courted fortune no further than was necessary to enjoy the pleasures and quiet of a literary life." He worked constantly until he was past seventy. He and his wife had four children, three sons and a daughter. In retirement, they lived with their second son, who was a canon of the cathedral in Boulogne.

People writing novels in the early eighteenth century did not proceed in the same way as novelists today. Most often they imagined a character and then imagined for that character adventures: *The Life and Strange Surprising Adventures of Robinson Crusoe, of York, Mariner* and *The History of Tom Jones, a Foundling* were late avatars. The structure was episodic; that is, each adventure was more or less self-contained. As opposed to later novels, there was little inner development in the protagonist—maybe a wising up at some point early on, maybe a token coming to religion or maturity later, but not much more. This kind of fiction, loosely picaresque, derived ultimately from a Spanish novella of the sixteenth century called *Lazarillo de Tormes*, in which a young rascal works for one bad master after another. The *picaro* or rogue is usually from the lower class, lives by his wits, casts a skeptical eye on a corrupt society, and makes his way through it as best he can. Generally realistic, often satirical, picaresque fiction was an alternative to romances in which noble gallants rescued threatened maidens, the model that inspired Cervantes to deep satire in *Don Quixote*. Characters are types in picaresque fiction—the venal clergyman, the lascivious matron, the doddering old man—but that does not mean they are incapable of surprise. The delight is in seeing how each episode plays out, as in commedia dell'arte: situations were given to the actors who then improvised their words based on the role they played. The sad clown, the lovers, the old man, and the rogue confronted one another in varying situations, always the same but always different. Some actors specialized, playing the same character for their entire career, and you can see traces of these types all over dramatic art, from pompous old Polonius in *Hamlet* to Mozart's clever servant, Figaro.

. *Gil Blas* is a picaresque novel, and I wondered how I could get through 758 tightly printed pages of such plotless fiction. I had to start four times before I generated enough momentum to attain the third chapter. Gil Blas of the town of Santillane in Spain is sent by his uncle, who has educated him, to Salamanca to further his studies. His uncle gives him a donkey and some money, plenty to get him started, but his journey has barely begun before Gil Blas is cheated of his money and his donkey. Some well-dressed men who promise to rescue him from his dire situation are merely bandits who imprison him in their underground hideout and make him work as a kitchen slave. I thought, I must give myself up to my bad fortune. I must not resist. Let Gil Blas be fooled over and over again, I will accept the blows. I will not protest, drop the book, and start again, hoping it has changed. I receive it for what it is. And just when I had made this Zen resolution, Gil Blas's fortunes (and mine as reader) began to turn. He resolves to act and not be acted upon. He escapes from the robbers—and takes another captive with him. And now, having learned a rudimentary skepticism, he begins his adventures, a succession of apprenticeships and service to different masters, through which we see a panorama of humanity. It's a world of fools and tricksters, gulls and con men. But Gil Blas himself, while willing to rob just about anyone, is basically good-hearted, open, and generous. He is great at getting other people to tell their stories, and in this world, everyone is ready to narrate—over a ragout and a bottle of wine or, while starving, to forget the hunger.

They all have stories. They have parents, are thrust into the world, fight to survive. Perhaps they steal. They fall in love or, more often, desire a conquest. They are insulted or a loved one is insulted. They defend their honor. They run someone through. They are forced to flee. They meet new people, hear new stories, are enslaved and eventually freed. They impose on others to get some money, which is soon taken from them by someone smarter, stronger, or more unscrupulous. Women like good-looking men; men like good-looking women. One story succeeds another. You forget who you're reading about. Is it Gil Blas himself or his friend, the notary's son? Or his brother, whom he meets in a tavern after not having seen him for twenty years? Or Don Alphonso? Don Raphael? Don Rolando? Whoever is telling his story is your friend. Whatever he's done, you back him. The raging self of nineteenth- and twentieth-century literature is nowhere to be seen. The focus is on what is perceived, not the perceiver; on society, types of human nature, not on the vulgar middle-class identity busily tweaking its own perfection. Whatever self there is in the picaresque novel is just a jack-in-the-box who pops up every now and then and always says the same thing: "BOO! I'm still around!"

A man named Don Raphael is captured by pirates and goes to work in the Sultan's seraglio, playing the guitar. He becomes the Sultana's lover. One day they are surprised by the Sultan, and the Sultana claims she is converting Don Raphael. The Sultan believes this, but Don Raphael is forced to convert. The Sultana showers him with gifts. One day at the slave market, he sees two Spanish ladies for sale, his mother and his sister. He buys them. His mother tells her story. She had been married three times; her third husband was Sicilian. After his death she was on her way to see the lands she inherited in Sicily, when their boat was captured by pirates and she was sold to her son. The wheel of fortune turns round and round.

Once you get into this book, it's hard to stop. It's like eating potato chips. Each little bit is so satisfying, you want just another. Forget what's happening in your own life. Nothing in this book will remind you of it.

Don Alphonso, deposited as a baby in a basket on the doorstep of the Baron de Steinbach, is now a grown man in love with Seraphina, daughter of the Count de Polan, but he cannot marry her because (a) he is illegitimate and (b) he has just killed her brother. One day he and Gil Blas discover a man and a young woman tied to a tree, at the mercy of villains who are drawing straws to see who gets the woman first. Gil Blas and Alphonso rescue the victims without knowing who they are and bring them to a nearby castle, which happens to belong to Alphonso's real father, who had had to abandon him for complex reasons. However, he has no other children and is now happy to acknowledge Don Alphonso—even to present him with a wife. "No, no," says Alphonso, whose heart is given to Seraphina. "At least see her," says his father. It *is* Seraphina, whom he has just rescued, along with her father, the Count de Polan, who forgives Alphonso for killing his son because he has saved him and his daughter.

This marriage makes everyone very happy, not least Gil Blas, who becomes the honest and commendable steward of the entire family. But a narrative like this does not rest long on happiness. Something has to destabilize it: in this case, the passion of Seraphina's old duenna for Gil Blas. Gil Blas is forced to leave.

His next job is as secretary to the archbishop of Grenada. This is one of the great set pieces of *Gil Blas*. The archbishop prides himself on his sermons, and when he hires Gil Blas, he insists on one thing: if ever the quality of his sermons falls off, Gil Blas must inform him. The archbishop hates it when people age without realizing that their powers have diminished. He makes Gil Blas swear to tell him when that moment has come so he may stop at the height of his powers. The archbishop has a stroke, and his sermons are affected. He begins to ramble and repeat. Gil Blas wrestles with himself about whether or not he should fulfill his promise to inform the archbishop of his decline and finally decides he must. He does it delicately and tactfully, but the archbishop is outraged, rejecting the idea that his sermons aren't as good as they used to be. The truth is that Gil Blas doesn't have the taste the archbishop thought he did. He tells Gil Blas to collect a hundred ducats from the treasurer and dismisses him. "I wish you all manner of prosperity with a little more taste" (*"toutes sortes de prosperités et un peu plus de goût"*). The archbishop's dismissal of Gil Blas for his lack of taste becomes a running joke in the novel, as well as a touchstone of behavior. Oliver Wendell Holmes wrote a poem about the self-deceptions of the old, called "The Archbishop and Gil Blas."

Clerics do not come off well in *Gil Blas*. Actors don't either. They are loose in their morals and stupid in their judgments. Gil Blas works for a famous actress but is so turned off by her profligacy that he leaves, a rare example of someone not being up to Gil's moral snuff. But the profession he hates more than any other is that of the physician, who bleeds the patient until he dies and then claims that the bleeding wasn't administered soon enough. Not many ways of life pass muster. Young men of pleasure are attractive and fun but vain and ruthless. Noblemen are elegant and generally well-meaning but out of touch.

As Gil Blas's merit is recognized by master after master, he rises to the position of private secretary to the prime minister, the Duke of Lerma, the most powerful man in Spain after the king. Gil Blas is devoted to this master, whose service he is proud to be in and whose friendship he enjoys. But there's a problem: the duke is so far removed from daily life that it has not occurred to him to pay Gil Blas, who is close to starvation. One day, master and servant, in a garden, hear two birds talking. The duke wonders what they are saying. Gil Blas asks permission to tell a story: Once, in Persia, a powerful vizier, Atalmuc, and his humble secretary, Zeangir, were in a garden and heard two ravens talking. The vizier wondered what the birds were saying, and the secretary said he had mastered the language of birds from a traveling dervish and would gladly translate. They are talking about us, he said. One bird said, "How happy is that secretary in serving a master that has so much affection for him!" The other bird replied, "Zeangir will die of hunger . . . The Grand Vizier . . . is content with entertaining favorable sentiments in his behalf, but leaves him a prey to poverty."

Gil Blas's pointed tale, a witty invoice to his master for services rendered, is so successful that he is not only paid but given permission by the duke to sell his influence and thereby get rich.

Gil Blas now grows very great indeed, no longer a common rogue, but a wielder of power, sometimes for good, sometimes for not so good. Morally, he is at his least attractive. His biggest coup is procuring a mistress for the Prince of Spain, part of a very complicated intrigue in which the Duke of Lerma is pitted against his own son. It brings Gil Blas to the height of wealth and influence but eventually leads to his patron's disgrace and to his own imprisonment in the tower of Segovia, with the loss of every single thing he has accumulated. Only his many friendships and his innate talents remain. His time in prison isn't wholly unwelcome: Gil Blas has grown disgusted with the court and its chicanery, and he uses his solitude to prepare himself for a smaller, better, deeper life. The fun lies in knowing that Le Sage will soon find a way to free him. And not just free him, but set him on the road to prosperity again. The buoyancy of this hero, the buoyancy of the narrative is what makes it irresistible. While acknowledging cruelty, menace, and vice, it radiates optimism, and the optimism passes to the reader. Reading this book, you feel you can take on anything.

But now the end is in sight. The bookmark has moved from showing all ahead to most behind. There are 258 pages left, and it doesn't seem enough. I don't want to stop reading *Gil Blas*. There is a moment in reading a book, not necessarily in the middle, when you shift from having it all depressingly before you to having most of it depressingly behind. You begin to dread the end, the disappearance of everything you've come to love. You begin to worry about starting all over again, getting involved in another story. Or not. Samuel Johnson wrote,

"There are few things not purely evil, of which we can say, without some emotion of uneasiness, 'this is the last.'" All endings remind us, in some way, of The Ending. A couple who never got along feel bad when the final separation comes, a place you've never liked you see for the last time with heaviness of heart. "The secret horror of the last is inseparable from a thinking being, whose life is limited, and to whom death is dreadful."

Six hundred pages in, only 158 to go, and Gil Blas still hasn't married and settled down. Well, he's settled down, in a glorious estate in the kingdom of Valencia given to him by his patrons Don Cesar and Don Alphonso de Levya, but he has not married. Fortunately, the estate includes a tenant with a beautiful daughter with whom Gil Blas falls in love. So now he is happily married. His faithful servant and friend, Scipio, is also happily married. The four young people live in perfect harmony. The two wives become pregnant, and Gil Blas is thrilled to be a father.

Not only the people of my family were rejoiced at the birth of my son; the inhabitants of Lirias likewise celebrated it by feasts, which showed that the whole village partook of their master's pleasure. But, alas! Our rejoicings were not of long duration: or rather, they were all of a sudden converted into groans, complaints, and lamentations, by an event which more than twenty years have not been able to make me forget, and which will ever be present to my thoughts: my son died, and his mother though safely delivered, soon followed him; a violent fever robbed me of my dear wife fourteen months after we had been married. Let the reader conceive, if possible, the sorrow with which I was seized.

This paragraph gives a good example of the pace of *Gil Blas*. Le Sage dwells on nothing—to such an extent that he challenges your assumptions about weight and depth in narrative. Traditionally, fiction assumes that an event like the death of a wife and child should be dramatized at a length appropriate to its gravity. Le Sage pivots from one state to another with no more than "But, alas!" and although Gil Blas tells us he couldn't eat, fell into a deep depression, and might have died if Scipio had not forced him to sustain himself, there is no plumbing the depths of his soul. We are left to imagine his anguish: "Let the reader conceive . . . the sorrow with which I was seized."

There is a certain wisdom to this approach in fiction, as in life. When a child dies, when a spouse dies, one feels the grief that one feels when a child dies or a spouse dies. There's no point in trying to describe it. How much does it hurt to have your arm pulled from the socket? It hurts as much as having your arm pulled from the socket. Just as some situations are beyond metaphor, some events are beyond dramatization. There's truth to life in the pace of events in Gil Blas. Bad things happen out of the blue. Everything changes in a flash. And life goes on. Within three pages, Gil Blas is up and running again and back at court. The king has died, a new king (the prince for whom Gil Blas found a mistress) has inherited the throne. Gil Blas's fortunes have changed again, and he goes on to be the confidant and private secretary of the new prime minister.

There is no plot in *Gil Blas*—only action, one thing after another. Yet it turns out that the absence of development and direction brings with it immense energy. It's like a wild river with rapids at unpredictable places versus a river dammed, whose energy is released in controlled bursts. The novel in its early days resembled an undammed river, unlike drama, which was tighter, more disciplined, classically had a beginning, a middle, and an end. The novel was inclusive—the loose, baggy monster that Henry James mocked but which was so inspiring to Defoe and Fielding, Dickens and Mark Twain. For E. M. Forster, serious fiction has to have plot, a meaningful sequence of events, and round characters, but much as I love good plots and round characters, reading *Gil Blas* has delighted me because it lacked them.

Le Sage wrote *Gil Blas* over the course of twenty years, while he was at work on many other things. The first two parts were published in 1715, the third in 1724, and the fourth in 1735. It's hard now to imagine a novel being published over the course of twenty years; think instead of a movie franchise like the *Star Wars* series, which began in 1977 and didn't conclude until 2005. People, like my son, who were five years old when they first saw *Star Wars*, had returned to college for their fifth reunion by the time a prequel called *The Phantom Menace* appeared in 1999. And I can measure my own growth by the James Bond series.

The pleasure of following a narrative over months or years, whether reading installments of a novel, watching a TV serial, or, as with mystery novels, coming back to the same character in a series of books, is the pleasure of meeting a beloved friend again and renewing your acquaintance. In life, we may go for years without seeing a friend of our youth and then enjoy a reunion, interested to see how our friend has changed with time but even more pleased by the fundamental continuity. In art, too, a character may change and still be recognizably the same. James Bond may even be played by different actors, but he is always James Bond, always British, always handsome, always well dressed, always successful with beautiful women, always cool, whether or not he drinks his martini shaken or stirred, and his sameness—the dependability of his character—is part of the pleasure. We do not expect or want growth from James Bond. We do not want him to grow self-reflective or tamped down with time (although every writer inheriting a successful series will inevitably try at least once to darken it). We want him to be Bond. The pleasure of watching *The Sopranos* week after week was to see Tony being Tony, Carmela being Carmela, no matter what surprising things they did.

At the same time that I was reading *Gil Blas*, I happened to be reading—in my off-shelf life—*Out of Sheer Rage* by Geoff Dyer. It describes trying to write a book about D. H. Lawrence and sort of failing, but sort of not, because what he did write really says a lot about D. H. Lawrence though even more about a certain melancholy-humorous attitude toward life that Geoff Dyer embodies and that I find immensely appealing. How do the British do it? They manage to be so deep and so funny at the same time. It's as though they've all been taught to take the most extreme position possible and assume that that's the standard, the received wisdom, and then to introduce the true and ordinary as a revelation. They begin with the high-flown what-ought-to-be and puncture that with the deflating edginess of what is. Dyer's description of packing for a trip to Greece—how Lawrence's poems are essential and therefore he decides not to take them, then decides he must have them, obtains them, brings them, and pays no attention to them at all—is a dazzling evocation of a range of human experience hardly ever described, the negative space, what is not done or is done perversely. Dyer is the master of defining the complex reasons we give ourselves for not doing things. His way of being both brilliant and funny, light yet deep, makes some of us feel ponderous.

Dyer sees novels as merely stations on the way to essays and letters, which are more personal and more revealing. He prefers *Sea and Sardinia*, a travel narrative, to all of D. H. Lawrence's other work, with *Studies in Classic American Literature* just behind. He craves unmediated bursts of personality such as are found in the letters, sometimes in poetry, but rarely in novels, with their elaborate dramatic lumber. His favorite novelists are Roland Barthes and Thomas Bernhard, who aren't conventional novelists at all. He likes Marguerite Yourcenar's notes to *Memoirs of Hadrian* better than the novel itself. He is searching always for direct contact with an author's mind. You don't find that in fiction, at least not in fiction formed by the conventions of realism: plot, character, scene, dialogue, and description. For Dyer, fiction has become a laborious translation of sheer personality into another language, the language of character and plot. His breezy iconoclasm reminds me of Sterne's belief that digressions are the sunshine of the novel. Life is one thing after another, none related, little prepared for, and that is the structure of books that feel modern, like Dyer's. And Alain Le Sage's.

*Ten*

# SERIAL KILLERS: DETECTIVE FICTION

I HAD BEEN READING MY WAY THROUGH THE SHELF FOR A year. In that year, friends with chronic sicknesses were sicker. Three friends died. At the same time, new life developed. My son and his wife, deeply in the throes of parenthood, were expecting another baby. My grandson had advanced from crawling to walking, from no speech to single words to primitive but potent sentences, like "Eli love Mommy." My nieces' and nephews' children were going to college. Archie, a new Yorkie in our orbit, was starting to learn to behave like a dog. The stock market was going nowhere, but the real estate market was picking up. I had passed my Kindle on to my husband and started reading books on an iPad. I had been able to focus for many undisturbed days on reading and writing. The only books left to read on my shelf were mystery novels.

If fiction by women is underrepresented on my shelf, detective fiction may take up more than its fair share of space. I have already read two works by Gaston Leroux that are detective novels, the ones featuring Rouletabille, to say nothing of *The Phantom of the Opera*, which began as a detective story. There are another two detective novels on my shelf by the prolific

Edwardian writer William Le Queux and five by John Lescroart, a contemporary American novelist. Le Queux's enormous output begins on the shelf above and spills two books onto my shelf. Lescroart leaves five books with me (one in multiple copies) before rushing on and covering much of the shelf below. Had the shelving been different, my formula would have kept me from this shelf, more than five works by one author being prohibited. When I started, there were exactly five Lescroarts, but now there are eight, as reshelving changes the landscape.

Detective fiction is so popular that the New York Society Library, in order to give its members what they want to read, routinely buys as many copies of this genre as it does all other fiction combined. Every month the library prints a brochure announcing its new books in the categories of nonfiction, fiction, poetry, and mysteries. In one recent month, there were sixty-five new volumes of fiction, including such popular titles as Danielle Steel's *Friends Forever* and Jennifer Weiner's *The Next Best Thing*, a first novel that received a lot of attention called *Seating Arrangements* by Maggie Shipstead, a collection of short stories by an up-and-coming writer, Alix Ohlin, as well as books by such established authors as Joanna Trollope, Patrick White, Stephen L. Carter, Chris Bohjalian, and Carlos Fuentes. In the separate category of "mysteries," there were another sixty-seven volumes, including former New York sex-crimes prosecutor Linda Fairstein's *Night Watch*, three books translated from Swedish and one from Norwegian, Scandinavian crime being particularly hot right now, and various other books featuring a continuing character: *A Pleasure to Do Death with You: A DI Christy Kennedy Mystery*; *Creole Belle: A Dave Robicheaux Novel*; *House Blood: A Joe DeMarco Thriller*; *Dark Heart: A Mariner Novel*; and *In the Shadow of Evil: A DCI Neil Paget Mystery*.

One of the most popular mystery writers, according to the Society Library staff, is Donna Leon, a New Jersey–born American who has lived in Venice for thirty years and has written twenty-four mysteries set in Venice, featuring Commissario Guido Brunetti. If you want your detective to be a titled Englishman, you can have that. If you want an old-lady detective who knits, you can have that. A Parisian detective who waxes his mustache? Nothing easier. A New Yorker, a Londoner, a Native American, a Venetian, a Roman—all these are available. I myself tend to read detective fiction for imaginative access, and where I travel—or want to travel—determines what mysteries I read. In the Southwest or yearning for the Southwest, I read Tony Hillerman, who was based in Albuquerque and whose deep knowledge of southwestern culture he embeds in his mystery novels about officers of the Navajo Tribal Police. In Egypt, I was accompanied by the Amelia Peabody mysteries of Elizabeth Peters. In South Florida, or missing it, I read Carl Hiaasen and James W. Hall. In any national park I try to read the appropriate novel by Nevada Barr. Her detective, Anna Pigeon, is a park ranger who is perpetually being reassigned and so has solved crimes in national parks all over the country. When I'm in Boulder, Colorado, visiting my son and his family, I like to read Stephen White, a clinical psychologist and novelist who lives in Boulder and whose therapist-detective, Dr. Alan Gregory, happens to live there, too.

John Lescroart (pronounced, his website says, "less kwah") lives in Davis, in Northern California, and sets his novels in San Francisco. He has written more than twenty novels in a career that spans about twenty years—a book a year. This is someone who writes novels the way an accountant does tax returns: it is his job. He prides himself on doing it well and on being able to make a living by it. Most of his mysteries feature a defense lawyer, Dismas Hardy, affable, Irish, married to the lovely redheaded Frannie, and his best friend, Abe Glitsky, a homicide detective, half Jewish, half black, taciturn, married to the lovely Treya. They are intelligent, workmanlike novels, and they have an audience in the millions.

For a special edition of his novel *The 13th Juror*, Lescroart wrote a preface that I think is a remarkably frank account of the life of a working writer, someone trying to earn a living from fiction. In the first novel of the series, according to Lescroart's account, Dismas Hardy was a bartender who had renounced his former professional life as a lawyer. But Hardy as a bartender failed to win a readership, and soon Lescroart had him "return" to criminal law. This more demanding career engaged Dismas in social issues that could be explored in court, and Lescroart felt his novels getting meatier. He was writing not mysteries exactly, but courtroom dramas, legal thrillers, the kind of novel written by Scott Turow and John Grisham. Unlike those two writers, however, Lescroart was not himself a lawyer, and he felt a little uncomfortable with the material. He relied on his friend Al Giannini, an assistant district attorney for the city and county of San Francisco, to help with both issues and details.

"I worked diligently with Al to get my facts right. But all of this research, rewriting, and revision, it seemed to me, added an entire extra level to the basic work of writing a good book, difficult enough in any event. In short, it was hard. Beyond that, all of the legal stuff felt once-removed from who I was. It wasn't a reflection of my own life experience. In a real sense, I felt I was channeling Al's world and trying to pass it off as my own."

He was on the verge of abandoning Dismas Hardy when a German publisher bought the first three Hardy novels to appear in translation. This in turn got his American publisher more interested in the series and prompted a request for another novel featuring the lawyer. "At this time . . . I was 44 years old, a part-time writer and full-time stay-at-home father. My wife, Lisa Sawyer, was supporting the family at a deficit of around a thousand dollars a month. If I could make any money at all writing one more legal thriller, I would do it." Lescroart, his wife, and his lawyer friend Al went out to a steak house, had a few drinks, and batted around ideas for what another novel might deal with, settling on the "burning bed" issue: a mistreated woman kills her husband—by actually setting on fire the bed in which he's sleeping, or some other way. Such murder cannot be considered self-defense, because it is not an immediate response to an immediate threat. "Burning bed" led Lescroart and his brain trust to thinking about battered women in general and produced the subject of *The 13th Juror*.

The complexity and power of this idea all at once trumped my reluctance to continue with legal thrillers. Suddenly I had a grand theme, a burgeoning and compelling social issue, a badly-flawed and wholly sympathetic female character who would be charged with her husband's murder and who would not admit that he had even beaten her.

He began interviewing witnesses and defendants in battered women's cases at the San Francisco Hall of Justice. He was shocked by what he discovered. Women who seemed composed, competent, and successful—one he met was a physician—would put up with terrible physical abuse from their lovers and husbands. They would have the greatest difficulty acknowledging that they were battered. They participated in what to Lescroart was a bizarre psychological ballet in which they needed to be abused in order to feel loved, until abuse reached the point of violence, after which it subsided for a time and they felt that everything was better, until the next round.

The first Lescroart I read, *Betrayal*, written some years after *The 13th Juror*, is about corrupt military contractors in Iraq, and Lescroart has clearly done his homework as well as he did it for the battered woman syndrome. Evan Scholler, a young reserve officer in the National Guard of California, is in Baghdad in 2003 doing dangerous duty, not at all what he had expected or been trained for when he signed up. Torn away from his girlfriend and career by the decision to send National Guard troops to fight a foreign war, he has been assigned to security subcontractors who are, essentially, mercenaries, profit-seeking cowboys making as much as eleven and a half million, we are told, on a twelve-million-dollar government contract. One particularly reckless mercenary, Ron Nolan, gets Evan's men killed and Evan himself gravely wounded. Not only that—on a visit home, he steals Evan's girlfriend. We are not unhappy that he winds up dead, but Evan is charged with the murder. Worse, he cannot remember whether or not he did it, because he is suffering from post-traumatic stress disorder.

I sat reading *Betrayal* one evening. The American Humvees were making their way through blocked streets of Baghdad back to the safety of the airport. The men are terrified of every civilian car approaching them. It could be an SVBIED, suicide-vehicle-borne improvised explosive device. (The acronym alone seemed worth reading the book for.) If a car gets too close to a convoy, it risks being fired on by jumpy reservists or aggressive mercenaries. The people in the car may be innocents who don't understand a warning shout in English or the significance of your hand gestures and noises. Or they may be suicide terrorists bent on blowing you up. Evan and Nolan are in an armored vehicle but feel totally exposed. A car approaches and doesn't back off when warned. Nolan fires. A woman and children are killed. This was so upsetting I actually put the book down. I closed my eyes and imagined the disaster, too dismayed even to go on reading. But I was, simultaneously, entertained. Emotions are like muscles. They like to be used and are strengthened by use. I felt angry, scared, guilty, pitying, appalled. That's a lot of emotion from one scene in a book no one would nominate for the Pulitzer Prize in fiction. Sitting in my living room, I have experienced the horror of modern combat, which is useful and, in Horace's formula for literature (*utile dulci*), sweet. It's a literary experience, provided by words a writer chose out of all possible words and arranged in one order out of all possible orders. It may not be the same complex pleasure as reading a passage of *Middlemarch*, but it is not a different experience entirely. I describe my reading experience in an effort to be completely respectful of this writer's work. I want to see it for what it really is.

The informational aspect of fiction (*utile*) dominates, but that doesn't bother me. Frankly, I'd rather find out about how subcontracting of military security works from Lescroart than by reading his source, T. Christian Miller's *Blood Money: Wasted Billions, Lost Lives, and Corporate Greed in Iraq*. I am grateful to all writers for the research they do and for fictionalizing matters that otherwise I wouldn't know enough about. My understanding of the politics of real estate development in Florida

comes entirely from Carl Hiaasen, everything I know about
fly tying from James W. Hall, my sense of the generative possibilities of a turkey baster from Scott Turow's *Presumed Innocent*.

But I am not typical of Lescroart's fan base. They do not
want to hear about military contractors in Iraq. They want
Dismas Hardy, and he does not enter the novel until the case
against Evan Scholler goes to trial. On Amazon, the reviews
voted "most helpful" were all negative. "For those of you expecting another great Dismas Hardy/Abe Glitsky novel, don't
be fooled by the book jacket. Hardy/Glitsky appear in the first
ten pages and then not for another 250-300 pages, reappearing
only for the last 110. This book should not really be advertised
as featuring these characters. I'm glad I got it from the library
or I really would have been unhappy." And "I like to read
about Dismas Hardy and his friend in SFPD, Lt. Glitsky. I do
not like political commentary on the use of contractors to fight
in a war in a novel I am reading for enjoyment." And finally:
"It's my opinion Lescroart had a mediocre story focusing on
government contractor corruption and found a way to weave
in his popular characters. Maybe my disappointment with the
lack of a Hardy/Glitsky focused story line biased my opinion."
These comments show what a fine line a writer like Lescroart
has to walk between finding new material to keep himself functioning imaginatively and maintaining enough of a focus on
familiar characters to satisfy his fans.

For many readers, a large part of the appeal of detective
novels is in the recurrence of the same characters—a primitive
but potent effect, which we saw at work in *Gil Blas*. I myself
explain this effect in psycho-economic terms. You make a certain investment of time and imaginative energy every time

you begin a piece of fiction. You learn the traits you need to know—about Glitsky, for example, that he is half Jewish, half black, and taciturn, and that his first wife, whom he adored, died. For every work of fiction you read, you incorporate information you need to remember and scope out the level of seriousness the author expects from you. You adjust to the author's style. This basic orientation to a work of fiction is demanding enough that some people shun short stories, which seem to return so little on their initial imaginative investment. Novels give more, and series give the most. Once you've mastered what you need to know about a fictional detective (so brilliant he is often bored, plays violin, takes cocaine, doctor sidekick, problem brother), you can read book after book with astonishing efficiency. This registers as comfort. You are happy to meet your old friends again, even if your old friends are cardboard.

I never developed this feeling toward Dismas Hardy and Abe Glitsky. Rather than old friends whom I looked forward to seeing again, they were the couple who were always inviting us for dinner and I finally had to accept, knowing we were in for a lackluster evening. I knew we would have to get past Hardy's battle-ax secretary/receptionist vexingly called Phyllis. We would again have lunch at Lou the Greek's, featuring the half-Greek, half-Chinese cuisine of Lou's wife, especially Yeanling Clay Bowl. Tedious Treya and tedious Frannie and their tedious children and their tedious friendship would all be back. What can I say? Different strokes for different folks. Many readers love these characters and want to spend time with them; they might hate walking around the Central Park reservoir with my best friend and me talking about Broadway musicals.

I suppose there is no more dependable rule in the emotional life than that the things we look forward to most disappoint us and the things we expect least of turn out to give us more than we imagined. This run of mysteries turned out to be the hardest slogging on my shelf. What bothered me most was the absence of plot, the very quality that had pleased me in *Gil Blas*. So little appeared to be happening. It was all so intellectual.

I was beginning to think that most detective novels consisted of little more than revelations: he realized, he learned, he discovered. The challenge for the writer seemed to be to deploy information in effective order and at the right pace. Take *Oedipus Rex*, often—and rightly—called the first detective story: the task given to Oedipus, to discover the murderer of Laius, is a detective's task. One person after another comes to him with information that eventually lets him figure out what happened. Tiresias, Jocasta, the Messenger, the Herdsman—each adds a piece to the puzzle until Oedipus realizes that it was he himself who killed Laius. Laius was killed at a point where three roads meet? Uh-oh. I killed an old man at a point where three roads meet. But he couldn't have been my father. Polybus is my father. *Uh*-oh? You mean Polybus adopted me?

The earliest mysteries were quite self-consciously exercises in information processing. Edgar Allan Poe's "The Mystery of Marie Rogêt," from 1842, one of his "tales of ratiocination," attends closely to newspaper articles reporting on a murder that actually took place in New Jersey and concerns logic as much as murder, the gap between a mathematician's reasoning and public opinion and between legal proof and philosophical truth. "The Murders in the Rue Morgue" and "The Purloined Letter" are also about how to discover—or, in the case of "The

Purloined Letter," to hide. The Sherlock Holmes stories dramatized deductive reasoning. Were it not for the riveting character of the scientist-aesthete, we would not put up with the clunky lessons in logic that constitute much of the stories: "I see from the way the path is swept that a ten-hand horse has been here" and "I conclude from the marks on the window that the murderer was a peg-legged baboon." Not all Sherlock Holmes stories follow that pattern, but those that do are exasperating, since you cannot process information you haven't been given. Poe himself pointed out the stacked-deck nature of the invention in his detective tales: "Where is the ingenuity in unraveling a web which you yourself . . . have woven for the express purpose of unraveling?" he asked.

In the second Lescroart novel I read, *The Hearing*, a woman is found dead in an alley with a junkie hovering over her body, his pockets loaded with her jewelry. He is accused of her murder, and Dismas is retained as his lawyer. The victim turns out to be Elaine Wager, Glitsky's unacknowledged daughter by U.S. senator Loretta Wager. "Turns out to be" is key. The backstory expands, but nothing happens. Mysteries multiply: a detective investigating the murder disappears, some papers Elaine had taken in an investigation of her own go missing. Pieces of information appear. Connections are made. My favorite "aha" moment came near the end of the book, when Glitsky saw he was wrong to assume that Elaine had been coming from a restaurant within a circular area around the spot where she died. Instead, Glitsky realized that if you took that point, the corner of Grant and Maiden Lane, drew a line between it and where her car was parked, the corner of Montgomery and Bush, and continued the line to the south, you would find where she had come from along the line or to the west of it. I was so impressed by the precision of this that I went to Google Maps and drew the line myself. It was possible to do, so accurate was Lescroart's San Francisco geography. I could not guess what restaurant she was coming from, but Lescroart convincingly could. The half-Jewish Glitsky and his quarter-Jewish daughter both frequented David's Deli on Geary Street. Establishing that Elaine had her last meal there, it was simple to go to the deli, find out who Elaine had been eating with that night, and then figure out who had murdered her. In this sort of game, the odds always favor the house. Could not the coroner just as easily have performed an autopsy, discovered a pastrami sandwich in the victim's stomach, and sent Glitsky off much earlier to David's Deli?

Knocking detective fiction is a favorite game of literary critics. Edmund Wilson did it first and best with a piece published in the 1940s whose title says it all: "Who Cares Who Killed Roger Ackroyd?" Wilson considered detective novels a minor vice ranking somewhere between smoking and crossword puzzles. W. H. Auden followed in the same vein with an essay called "The Guilty Vicarage." Mystery fans have been outraged ever since, and this ancient battle continues because it's so much fun to upset mystery fans and so easy to do it. Not long ago, *The New Yorker* published a piece by Arthur Krystal with the Ackroyd-worthy title "Easy Writers." It ran just before the summer, and one reader thought that wasn't accidental: "a gigantic wet blanket" on our beach reading. But I thought it was not a wet blanket, just another delightful essay, like Wilson's, savoring detective fiction, if only to put it back in its (alleged) place at the end, thereby getting up the dander of the feisty and articulate genre fans. There's really no point in making fun of detective fiction beyond the fun of doing it. Nothing will stop people from reading mysteries, and anyway, why would you want to?

I surveyed some of my mystery-fan friends about the nature of their passion. All of them used the word "puzzle." Nobody used the word "literature." "There has to be a sense of rightness when you find out who the murderer is," said one. "Some writers cheat, and pull a character out of nowhere and nail him as the murderer. That's maddening, and I never pick up a book by that writer again." "Coming up with the answer," said another, who added that someone she knew had known someone who wrote mysteries and that person had gotten started by lying in bed and planning how she could kill her husband. No one seems to feel ashamed about spending time reading mysteries. Even the president of Harvard, while supplying a list of current reading to *The New York Times*, can admit that she is a detective story addict without compromising *veritas* or *gravitas*. Readers understand without much argument that there's room in their heads and hearts for many different kinds of literature, and of all the parts of our reading life, what we read for escape is most personal.

Then too, a lot of it is timing. Just as the best thing you ever ate was what you ate when you were hungriest, the best mystery novel or thriller is the one that appeared when you most needed it.

I had to read one more John Lescroart novel. I wasn't hungry, but I had to eat. Just one more novel, and I would have finished my self-imposed task. Every goal, no matter how arbitrary, is an opportunity for satisfaction. When Shackleton decided to mount his expedition to Antarctica, he had no real purpose. The South Pole had already been reached. There were no useful surveying or exploration tasks to perform. He determined to do the only thing that had not been done: to be the first to cross the continent. A pointless objective, and he did not achieve it. His expedition failed in its stated purpose. His real goal emerged only when he was overwhelmed by the disaster. It was to save his men. Imagine if he had said at the beginning, "My goal is to dig myself into a deep hole and out again." Who would have signed on for the enterprise?

The hurricane of 2012, Sandy, proved to be a monster. Its enormous bulk moved up the East Coast and then pushed inland just about at New York, with catastrophic effects on the shoreline of New Jersey, Staten Island, Brooklyn, and Queens, with the Rockaways—where Rhoda Lerman and I were children—particularly hard-hit. The boardwalk we both recall with such fondness, remembering the smell of the ocean, the burning of swallowed water, the scratchy feel of sand in our shoes, was utterly destroyed. Houses were battered to pieces or washed away, people drowned or killed by falling trees, hospitals inundated. The suffering was appalling. My husband and I sat in our apartment, bathtub filled with water, pantry stocked with cans of tuna fish, and watched the devastation on television. We never lost power for a minute, but much of the rest of the city remained without electricity for days, some areas for weeks and even months. People moved out of downtown apartments and camped out with friends or relatives until the power came back on. The city was out of commission. There were no subways or buses to get to work on. Taxis were afraid to take fares, because they didn't have gas. For the same reason, people from the suburbs couldn't drive into the city. Life was so hard for everyone that if you offered help, people were likely to fall into your arms crying.

That the library was closed for three days was the least of it, but it forced me to read the one John Lescroart I had actually purchased. I bought it at a Monroe County Public Library book sale in Key West, paying $2.50, half the previous markdown price. It was part of the flood of superfluous books that the library sells off once a month in season, its palm-studded patio filled with utility tables bearing row upon row of books, rivers of books. Samuel Johnson said, "No place affords a more striking conviction of the vanity of human hopes, than a public library," but that's because he hadn't seen the Key West library book sale. This flood had deposited a Lescroart novel on the alien shore of my personal library, a shelf in my study with other books I'd recently read or planned to read. Title? *A Plague of Secrets*. Victim this time? The manager of Bay Beans West, a coffeehouse in San Francisco, who's dealing pot on the side. Who is wrongly accused? The owner of the coffee shop, a wealthy socialite who also happens to be the mayor's niece. Why is she running a coffee shop and paying the manager much more than he is worth? Ah, to know that, we have to go backward. Who really did it and why? Truthfully, right now, a couple of weeks after reading the book, I can't remember.

This is what I've learned: if you don't like the characters, and there isn't a compelling narrative (what I would call a plot), and you're resistant to the puzzle-solving element in mystery novels, then you *have* to be reading for the direct contact with the writer that is the quality Geoff Dyer talked about. But that quality, "voice," is the hardest thing to achieve in literature. It requires that a writer fight against every sentence, resisting the pressure of convention and conformity, resisting his or her own impulses toward banality and the easy way. Unsurprisingly, not many writers do this. They just shuffle around the same old words, the same old ways of thinking, into a semblance of something new: new information, new settings, a new kind of detective. Most genre writers choose to write genre fiction because will, determination, and very hard work are enough to see them through. Although some writers achieve it, authenticity is not required.

I have reached the point in my project equivalent to four o'clock on a winter afternoon in the snowbelt, when you're tired but your day is far from over. You still have to get home, shovel the driveway, keep the kids happy, and cook dinner. One way or another, you've brought this on yourself. As for me, I wanted to survey the actual ground of literature, and it turns out that much of that ground, or shelf space, is detective fiction, the genre that, while most appealing in its own time, ages worst, its great successes destined to be replaced by newer, more efficient models. For much detective fiction resembles a machine—a household appliance—more than it does the thing of beauty that's a joy forever, and who wants to lug a samovar through life when they can have a new Nespresso machine? Unless it has slipped the bonds of its genre and established its literary value, nothing on a library shelf is less likely to be read with pleasure than another era's detective fiction.

My own take on mysteries, finally, is pseudoscientific. I am willing to bet that the brain has an inherent need to find what $x$ equals, to reach certainty at the end of a sequence of possibilities. Science will probably discover that at the moment of solving an equation or finishing a mystery novel, the brain releases endorphins. This will explain once and for all the popularity of detective fiction.

•

It is time to come clean about something I've hinted at. I have had, this past year, a secret life. I have snuck into my days and nights moments with books not on my shelf in the Society Library. Geoff Dyer, Alice Kaplan, Suzanne Collins, Janet Malcolm—I was not supposed to be reading you. This is one of the many benefits of an arbitrary undertaking. Define what you are supposed to be doing, and you immediately establish a whole range of things you should not be doing. These otherwise ordinary activities are thus transmuted into guilty pleasures, and their value grows correspondingly.

A month after Hurricane Sandy, I was involved with Alan Furst. Furst writes spy novels set at the time of World War II. Spy novels are quite different from mysteries and legal thrillers, although they are often put into the same category, and they are more to my taste. I began with Furst's latest, *Mission to Paris*, about an American movie star making a film in Paris just before the war who gets caught up in political warfare. I liked this so much that I immediately—and I mean immediately—began another, like someone lighting a second cigarette from the first. It was close to midnight. In the olden days I would have had to wait until morning to go to the library or bookstore to get the next book by Furst, fingers crossed that I could find the book I wanted. But now, in bed, I was able to download it, acquiring it magically from the heavens, it seemed, and not just the first in the series, *Night Soldiers*, but the two after that, *Dark Star* and *The Polish Officer*. I was off in another world, Bulgaria in the 1930s, until one in the morning, when I finally turned my light out, exhausted, like one of the twelve princesses in the fairy tale who disappear every night to a magic kingdom underground and dance themselves silly. My husband would have been justified to complain about my thing with Alan Furst. For several days I even snuck away in the afternoon to spend an hour with him. When the workday was over, I brought along my iPad and read as I drank my vodka. I raced us through dinner and left my husband with the dishes so I could return to Bulgaria or Russia or Poland.

Alan, I have to admit to myself, much as I love him, does not always manage to achieve a unique voice. But he is knowledgeable; I learned a lot from him about World War II, such as the effort to convince the obtuse French military establishment that Hitler would attack through the forest and the effort to keep the Nazis from getting oil to run their tanks. His protagonist, who is technically different in every book—Bulgarian or French, NKVD spy or film producer—is always at bottom the same, a guy who likes women and has sex regularly in a way non-creepy to a female reader, a guy who is politically reasonable whether he is Bolshevik or Gaullist, a guy who is up to everything life throws at him, about whom you never have to worry. He is somewhat under-characterized, which is part of what makes him pleasant to spend time with. Dismas Hardy and Abe Glitsky had driven me into his arms. They may be very good men, but they are not right for me.

Every time you read a work of fiction, you are committing an *acte gratuit*, a gratuitous act that proves your freedom. Novels and stories, as Jane Smiley has pointed out, can only attract, never coerce. "To read fiction is to do something voluntary and free, to exercise choice over and over." Of course, some of us get the habit of reading in school, where reading is the reverse of free: it is assigned and required. So freedom has to be acquired or reacquired in later life. But instead of urging us to venture forth on our own, our consumer culture tries to persuade us always to sign up for guided tours, to do what someone else may profit from our doing. Only libraries promote random reading through their open stacks and that ultimately random system of organization, alphabetical order. Otherwise, in all realms, literary and literal, the guided tour prevails. We are even offered the chance to pay in order to reenact my favorite gratuitous voyage: a professional crew of Australian adventurers will re-create Shackleton's journey from Antarctica to South Georgia Island in a lifeboat exactly duplicating Shackleton's *James Caird*. For twenty thousand dollars per person you can follow in a support vessel along with Shackleton's granddaughter, Alexandra.

More people should visit Antarctica, metaphorically speaking, on their own. That is one of the conclusions I have reached, one of my recommendations: explore something, even if it's just a bookshelf. Make a stab in the dark. Read off the beaten path. Your attention is precious. Be careful of other people trying to direct how you dispense it. Confront your own values. Decide what it is you are looking for and then look for it. Perform connoisseurship. We all need to create our own vocabulary of appreciation, or we are trapped by the vocabulary of others. Intensity, uniqueness, variety, specificity—these are qualities I value, but perhaps you will not. Size is important to me: capaciousness in a work of fiction, length in a career. What do you value? Why? Does reading have more merit than any other way of passing time? Is it useful to read randomly? alone? in discussion groups? bad books? old books? new? I wish that literary criticism could be built back up on the grounds of experience, closer to book reviewing than to academic theory, with a bias toward enthusiasm, with new Matthew Arnolds putting in their two cents about the best that was ever thought and said and new Nabokovs and Wilsons puncturing cant.

## Eleven

# IMMORTALITY

I HAVE NOT YET REPORTED ABOUT WILLIAM LE QUEUX—
whose name is pronounced "Le Q." He was one of those
writers who possess a torrential imagination but no feel for
literature. I was trying to end this book without writing about
him, because he is so bad. Hands down the worst book on the
shelf is Le Queux's *Three Knots*, a mystery that reads as if it
were written by an eight-year-old on Percocet. Still, you have
to respect Le Queux's imagination as you respect Niagara
Falls. In a forty-year career, he wrote more than two hundred
books. It seems impossible, but in 1922 alone, he published five
titles, including the two that ended up on my shelf, *The Young
Archduchess* and *Three Knots*. This was the year that saw the
publication of two of modernism's central texts, *Ulysses* and
*The Waste Land*. There was no formal innovation in Le Queux's
work, however, almost no form, just mad invention. He couldn't
turn it off.

I thought it would be useful to keep in our minds, exploring the ground of literature, that Le Queux was a conspicuous
and successful writer, however awful his work. Although his
name is now unknown and his books unread, he has also had

an influence on our collective imagination in a way I will explain. It might be fitting to end my trek with the worst writer on the shelf and humbling to consider both how successful he was and how completely he has been forgotten.

Le Queux was principally known for his espionage fantasies, including *The Invasion of 1910*, published in 1906, which imagined a German invasion of Britain prepared for by a hundred well-placed German spies. They identified weak spots in Britain's defenses so that the German invasion flotilla could land, and then they aided the army's advance by sabotage, blowing up railway bridges, cutting telephone and telegraph lines, and so on. This novel was tremendously popular, raising the circulation of the newspaper in which it first appeared and then selling more than a million copies when it was published in book form six months later, one of the first books ever to sell at that level. *Spies of the Kaiser* returned to the theme in 1909, but now the small cadre of German spies had grown to thousands, coordinated by a spymaster embedded in London but in constant secret contact with the chief of the "German Intelligence Department" in Berlin.

Le Queux insisted that these novels were based on fact, and they helped stir up anti-German and pro-war sentiment in the years before World War I, although many people found them risible. A. A. Milne parodied *Spies of the Kaiser* for *Punch*. "Last Tuesday a man with his moustache brushed up the wrong way alighted at Basingstoke station and inquired for the refreshment room. This leads me to believe that a dastardly attempt is about to be made to wrest the supremacy of the air from our grasp." But many more people believed Le Queux's fantasy of a country filled with German spies riding around on bicycles and embarked on walking tours, noting the location of every country lane and grocery store and transmitting the information methodically back to Berlin.

One believer was the head of a special section concerning military counterespionage within the British War Office, Lieutenant Colonel James Edmonds, whose reports of spy activity, most of which were nonsense, fueled Le Queux's imaginings, which in turn were seized upon by Edmonds as substantive reports. For example, Le Queux sent word to Edmonds that he had discovered a barber with a French name who was actually German and wore a wig. This was deeply suspicious. Or a man on a bicycle was looking at a map and, when accosted, swore in German. It is straight out of A. A. Milne's parody. Yet Edmonds's ideas, and his frustration that the British government would not back his counterespionage activities with more money, informed Le Queux's fiction, which acted as proof of Edmonds's ideas. The less evidence of a spy network that actually existed, the more subtle and fiendish it appeared! According to British historian Nicholas Hiley in his introduction to a new edition of *Spies of the Kaiser*, the counterespionage group Edmonds headed was in 1916 renamed MI5. Hiley says, "Some may think it fitting that MI5 should have had its origins in the pages of a novel, and such a wonderfully bad novel at that, for much of the subsequent history of that unit has seen the blending of truth and rumour into a heady cocktail of suspicion and allegation." It was through Le Queux, according to Hiley, that we first learned the pleasure of "watching with horror as a complacent government and a trusting people are undermined by the ruthless agents of a foreign power."

By the time the war started, Le Queux had become convinced that he was being targeted by the Germans for having revealed their plans, and he demanded special protection from the police. They refused to supply it, saying that Le Queux was a person "not to be taken seriously." Le Queux began carrying a revolver for his own protection. He seemed genuinely to believe his own paranoid fantasies.

Born in 1864, Le Queux was a few years older than Gaston Leroux, and like Leroux, he was a literary celebrity in his time. His payment per word was as high as that of the best-paid English writers of the day, Thomas Hardy and H. G. Wells. Wells's *The War of the Worlds* (1898), in which Martians attack Earth, was inspired by the invasion literature of the 1890s, of which Le Queux's *The Great War in England in 1897*, published in 1894, imagining an invasion of Britain by France and Russia, was one of the most popular. Le Queux's huge readership included members of the Royal Family, Prime Minister Arthur Balfour, the young Graham Greene, and the young Ian Fleming. His were the novels that helped form the younger and better writers' imaginations. Le Queux's debonair spy, Duckworth Drew of the Secret Service, with his good looks and cosmopolitan ease, his fondness for high-tech and intricate weaponry hidden in small packages, his beautiful, well-dressed girlfriends, often under the influence of the villain, was certainly the godfather of 007. His name may have inspired that of Bond's weapon master, "Q." There is a line going back from my beloved Alan Furst to Graham Greene and from him back to William Le Queux, a lineage of little boys and lonely teenagers burying themselves in books, and from this tradition has come some of our greatest pleasures—and deepest fears. One of Graham Greene's characters, observing how daily life had come more and more to resemble the fevered imaginings of the spy thrillers of his youth, said, "The world has been remade by William Le Queux." Americans who cannot travel through airports without taking off their shoes, and without sequestering liquids in containers of a few ounces, surely live in a world remade by spy novels. We are caught up every day in a battle against an unseen, malignant, perhaps invented enemy with a fiendish imagination generating new and cleverer ways to destroy us.

I'm glad the New York Society Library gives William Le Queux and his ever-timely paranoia space on its shelves. But alas, there are no spy novels or invasion fantasies by Le Queux on my particular shelf. There are only two of those early detective novels, a genre familiar to us from the work of Gaston Leroux, in which the detective is a skilled actor or actress capable of disguise and the murderer is some arbitrarily chosen person whose discovery gives us no satisfaction at all. Of the books by Le Queux actually on my shelf, the better of the two is *The Young Archduchess*, which contains the single line I would most like to have occasion to utter in my life: "I am going to stay at Claridge's till I find a pied-à-terre." For the legions of people who wish they had been born into the English upper class in the years before World War I (fans of *Upstairs, Downstairs* and *Downton Abbey*), this is the right stuff.

At the start of *The Young Archduchess*, a glamorous group is gathered at Colonel Ashdown's dinner table. The host mediates between the two lovely ladies beside him—the witty and intelligent Lady Gertrude and the beautiful but dim Mrs. Mabel Somers. The ladies are funny and direct: " 'One can't have everything, dear Mabel. There were plenty of good fairies at your christening. Don't grumble if one or two failed to turn up.' It was a left-handed compliment, but the beautiful woman was not subtle or exacting." Genial Colonel Ashdown loves everyone at the table except his own appalling son, Hugh, who inherited Mrs. Ashdown's family history of shameful behavior. These things are related bluntly, the writer comfortable with his own authority. His prose style, with its Latinate and Augustan balance, bespeaks an upper-class boarding-school certainty. This of Hugh, for example: "Idle, vicious, and insubordinate, he was equally unpopular with his schoolfellows . . . and his masters." But after its Trollopean beginning, the novel descends into melodrama and absurdity. Le Queux lacks the patience to keep up the style and the discipline to rework what he's written. What spills out of him is what we get.

Colonel Ashdown is summoned to Paris to the deathbed of an old friend from his days as a military attaché in Vienna. The old friend is the Archduke of Montenero, wealthy, healthy, and ebullient when Ashdown last saw him, now wasted away, having lived in obscurity and fear for many years. His wicked brother, Prince Louis, has been trying to kill him and take all his money. Now, on the point of death, the archduke's only concern is for his daughter, living humbly under an assumed name in England. He begs Ashdown—his dying wish—to take her in, protect her, see that she marries a good English gentleman.

Geradine [sic], the young archduchess, is soon living happily with the Ashdowns. Handsome Monsieur Vincent, a gentleman who has adopted the ungentlemanly profession of private detective, visits often and keeps the colonel informed about Prince Louis's movements. Perhaps Geradine will marry him. In books like this, every young man is a potential husband, but it doesn't seem a brilliant match. He is a detective and no Lord Peter Wimsey. Mr. and Mrs. Somers warn Geradine that as a foreigner, she may not be able to evaluate Englishmen properly, and Geradine acknowledges the truth of this: "She did not really know a proper English gentleman from a counterfeit."

Automobiles play a big part in this novel, and we understand that "motoring" is a sport, like hunting or riding. A car is a dangerous and unreliable animal. You have to know how to handle it, or it will throw and maim you. Geradine is out motoring when an accident occurs. Another motorist stops to help. Can it be? Yes, it is! A genuine English gentleman, "Basil Long, son of the eminent judge, and one of the most prominent jurors at the English bar." The White Knight has arrived, not a déclassé detective, but a gentleman, a juror, a man who spends his holidays motoring! Soon Geradine decides to trust Basil and share with him the secret of her birth. "Proud as he was of her confidence, the narrative had depressed him. He was very much in love with her . . . As a girl of ordinary, even noble Italian descent, he might have wooed and won her. But the knowledge of her royal blood dashed his hopes to the ground."

Meanwhile the detective Vincent and the beautiful Mrs. Somers bump into each other in a country lane and are seen talking by Mr. Somers. Disaster! Ruin! Her husband demands a separation. How awful!! And yet . . . Mrs. Somers goes to London and cheers up to hear that her friend Geradine will also be there. My favorite sentence in the book follows, and I seize the chance to repeat it: "I am going to stay at Claridge's till I find a pied-à-terre." Vincent eventually pays a call on Mrs. Somers in London, and they confess to each other their mutual feelings. He proposes a relationship. She declines. She is bound to her husband, although they are separated. Just then a note arrives. Her husband has been killed in a car accident. Hurrah and thank heaven for motorcars! Vincent and Mabel get together, Basil and Geradine get together, the obnoxious son is murdered, I forget how or why or who does it, and the threat of Prince Louis evaporates, again I forget how or why. In other words, this is a high-society romantic comedy shoehorned into a detective format, typical of the sloppy construction and continuity of William Le Queux.

This book tells me nothing about reality, nor is it a well-constructed Nabokovian *objet*. Yet I enjoyed reading it. It took me out of myself. It focused me outward, like yoga or a good game of solitaire. It has no depth, the voice is limited and shallow, yet it has a kind of authenticity. It is an authentic trifle, a genuine piece of Edwardian fluff, nodding to high life and low life, seeding romances that will flower by the novel's end, creating a country-house world full of jabbering people, fun to visit for the weekend. Le Queux could toss off this kind of fiction without thinking twice, and there is no evidence he ever did think twice about any of it or he might have noticed that motorcar accidents were entirely too useful in his plotting.

And now we descend into the belly of the beast, the worst novel on the shelf. I don't blame you if you don't want to follow me. You may skip the next four paragraphs. I'll understand. But should you want to know the worst, I feel bound to give you a taste of it. What is a truly awful novel like? It is like a bad dream. Things happen that make no sense and are never explained. The scene shifts abruptly and for no reason. One minute you are finding hotel rooms in Paris for a troop of Boy Scouts, the next you are announcing the Harvard-Yale game, and the next you are begging someone to pour coffee in your watch. Being thrust so quickly from one improbability to another produces a form of motion sickness.

A young woman is murdered, strangled by a cord with three knots. Her mother, her fiancé, everyone in the small town in which they live is completely mystified. Why would anyone want to kill this lovely woman? The fiancé, Gerald Grey, hires a detective to solve the mystery, the extraordinary Irene Baxter. Irene Baxter is a master of disguise. She can even change her voice so that she seems to be a man. The resemblance of the name Irene Baxter to Conan Doyle's striking character Irene Adler of "A Scandal in Bohemia" is surely no more accidental than the reappearance of the name Ashdown (now with an *e*) as the family name of the murdered girl. It shows just how little trouble Le Queux put himself to to ensure originality. He took whatever names came to mind first.

Mrs. Ashdowne, mother of the murdered girl, Ella, goes away after the murder and comes back with Ella's twin sister, Polly, who looks like Ella but is her opposite in character. Everyone distrusts her. Everyone except the reader. There seems no reason to distrust her, as she has no character. Mrs. Ashdowne, on the other hand, is always fainting and acting guilty. She is suspected of her daughter's murder. Why has she kept her other daughter, Polly, hidden away all these years? Why indeed! We never learn. One night Polly finds her mother sandpapering a spot on the floor of the room in which the murder took place. But who is arrested for the murder? The good Gerald Grey, Ella's fiancé. Why? Why indeed. Irene Baxter, previously disguised as the Ashdownes' obese cook, now reappears as a loathsome wastrel youth and says, "I'm only surprised it didn't happen earlier." Since everything is possible and Irene can convincingly disguise herself as an obese cook one minute and a wastrel youth the next, nothing in this story astonishes us. Irene next appears as a California gold miner and after that as an English widow. As an English widow, she meets and cultivates a man named Octavius Milo and taunts him with the information she supposedly got as the California miner. Irene is so busy disguising herself and investigating peripheral matters that she has made no progress on solving Ella's murder. Gerald wants to fire her. But she has fallen in love with him and tells him so. They kiss. Jesus! This stuff gives novels a bad name. It's a different kind of bad from the overworked prose of the Rhoda Lerman novel I disliked or of Lisa Lerner's first draft of *Just Like Beauty*, in which she tried too hard to prove her seriousness. This is the badness of tossing it off.

A dancer from San Francisco turns up at a garden party in Devon. You immediately suspect it's Irene again, but no, Irene, disguised as a comely dark-haired youth, is now the dancer's half brother. They have come to examine a cave. Disguised as an elderly drunk, Irene listens to workingmen's late-night tavern talk. The tavern is crawling with sailors from Newfoundland. Two women converse. Who about? Wal Marner? And who is Wal Marner? Oh well. One woman says to the other, "Remember that odd way he had of tying knots?" (Aha!) "He said they used it in New Guinea to strangle children." (Aha!!) "He said the only other places that knot is used is in Iceland and Newfoundland." (Aha!!!) Now at least we understand why the tavern is filled with sailors from Newfoundland.

*Three Knots* features a detective adept at disguise, but she has nothing whatever to do with solving the mystery. There is an old man with a dark past, but he is irrelevant also. The murderer turns out to be someone in plain sight all along, but he is such an uninteresting and insignificant character that you couldn't possibly care that he turns out to be the murderer. It's the chauffeur. It might just as well have been the obese cook or the Icelandic gardener.

How can a book be so bad? It helps to remember that *The*

*Young Archduchess* and *Three Knots* were published in the same year—and these two were not all Le Queux published that year. He was writing an average of five books a year, a book every two months or so. Great books have been written in less time. *The Charterhouse of Parma* was written in six weeks. Georges Simenon often turned out Inspector Maigret novels in two weeks of night-and-day concentrated work. But these were occasional feats. Le Queux kept up his output year after year. If you put Shakespeare in a room and made him write for ten hours a day, year after year, eventually even he might sound like a monkey.

Viewed in a purely Darwinian light, the quantity of Le Queux's output gives it an edge. Some of it will survive simply because there was so much of it. Amazon has 505 paperback entries for Le Queux and 230 hardcover. Forty-six of his titles exist in electronic editions. His is a different strategy for immortality from that of Etienne Leroux or Alain Le Sage or Mikhail Lermontov. Overproduce, and something, fit or unfit, may survive. There's something to it. As with any human endeavor, it's easy to produce nothing and congratulate yourself on the high standards to which you hold yourself. As far as writing goes, "Bash it out" may be the best advice. The worst you can be is William Le Queux, who seemed to have bashed it out, never given it a second thought, sold millions, and, however anonymously in the long run, helped make the world we live in.

After all, I preferred not to end with the worst. There was that new translation of *A Hero of Our Time* by Natasha Randall, published in 2009, five years after the one by Marian Schwartz. It appeared on the shelf somewhere in the middle of my project, and I had not wanted to read it at that time, having had my fill of translations of Lermontov and wanting to get on with my other reading, but now I welcomed it. First of all, I didn't want my project to end. And *A Hero of Our Time*, which I had struggled with, was already different in retrospect. It seemed unique, a masterpiece, a star of my shelf. In the same way that a vacation which had its ups and downs as you were taking it can coalesce, in retrospect, into a succession of glorious moments and a radiant whole—Istanbul, let us say, or that perfect place visited in memory which Proust called "Balbec"—a novel can improve when the moment-by-moment distraction of actually reading it is in the past. I wanted to read this book again and to end my adventure with the taste of excellence on my tongue.

Once again I was traveling post from Tiflis. The entire load of my cart consisted of one valise of average size, half filled with my travel notes about Georgia. The Ossetian cart driver sang songs at full voice, urging the horses onward so we could climb the mountain before nightfall. How beautiful this valley is! How thrilling are the jagged peaks, the mountain streams!

I am happy to be back with the traveler and the staff captain as they make their precarious way through the Caucasus, happy to meet up with Pechorin again. His youthful posturing pleases me. I am tickled by the way he protests his boredom while showing such a keen interest in everything. This time, I feel the extent to which the book represents an almost anthropological examination of a strange and beautiful culture, deeply exotic to the Russian soldiers banished to its midst. We witness a Circassian wedding, with all the showing off of the *dzhigits*, stunt riders on horseback, and the ceremonial declaiming through which young women and men converse. A lovely girl of sixteen comes to face Pechorin and chants her thoughts in spontaneous poetry: "Our young dzhigits are strapping, and their caftans are covered in silver, but the young Russian officer is more strapping than they, and the galloon he wears is in gold. He is like a poplar among them." This is Bela, traded to Pechorin later by her brother in exchange for a horse—Bela, whose captivity bothered me so on my first reading, and still does, but less. In this world, men prize spirited horses more than the best of wives. That is nasty, but that's how it is. The man from whom the treasured horse is stolen by Bela's brother will kill Bela's father in revenge, and the captain remarks: "Of course in their terms, he was absolutely right." The traveler is struck by the old soldier's Russian flexibility and "that clear common sense, which forgives evil where it seems unavoidable, or impossible to destroy."

It's the opposite of Petersburg salons, where appearances reign. According to Lermontov, "Drawing near to nature, we become children without meaning to, and everything that has been acquired falls away from the soul." For nineteenth-century Russians the Caucasus was what the West was for Americans, and the mountain people in their national myths play the role of America's Indians. Young men like Lermontov and his fictional alter ego Pechorin experienced in the southern mountains a way of life completely at odds with their upbringing, a life seeming close to nature, whose often brutal values were in some ways appealing.

This time, as never before, I understand the author's scorn for the life he led in society, his resentment of its conventions, the unexpressed, inexpressible hatred of the autocratic government he lived under. The mountains are freedom. His ecstatic descriptions of them evoke exhilaration and transcendence. This time I feel all the romantic fervor, at once existential and political, reminiscent of the poetry of Wordsworth and Byron, yet this is prose, a novel, which is, frankly, so much more fun. I understand why the Russians rejoice to have this book at the start of their national literature. It is youthful, fresh, the literature of a rising country.

This time, I particularly appreciate the story "Taman," about the smugglers on the Sea of Avov, as harsh and uncompromising a story as any I've read: Pechorin stumbles upon a smoothly functioning, benign group of petty smugglers and, by thoughtlessly threatening to expose them, forces them to give up everything they've built and start all over in a new place. He is aware of how outsized an effect he has had on their lives by his thoughtless action, and he regrets it. All the more striking that in the next story, "Princess Mary," he feels no remorse for his callous, carefully planned destruction of the young princess's happiness by making her love him and then rejecting her, and for his taking away of the happiness—and the life—of her admirer, Grushnitsky.

I begin to feel the emotional logic of the narrative, the fury that conventional society arouses in Pechorin. At Pyatigorsk, he spends part of the day taking the mineral waters with the other Russians, part of it playing at seduction, but the best part riding madly on the Steppes. There he feels free. He prides himself on riding in the Circassian way. He has gone native. "Princess Mary," with its disdain for women in polite society, its unforgivable cruelty, makes some emotional sense if we remember Pechorin's attraction to the harsh sexual customs of the Steppes, including bride kidnapping. Like his descendant Humbert Humbert—a Pechorin still alive in middle age—Pechorin is a very bad boy. Yes, the picture of the male ego is unattractive—everything and everybody fodder for self-esteem—but we Russians know how to forgive evil where it is impossible to destroy.

As I read *A Hero of Our Time* again, I was struck by the clarity and elegance of this translation by Natasha Randall, but when I went back to Marian Schwartz's translation and compared it with Randall's, I found that there wasn't all that much difference. Why does the Lermontov seem so different to me from one reading to the next? Texts change with the circumstances of the reader. I don't mean this in some fancy, deconstructive way, but rather simplemindedly. Reading *A Hero of Our Time* at the start of my project, I was a different reader with different needs and expectations from the one I am at the end of my project. At the start, I began the book knowing that this was a classic, "my" classic. I was worried that I wouldn't respond to it, and to my horror, I didn't. I began with the novel on the defensive, needing to prove itself to me. Why did the Russians love it so much? At the end of my project I return to it as a friend. Its familiarity is pleasing. I know what ground we will cover together. I look forward to experiencing again the unique things it has to offer, happy to be away from sick children and depressive detectives, intractable problems and phony mysteries, and in a world where duels are fought, horses and women are stolen, and a man tests predestination by firing a loaded pistol into his head. I feel I could read this novel again and again, and every time I would find something different in it because I would be a different person. Mikhail would talk to me, and all the different *mes* in time would reply to him differently, as in conversation, you can say one thing, the same thing, to a roomful of people—"My water heater is broken" or "How about the pope's stepping down?"—and get a roomful of different reactions.

Reading a great novel is talking to the dead. There is no need for a psychic. When you read the words of a dead or absent master, they sound in your brain and he or she is present in the room with you. I hear Lermontov clearly. I will tell you exactly what he says.

"Enough people have been fed on sweets: their guts have rotted from them. What is needed is a bitter medicine, the pungent truth."

"Mikhail, you're so right," I reply, the grandmother of two boys now. "I know just how you feel. So much of what surrounds us is cant and sentimentality. But Mikhail, life gets better. It develops meaning. Don't throw it away in a duel. Don't let your silly joking get you in trouble. Watch your tongue. Get married. Have children. You'll see. The pain will lessen. You have so much to give. You have energy, elegance, genius, passion. Don't be so reckless. You will only live once."

But he didn't listen. He threw his life away in a duel. He died at twenty-six.

The stupidity of it was monumental. The duel took place at Pyatigorsk, the spa town in the Caucasus where Lermontov set Pechorin's duel with Grushnitsky. A young officer named Martynov liked to dress in Circassian clothes, with an enormous dagger in his belt. Lermontov considered him a fool and made fun of him in the French used by upper-class Russians of the time, calling him *"le montagnard au grand poignard,"* the mountaineer with the big rapier. He and a lady were sitting and chatting at a party; Martynov was listening as Prince Trubetskoy played the piano. The piano fell silent, and Martynov heard Lermontov's quip. In truth, Lermontov's constant mockery was disagreeable to many people. "For all his genius, Lermontov was clearly a quite insufferable character and a pain in the neck to all those who associated with him, friend and foe alike," wrote a descendant of Prince Vasiltchikov, who would be Lermontov's second in the duel.

On this occasion, in the summer of 1841 in the mountain resort, Martynov rebuked him.

"How many times have I asked you to abandon your jokes, at least when ladies are present?"

Lermontov had known Martynov a long time and thought nothing of this, but before they left the party, Martynov repeated his remark.

Lermontov couldn't believe it.

"Are you really going to challenge me to a duel for this?" he asked, and Martynov said yes.

There are other versions of the quarrel. Most agree there was a slight insult, typical of Lermontov, and a touchy response by Martynov.

The duel followed on the afternoon of the next day. That morning, Lermontov took a walk with his cousin Ekaterina Buikhovetz and spent the day with her, talking deeply and, according to her, with a sadness that was his manner when they were alone. He didn't mention a word about the duel, but kissed her hand upon leaving her and said, *"Cousine*, my darling, there will not be a happier day than this in my life."

The duelists and their seconds rode up Mount Mashuk a little way until they came to a meadow, which they chose as the dueling ground. There was no doctor with them, for which various reasons have been given: no doctor wanted to be involved in such a tawdry affair; no doctor wanted to come, because it was raining; no doctor would be needed, because Lermontov had already said that he didn't intend to fire at

Martynov, and no one imagined that Martynov, in those circumstances, would fire at Lermontov.

The seconds, Glebov and Vasiltchikov, measured off thirty paces and laid swords down to mark the barrier, then ten paces beyond for each antagonist to take his place. At the given signal, each walked the ten paces to the barrier to fire. Lermontov, covering his chest with his arm and elbow in the appropriate fashion for dueling, cocked his pistol and then raised the muzzle to the sky, indicating that he declined to shoot. But he could not keep quiet and said clearly, "I will not fire on that fool." Martynov, infuriated, fired and killed him.

Dueling was illegal, and to shoot at a man who had refused to shoot was very close to murder, but Martynov was not severely punished. He spent four penitential years in the monastery of Kiev, and when he came out, he married the daughter of a wealthy general of that city. They had eleven children. He was a mild, unextraordinary man who, by all accounts, felt awful to the end of his life about having robbed Russia of one of its greatest writers in a youthful fit of anger. One of Martynov's descendants, Dr. Cyril E. Geacintov, was present in Moscow in 2004 at a celebration of the 190th anniversary of Lermontov's birth to put flowers on the writer's grave. Some people feared that his presence would set off a disturbance, but fortunately, no one knew who he was. Dr. Geacintov lives in the United States, where he is the head of a global medical-equipment development-and-manufacturing company and president of the Russian Nobility Association.

Lermontov's descendants include everyone who reads him. That astonishing truth explains why people will go on trying to be writers, even as authorship gets more demanding and the rewards fewer. To have reason to hope that you will continue

to speak to people even from beyond the grave—that one reward is worth it all.

Twenty-three books. Eleven authors. Short stories and novels.
Realistic and mythic. Literary fiction and detective fiction.
American and European. Old and contemporary. Highly
wrought and flabby fiction. Inspired fiction and uninspired. My
shelf covered a lot of ground. Guided by the alphabet, I broke
through categories to read a famous book I didn't think I'd like
but did (*Gil Blas*), a book I thought I'd like but didn't like as
much as I'd expected at first and later came to love (*A Hero of
Our Time*), novels by a first-rate writer who isn't sufficiently
appreciated (Rhoda Lerman), a powerful narrative that has
evolved into a masterpiece in other forms (*Phantom*), work by
two writers from beyond the New York–Paris axis from which
most of my reading is drawn (Lernet-Holenia and LeRossignol),
and writing by women that I probably would not have chosen
otherwise (Leroy and Lerner). I got to spend imaginative time
in South Africa, San Francisco, and the Caucasus. I talked a
great deal to Vladimir Nabokov in my head. Via the Internet, I
contacted editors and book designers, writers and old friends,
many people who love books and are open to discussing them.
I read *Salon*, *Slate*, *The Millions*, and reviews in papers from *The
Guardian* to the *San Francisco Chronicle* to see what other people
thought about what I was reading. I discovered the fun of par-
ticipating in a virtual conversation about literature at any moment of the day or night. I think this is a good time for reading
in many ways, not the least technological. When my mother
lost her vision, we got her a huge and very expensive machine
that projected a larger version of printed texts onto an unwieldy

screen. Now anyone with eighty dollars can get an e-reader that enlarges type with a click.

I met eleven people, none of whom I had known at all before. In some cases, I made their acquaintance quite literally. Rhoda Lerman came to stay with me for several days. Lisa Lerner I count as a friend now, too. After Rhoda and Lisa, I may feel closest to James LeRossignol, the author of *The Habitant-Merchant*. I think of him with pleasure, teaching, writing, reading, keeping up his German, leading the life of a man of letters, a midwestern Montaigne, without Montaigne's genius or ultimate success but with some of his satisfactions. Busy Gaston Leroux, the plucky journalist, and even busier William Le Queux, earnest Margaret Leroy, hardworking John Lescroart, and mysterious Lernet-Holenia, I am fond of all of them. Lermontov, my reckless young friend, stays in my mind along with the wise, worldly Alain Le Sage, living out his life in a cathedral close, and Etienne Leroux, who fought the good fight in South Africa in ways too obscure for me to comprehend, although the image of his grave on a windswept hilltop remains with me as an image of gallant effort in a hostile world.

What I've learned from my experiment is respect for the whole range of the literary enterprise—for writers of all sorts, from those who write to make a living to those with something to say and issues to explore (not necessarily mutually exclusive), from those who aspire to create a beautiful aesthetic object to those who want to create a clever machine. They are all workers in words, creators of verbal reality. The work they do demands, besides a defining delight in the lexicon, a tricky combination of solitude and sociability, detachment and engagement. Writers' lives are not easy, and most of them, if they are lucky enough to have a moment of people's attention at all, will probably live to see that moment pass, like other figures in the public's view. All writers seem to me in some way valiant, whether or not I put their work on the inner shelf of texts that accompany me through life, a shelf that includes Keats's poetry and Shakespeare's plays, *Middlemarch* and *David Copperfield, Mrs. Dalloway* and *The Charterhouse of Parma, Jane Eyre* and *Ulysses, Pale Fire* and *Wuthering Heights, The Diary of Anne Frank* and *In Search of Lost Time, Tristes Tropiques* and *A Room of One's Own, Memoirs of Hadrian* and *Out of Sheer Rage, Getting Even* and *Native Tongue, Slouching Towards Bethlehem* and *Coming of Age in Samoa, Teaching a Stone to Talk* and *Against Interpretation, The Duke of Deception* and *Father and Son, Fierce Attachments* and *Foreign Affairs, Memories of a Catholic Girlhood* and *Memoirs of a Dutiful Daughter, Gone With the Wind* and *The Winds of War,* Barthes's essays and Montaigne's, Colette's tales and Dinesen's, Trilling's criticism and Dorothy Van Ghent's, Matthew Arnold's and Janet Malcolm's, George Saunders's stories and Alice Munro's, Hemingway's and Grace Paley's, Joyce's and Ann Beattie's, Borges's and Amy Bloom's, Chekhov's and Annie Proulx's, Virginia Woolf's diary and Andy Warhol's, Woolf's letters and Jane Carlyle's, Trollope's Palliser novels and Updike's Rabbit novels, Samuel Johnson's essays, Denis Johnson's stories, *Super Sad True Love Story, My Mortal Enemy, Middlesex, Nisa, Portnoy's Complaint, Tess of the D'Urbervilles, Cousin Bette, Tristram Shandy, The Canterbury Tales, O Pioneers!, The Odyssey, Endurance, The Yearling, Patrimony, A Flag for Sunrise, War and Peace, Mapp and Lucia, Their Eyes Were Watching God, Death Comes for the Archbishop, The Unbearable Lightness of Being, I Know Why the Caged Bird Sings, Sense and Sensibility, Pride and Prejudice, Persuasion, Emma, Huckleberry Finn, Ethan Frome, My Friend Flicka, Treasure Island,*

*Goodnight Moon, The Story of Babar, Babar the King,* Grimm's fairy tales, Mother Goose, *A Child's Garden of Verses,* the Old Testament, and *The Corrections,* to cite just a few. From this experiment my return has been rich. I've found three texts to keep me company through life: *God's Ear, Gil Blas,* and *A Hero of Our Time.* If *The Shelf* brings other readers to these novels, I will be happy, but even happier if it sends them into the stacks of libraries to find favorites of their own and to savor the beauties of what I hope is not a vanishing ecosystem.

# NOTES

## 1. THE EXPERIMENT BEGINS

3 *Extreme Reading*: "Extreme sports by their nature can be extremely dangerous, conducive to fatalities, near-fatalities and other serious injuries, and sometimes consist in treading along the brink of death . . . One common aspect of an extreme sport is a counter-cultural aura—a rejection of authority and of the status quo by disaffected youth." *Wikipedia* entry on "Extreme Sports."

3 *reduced to eating the sled dogs*: See Alfred Lansing's great adventure book *Endurance: Shackleton's Incredible Voyage* (New York: McGraw-Hill, 1959).

12 *the rules themselves are malleable*: Oulipo, a French organization of writers and others interested in experimental fiction, has focused on the connections between limitation and creativity. Write a novel without the letter *e*. Why? Because otherwise you think in the old, stale way about representing reality. Leaving out the *e* shakes you up, reawakens your inventiveness, forces you to new meanings.

19 *preceded it*, Seven Days at the Silbersteins: What came to be called the Welgevonden Trilogy was published in English by Penguin in 1972. The three novels together were titled *To a Dubious Salvation*.

22 *his funeral in 1989, broadcast in Afrikaans*: www.youtube.com/watch ?v=am7yKJcYrRo. Much of what I find so moving about Leroux's life and situation is also captured in this portrait of him by David Goldblatt, the great South African photographer, made at Koffeefontein in 1965 and published in *Some Afrikaners Photographed* (Cape Town: Murray Crawford and Struik, 1975), reprinted in 2007 and 2009 as *Some Afrikaners Revisited*.

## 2. THE MYTH OF THE BOOK: *A HERO OF OUR TIME*
25 *masterpiece of graphic design:*

## 3. LITERARY EVOLUTION: *THE PHANTOM OF THE OPERA*

43 *the most successful "entertainment venture":* "The Study Guide for *The Phantom of the Opera*" by Peter Royston can be downloaded at: www .thephantomoftheopera.com/wp-content/themes/phantom/pdfs /phantom-study-guide.pdf. As of March 21, 2013, *The Phantom of the Opera* had grossed $5.6 billion since 1985, *The Lion King*, $5 billion since 1997, according to Patrick Healy in *The New York Times*. http:// theater.nytimes.com/2013/03/24/theater/matilda-arrives-on-broadway -with-big-dreams.html?pagewanted=all.

49 *gaston-leroux.net*: The official site of "*les ayants droit*" of Gaston Leroux. "*Ayants droit,*" which translates as "rights holders," loosely means the heirs or estate of Gaston Leroux. *Phantom of the Opera* has been in the public domain since the mid-1980s, before Andrew Lloyd Webber's stupefyingly successful adaptation, so the heirs cannot have profited much from its success. Still, with no apparent self-interest, they have put together an excellent tribute to their ancestor, sharing news as it comes up. The latest news came in 2008, when a grandson of Gaston Leroux's discovered the manuscript of *The Mystery of the Yellow Room* in a trunk in the attic of a family home. It was donated to the Bibliothèque Nationale.

53 *a cache of phonograph records*: The records were dug up, as planned, after a hundred years, in 2007, and EMI has put the music onto three CDs, called *Les Urnes de l'Opéra*.

60 *the best way to get a feel*: Or go online for a virtual visit. www.operade paris.fr/L_Opera/Palais_Garnier/visite_virtuelle.php#BPythie.

61 *shot on the Universal Studios stage*: They realized it would be possible to reproduce the Paris Opera House after successfully building Notre Dame for *The Hunchback of Notre Dame*, also with Lon Chaney. See the excellent website about the 1925 *Phantom* stage set, written by Chaney's biographer, Michael F. Blake, www.silentsaregolden.com /featurefolder2/phantomstagearticle.html.

62 *Phantom leads her down a stone staircase*: The current Broadway production of *Phantom* ingeniously reproduces this effect. Indeed, much of this excellent production seems influenced by the silent film and by the book illustrations of André Castaigne.

62 *Jeanine Basinger: Silent Stars* (New York: Knopf, 1999), 358. Also, Mordaunt Hall, *The New York Times,* September 7, 1925. The *Phantom* Study Guide quotes the British critic.

63 *the playwright Arthur Kopit:* This version has many fans. See www.ny times.com/2012/09/02/nyregion/a-review-of-phantom-in-bellport -ny.html.

67 Danse Macabre *to a large audience:* This actually took place on April 2, 1897. A hundred people received invitations to gather at the entrance to the catacombs and descend underground for a funereal concert.

67 The Phantom Clue, *the other:* http://mysteryfile.com/blog/?p=7486.


## 4. THE UNIVERSE PROVIDES: RHODA LERMAN

72 *"Sometimes, if my child": Call Me Ishtar* (New York: Henry Holt, 1973).

75 Fear of Flying: The two novels appeared not only in the same year, 1973, but from the same publisher. However, a friend in publishing who remembers the coincidence says that the two books, which had different editors, were not aimed at the same audience. *Call Me Ishtar* was marketed as "literature."

84 *"It is soon told . . .": The Book of the Night* (New York: Henry Holt, 1984).

87 *a little boy in India:* This once-classic book was *Little Black Sambo,* written by Helen Bannerman, a Scotswoman living in India, and published in 1899. Its Indian setting didn't stop it from inspiring noxious stereotypes of black Africans and provoking many people to shun it for racism.

89 *floating mah-jongg:*

90 *She was happy to talk*: Interviews, New York City, March 18, 2012, March 22, 2012, and June 2, 2012.

92 *"only invocations of myth . . ."*: William Irwin Thompson, *The Time Falling Bodies Take to Light: Mythology, Sexuality, and the Origins of Culture* (New York: St. Martin's Press, 1981), 94.

96 *J. M. Barrie immortalized his Newfy*: But popular culture (starting with the Disney animated film of *Peter Pan* in 1953) has morphed her into a Saint Bernard.

97 *She has a full other life*: Rhoda has since published another book about dogs, *Elsa Was Born a Dog*. That book and *In the Company of Newfies* can be ordered directly from the Blue Heaven Kennels website or from dogwise.com in various electronic formats. See http://bornadog .com/hard-cover-book-pricing-and-alternate-digital-options/.

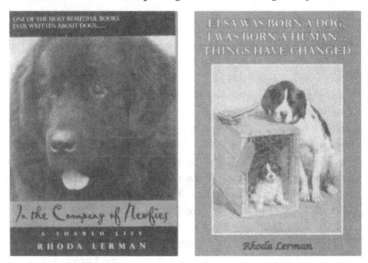

## 5. WOMEN AND FICTION: A QUESTION OF PRIVILEGE

99 *VIDA began surveying*: See www.vidaweb.org/the-count-2010; www .vidaweb.org/the-count; and www.vidaweb.org/the-count-2012.

100 *raised in* A Room of One's Own: Online calculators tell us that a British pound in 1927 was worth about $3 U.S., making Woolf's 500 pounds worth $1,500, which would be worth about $20,000 in current value. This is an interesting figure because one could not support a family on $20,000. Woolf was probably calculating how much money a woman needed to give her psychic independence from a

family that existed, economically, without her. See www.likeforex
.com/currency-converter/fxconverter.php?f=british-sterling-pound
-gbp&t=usd-us-dollar&amt=1928 and www.dollartimes.com/calcula
tors/inflation.htm, and, for a more complex view, Measuring Worth:
www.measuringworth.com/calculators/uscompare/index.php.

102  *V. S. Naipaul*: Amy Fallon, "V. S. Naipaul Finds No Woman Writer
His Literary Match," *The Guardian*, June 1, 2011, www.guardian.co
.uk/books/2011/jun/02/vs-naipaul-jane-austen-women-writers.
The editor Naipaul dissed was Diana Athill and her memoir, *Somewhere Towards the End* (London & New York: Granta, 2008).

103  *"I was going on about some novel"*: Chris Jackson, "All the Sad Young
Literary Women," *The Atlantic*, August 20, 2010, www.theatlantic
.com/entertainment/archive/2010/08/all-the-sad-young-literary
-women/61821/.

105  *"So much of reading is sustained"*: Jonathan Franzen, quoted by Ruth
Franklin, "The READ: Franzen Fallout," *The New Republic*, September
7, 2010, www.tnr.com/article/books-and-arts/77506/the-read-franzen
-fallout-ruth-franklin-sexism.

105  *the current male contenders*: See Elaine Blair, "American Male Novelists:
The New Deal," *The New York Review of Books* (June 12, 2012), 19–21.

106  *reading habits of men and women*: Lisa Jardine and Annie Watkins, "The
Books That Move Men," *The Guardian* (April 5, 2006), www.guard
ian.co.uk/world/2006/apr/06/gender.books. *Jane Eyre* is far and away
English women's most treasured novel, but after that, their favorites
are immensely varied, including *The Lord of the Rings, Catch-22, Gone
With the Wind, Heart of Darkness, Rebecca, The Hitchhiker's Guide to the
Galaxy, Mrs. Dalloway, Anna Karenina, Beloved, The Handmaid's Tale,
Pride and Prejudice*, and *The Golden Notebook*. The men surveyed by
Jardine and Watkins all tended to cite the same books, *The Stranger,
The Catcher in the Rye, Slaughterhouse-Five*, and *One Hundred Years of Soli-
tude*. Only one novel by a woman made it into the men's top twenty, *To
Kill a Mockingbird*.

106  *as though the novel were a handbook*: This study doesn't mention it, but
Ralph Ellison claimed that he learned to hunt from reading Hemingway.

107  *"female chacma baboons"*: Natalie Angier, "The Spirit of Sisterhood Is in
the Air and on the Air," *The New York Times*, April 23, 2012, www
.nytimes.com/2012/04/24/science/how-hbos-girls-mirrors-the
-spirit-of-sisterhood-in-nature.html?pagewanted=all.

108 *"deep-seated double standard"*: Weiner quoted by Ruth Franklin, "The READ: Franzen Fallout."

108 *another strike that they sell*: It took Stephen King to single out Jodi Picoult as someone who really writes well, "with unassuming brilliance."

109 *Joanna Russ*: How to Suppress Women's Writing (Austin: University of Texas Press, 1983).

110 *J. K. Rowling's publisher*: On *60 Minutes* (1999), Rowling told Leslie Stahl that she had submitted the manuscript with "Joanne Rowling" as the author's name, and the publisher asked if they could use only initials, as boys did not like to read books by women. www.cbsnews.com/video/watch/?id=7045170n.

110 *test in which one could match*: www.guardian.co.uk/books/quiz/2011/jun/02/naipaul-test-author-s-sex-quiz.

112 *Willa Cather has been a special case*: See my "Modernism: The Case of Willa Cather," in *Modernism Revisited*, edited by Robert Kiely, assisted by John Hildebidle (Cambridge, MA: Harvard University Press, 1983), 123–45, reprinted in my collection *Writing of Women: Essays in a Renaissance* as "The Case of Willa Cather" (Middletown, CT: Wesleyan University Press, 1985), 142–58.

113 *a piece he wrote on Edith Wharton*: "A Critic at Large: A Rooting Interest," *The New Yorker*, February 13 & 20, 2012, 60–65.

115 *"It is as primitively powerful"*: Dorothy Van Ghent, *The English Novel: Form and Function* (New York: Rinehart, 1953).

115 *a theory and a vocabulary*: To someone who wants to understand how academic reputations work and how the study of literary criticism in universities changed in the second half of the twentieth century, I recommend Alvin Kernan, *In Plato's Cave* (New Haven, CT: Yale University Press, 1999).

116 *the process takes a long time*: As much as it may have called attention to the problem of gender bias in reading, I doubt that a generation's worth of gender studies has done much to change it, since gender studies courses tend to preach to the converted. Nor do I see a quick way out of the dilemma, unless it's something as crude as Really Good Guy's self-help program, each man vowing to read one book by a woman for every book by a man. The problem, let's not forget, is to get men to read women, not to turn women off to books by men.

116 *Prospero's Daughter*: Elizabeth Nunez beat me to this phrase for the title of her 2006 novel, which is worth reading but has nothing to do

with my imagined figure of Prospero's daughter. My Prospero's daughter was inspired by Lisa Jardine, daughter of Jacob Bronowski, and borrows heavily from a two-hour videotaped interview she did with Alan Macfarlane in 2008, available on his website: www.alan macfarlane.com/DO/filmshow/jardine1_fast.htm. Lisa Jardine is a professor at the University of London, the author of many books about the Renaissance, and a frequent radio commentator for the BBC. She came to my attention as the coauthor of the study of male and female reading habits in Britain that I cited earlier.

117 *women instructors who had been trained*: They had no formal degrees, because Oxford and Cambridge could not give them to women until 1948.

119 *Motherhood and their personal lives*: There is still a gap between what men and women are paid for the same work. Apparently, the women's movement had a big effect at first; the difference in pay between men and women dramatically lessened. But in the past twenty years the pace of improvement has slowed. The explanation is not that employers pay women less than men for the same job, but that women and men take different jobs and follow different career paths. Women make different choices from men, weight their time differently, taking their family into account, and these choices affect their pay. Women doctors tend to choose to be lower-paid pediatricians more often than to be cardiologists, for example. See Eduardo Porter, *The New York Times*, June 13, 2012.

In a controversial article in *The Atlantic*, Anne-Marie Slaughter addressed the issue of how women in high-power jobs balance the demands of family and work. She decided that she could not work at the pitch required for a top government position (assistant to the secretary of state) and resigned until her children were older and needed her less. Slaughter argues that women should be frank about their family obligations and cite them as reasons for not being able to fulfill professional responsibilities, which is exactly the opposite of what ambitious women have been trained to do for at least two generations. She argues that society won't change until such acknowledgment is made.

An interviewer asked the writer Jayne Anne Phillips why she decided to take such a long time between novels, and Phillips replied, "It wasn't a decision! I live numerous lives at once—like most of us. Teaching is very involving, as is parenting. The space and quiet required for writing isn't always available." Jessica Roy, interview with

Jayne Anne Phillips, *NYU Local* (February 3, 2009), http://nyulocal
.com/entertainment/2009/02/03/interview-with-jayne-anne-phillips
-author-of-lark-and-termite/#ixzz1zToXTNqC.

119 *hair done twice a week*: I'm referring to beloved Nora Ephron. See www
.nytimes.com/2012/06/27/movies/nora-ephron-essayist-screen
writer-and-director-dies-at-71.html?pagewanted=all.

## 6. DOMESTICITIES: MARGARET LEROY AND LISA LERNER

121 *past the title of* Yes, My Darling Daughter: The book's original title, in
Britain, was *The Drowning Girl*. You can see why the American publishing team might have thought that title was a turnoff.

123 *Victoria Holt*: One of several pen names of the British writer Eleanor
Hibbert (1906–93), who also wrote as Jean Plaidy and Philippa Carr.
As Victoria Holt, she wrote thirty-two novels, and under her other
names, especially Plaidy, the name she used for her historical novels
about royal families, dozens more. Her books have sold hundreds of
millions of copies.

124 *"Sleep is a door"*: Margaret Leroy, *Yes, My Darling Daughter* (New York:
Farrar, Straus and Giroux, 2009), 96.

137 *interviewed by Ellen DeGeneres*: www.youtube.com/watch?v=w79-Cp
zuPMI.

## 7. SMALL WORLDS: THE NIGHTINGALE
## AND THE LARK

141 *"At a recent reception"*: Alexander Lernet-Holenia, *Count Luna: Two Tales of the Real and the Unreal*, introduction by Robert Pick. *Baron Bagge*, translated by Richard and Clara Winston; *Count Luna*, translated by Jane B. Greene (New York: Criterion Books, 1956), 18, 23.

147 *toads he used to kill*: *Mars in Aries*, translated by Robert von Dassanowsky and Elisabeth Littell Frech (Riverside, CA: Ariadne Press, 2003), 103, 140–41.

148 *Viennese fascination with dreams*: See Robert Pick's introduction to *Count Luna*, p. 10. Also Leo Lensing's edition of Arthur Schnitzler's dream journal, *Träume: Das Traumtagebuch 1875–1931* (Göttingen: Wallstein Verlag, 2012).

149 *Marjorie Perloff: The Vienna Paradox: A Memoir* (New York: New Directions, 2004).

151 *Ernest Jones*: Elisabeth Young-Bruehl, *Anna Freud* (New York: Summit Books, 1988).

152 *The story of this painting*: Anne-Marie O'Connor, *The Lady in Gold* (New York: Alfred A. Knopf, 2012). Also, Carol Vogel, "Lauder Pays $135 Million, a Record, for a Klimt Portrait," *The New York Times*, June 19, 2006. www.nytimes.com/2006/06/19/arts/design/19klim.html ?ref=carolvogel&pagewanted=all.

153 *"German editors have always tried to adapt"*: Daniela Strigl, "Literary Perspectives: Austria (Anything but a German Appendix)," *Eurozine*, June 6, 2008. www.eurozine.com/articles/2008-06-10-strigl -en.html. Her list of contemporary Austrian novelists will be cited in the text below.

154 *Robert Pick, an editor*: According to Krishna Winston, daughter of the great translating duo, Pick had successfully lobbied Knopf to publish Heimito von Doderer, another Austrian writer, and persuaded the Winstons to translate him. So it's very likely he was also responsible for the English translation of Lernet-Holenia. On Hermann Broch and Robert Pick as Don Giovanni and Leporello and the friendship of the two Austrians with Hannah Arendt and her husband in New York, see Elisabeth Young-Bruehl, *Hannah Arendt*. Besides Pick, the other champion of Austrian literature in the United States is Robert von Dassanowsky, professor of German and film studies at the University of Colorado at Colorado Springs. He is the author of *Phantom Empires: The "Austrian" Novels of Alexander Lernet-Holenia* (Riverside,

CA: Ariadne Press, 1996); the translator, with Elisabeth Littell Frech, of *Mars in Aries*; and a member of the advisory board of Ariadne Press, which is devoted to "studies in Austrian literature, culture, and thought."

156 *David Brooks*: "The Power of the Particular," *The New York Times*, June 25, 2012, www.nytimes.com/2012/06/26/opinion/brooks-the -power-of-the-particular.html.

157 *Libraries make strange bedfellows*:

157 *called* The Habitant-Merchant:

J[ames] E[dward] LeRossignol, *The Habitant-Merchant* (Toronto: Macmillan, 1939).

159 *"a model father, a gregarious, fun-loving man"*: John Christie Stockdale of Laval University, Quebec, in *The Dictionary of Literary Biography* (Gale Research). www.bookrags.com/biography/james-le-rossignol-dlb/. Genealogical information for prominent Nebraskans available at www.usgennet.org/usa/ne/topic/resources//OLLibrary/Nebraskana/pages/nbka0170.htm.

## 8. LIBRARIES: MAKING SPACE

162 *Its life was prolonged by*: Its physical chances of survival in the future are vastly increased by technology. Via Google Books it is now possible to see the original 1901 edition with an introduction by Henry Lawson and also glimpses of a 2008 scholarly edition, with maps of Australia, an extensive historical/critical introduction, and an appendix with correspondence between Lawson and Franklin, Pinker and Blackwood, Pinker and Franklin.

164 CREW *manual*: *CREW: A Weeding Manual for Modern Libraries*, revised and updated by Jeannette Larson (Austin: Texas State Library and Archives Commission, 2012), 9, 42–43. www.tsl.state.tx.us/ld/pubs/crew/index.html.

167 *weeding on a scale*: This and other cautionary tales of library design are told by Nicholas A. Basbanes in *Patience & Fortitude* (New York: HarperCollins, 2001), which should be required reading for all trustees of libraries—and library architects.

168 *"a plant that interferes"*: J. M. Torell, *Weeds of the West* (Jackson, WY: The Western Society of Weed Science, 1992), ix.

168 *the fortunate position of not having to worry*: Some libraries are in the even more fortunate position of never having to weed at all. Once a book enters the Princeton University Library, for example, it never leaves. It may be moved to off-site storage but will never be deaccessioned.

169 *The Wesleyan University library*: The exact criteria for initial weeding may be found at http://weeding.blogs.wesleyan.edu/sample-page/. A whole website exists to document the project and make it as transparent as possible. Adina Hoffman, who knows how interested I am in weeding, sent me pictures of shelves of books that are being weeded out of the collection, calling them "crime scene photos." Hoffman, with Peter Cole, is the author of the invaluable book *Sacred Trash: The Lost and Found World of the Cairo Geniza* (New York: Schocken Books, 2011), which describes the discovery in the nineteenth century of a

cache of ancient manuscripts preserved in Cairo thanks to the medieval Jewish belief that every scrap of writing is too precious to destroy. This book is itself a potent and poetic argument against dismantling libraries.

Weeded books, Olin Library

171   *"dull in a pretentious"*: Orville Prescott, *The New York Times*, August 18, 1958. www.nytimes.com/books/97/03/02/lifetimes/nab-r-booksof times.html. For more, see *Rotten Rejections: A Literary Companion*, ed. André Bernard (Wainscott, NY: Pushcart Press, 1990).

171   *"invisible to the average reader"*: Laura Miller, "The Case for Positive Book Reviews" (*Salon*, August 17, 2012), www.salon.com/2012/08/17 /the_case_for_positive_book_reviews/. See also www.theawl.com /2012/06/book-reviewings-long-decline (Jane Hu) and http://nplus onemag.com/against-reviews (Elizabeth Gompert). Cheerleading, although it is what authors crave and arguably what the book business needs, doesn't win much respect for the cheerleader, unlike gatekeeping. For some reason, harsh reviews tend to be considered more useful for vibrant cultural discussion. Personally, I consider this a macho and probably masculine cover for innate aggressiveness and unattractive careerism.

An old and solacing adage holds that no review is a bad review. Any attention drawn to a book is useful, and a Stanford Business School professor's study showed that there is much truth in this. For unknown novelists, even bad reviews get their work attention, and some people try it as a result. But for established novelists a bad review is bad. It inhibits a purchase by readers who usually buy the author's work. In the language of the social scientist, "Bad publicity, while damaging to well-known products, provides lesser-known products with more consumer exposure." Jenny Thai, February 23, 2011. www.stanforddaily.com/2011/02/23/bad-publicity-may-boost-book -sales/. See http://mktsci.journal.informs.org/content/29/5/815.ab stract. An earlier study of the same subject had slightly different results: www.forewordreviews.com/media/pdf/stanford-study-book -reviews.pdf.

172 *"The merchandise of the information economy"*: James Gleick, "How Google Dominates Us," *The New York Review of Books*, August 18, 2011.

174 *What the rating says to me*: Compare, with these tortuous deductions, the straightforward experience of shopping at a local bookstore, as I do at Crawford Doyle on Madison Avenue, where I can ask for a book and have it handed to me within a minute by someone who may have read it.

174 *guessing the weight of an ox*: See James Surowiecki, *The Wisdom of Crowds* (New York: Doubleday, 2004).

176 *"Once a populist gimmick"*: David Streitfeld, "Giving Mom's Book Five Stars? Amazon May Cull Your Review," *The New York Times*, December 23, 2012, www.nytimes.com/2012/12/23/technology/amazon -book-reviews-deleted-in-a-purge-aimed-at-manipulation.html.

176 *subject to manipulation*: English economist John Kay wrote what he calls a parable of the stock market, based on Galton's experiment, with people seeking inside information about the ox, a regulatory agency requiring official reports on the state of the ox, analysts parsing those reports and selling clients their opinions about the state of the ox. See www.johnkay.com/2012/07/25/the-parable-of-the-ox.

176 *"We do not require people"*: www.nytimes.com/2012/12/23/technology /amazon-book-reviews-deleted-in-a-purge-aimed-at-manipulation .html.

177 *currently under attack*: www.ncac.org/Books-Removed-in-Katy-TX -After-Parental-Complaints.

180 *Nabokov's scorn*: John Updike, "Introduction," to Vladimir Nabokov, *Lectures on Literature*, ed. Fredson Bowers (New York: Harcourt, Brace, Jovanovich, 1980), xxiii. The discussion with Wilson over the course's content can be tracked in *The Nabokov-Wilson Letters* (New York: Harper & Row, 1978). Updike's wife, Martha, took Nabokov's course in European literature at Cornell and never after valued Thomas

Mann. According to Updike, she remembered throughout her life the central credo of Nabokov's teaching: "Style and structure are the essence of a book; great ideas are hogwash."

Nabokov is a piquant stand-in for Socrates dissatisfied in the realm of literature. "Many accepted authors simply do not exist for me," he wrote. "Their names are engraved on empty graves, their books are dummies, they are complete nonentities insofar as my taste in reading is concerned. Brecht, Faulkner, Camus, many others, mean absolutely nothing to me, and I must fight a suspicion of conspiracy against my brain when I see blandly accepted as 'great literature' by critics and fellow authors Lady Chatterley's copulations or the pretentious nonsense of Mr. Pound, that total fake." Dostoyevsky was "a third-rate writer," Eliot "a fraud," Colette a writer of "second-rate vocational literature," Thomas Mann a "tower of triteness." Nabokov could go on and on like this: *Death in Venice* was "asinine," *Doctor Zhivago* "melodramatic and vilely written," and Faulkner's novels "corncobby chronicles." See "The Art of Fiction, No. 40," *The Paris Review*, Summer-Fall 1967, interview by Herbert Gold. The alliterations and assonance ("corncobby chronicles," "tower of triteness," the "flimsy little fables" of Borges) show how much of a game these insults were to Nabokov. Saul Bellow got the joke. Nabokov called him a "miserable mediocrity," and Bellow hurled back at Nabokov the (pathetically feeble) epithet "wicked wizard."

182 *Mark and Steve knew the collection*: Mark and Steve also gave me a new way of measuring a book's endurance by introducing me to WorldCat. An online catalog of books in libraries worldwide, WorldCat tells you the nearest library (or farthest) that stocks the book you're interested in and the number of libraries that hold a copy worldwide. Mark warned me that WorldCat was not completely accurate because libraries had to pay to list their books, and some libraries, including the Society Library, chose not to. So there may be more copies out there than are listed in WorldCat, but for my purposes it provides a rough measure of how any given title is valued. For example, you can easily see the relative popularity of Rhoda Lerman's novels by looking at their WorldCat statistics:

*Call Me Ishtar* 226
*The Girl That He Marries* 253
*Eleanor* 600

*The Book of the Night* 180
*God's Ear* 298
*Animal Acts* 206

With the exception of *Eleanor*, which was evidently raised above the others by its subject, her novels have made their way to some two hundred libraries worldwide, from Columbia University to the University of Western Australia. That's comparable with Etienne Leroux's *Seven Days at the Silbersteins*, 253, and Lisa Lerner's *Just Like Beauty*, 322. By contrast, currently popular or classic books are to be found in thousands of libraries. The 1911 American edition of *Phantom of the Opera*, which I read, exists in 3,010 libraries, including one in Afghanistan. Nabokov's translation of *A Hero of Our Time* is in 1,724 libraries, and John Lescroart's *Betrayal* is in 1,827. At the other end of the popularity-and-survival spectrum, Lernet-Holenia in English has made it to only 64 libraries, none out of the United States, and some of William Le Queux's books have become (deservedly) rare, *The Young Archduchess* existing in only 14 WorldCat-cataloged copies worldwide and *Three Knots* in 7.

### 9. LIFE AND ADVENTURES: *GIL BLAS*

193 *can measure my own growth*: Beginning with *Dr. No* in 1962, which I saw with my parents on a visit home from college, Sean Connery playing Bond, I have been watching James Bond films my entire adult life: through my first marriage and the birth of my son (*Live and Let Die*, 1973, Roger Moore as Bond), into a second marriage and the death of my father (*License to Kill*, 1989, Timothy Dalton), through the end of middle age and the death of my mother (*The World Is Not Enough*, 1999, Pierce Brosnan), and into my later years (*Skyfall*, 2012, Daniel Craig).

### 10. SERIAL KILLERS: DETECTIVE FICTION

200 *For a special edition of his novel*: *The 13th Juror* (Davis, CA: Willowbank Books, 2012). This edition of 250 copies, signed by Lescroart with a new introduction by him, is part of Willowbank's Breakout Books Series. Many thanks to Max Byrd, cofounder of Willowbank, for bringing this piece to my attention.

203 *Horace's formula: Omne tulit punctum, qui miscuit utile dulci, lectorem delectando pariterque monendo,* Ars Poetica. *Utile dulci,* mixing instruction and entertainment, has been a winning strategy in literature since ancient days. In 18 B.C. Horace wrote, "He who mixes the sweet and the useful wins every point, entertaining and informing the reader equally."

204 *the generative possibilities:* After seeing the film *Last Tango in Paris,* with its notorious scene of butter-assisted sodomy, Julia Child reportedly said, "I thought I knew everything that could be done with butter." And how many women growing up in the 1950s first learned about diaphragms from Mary McCarthy's *The Group?*

207 *"Where is the ingenuity":* Letter to Phillip Pendleton Cook, www .eapoe.org/works/letters/p4608090.htm.

208 *I went to Google Maps:*

208 *Arthur Krystal:* "Easy Writers," *The New Yorker,* May 28, 2012. See also Lev Grossman's reply, http://entertainment.time.com/2012/05 /23/genre-fiction-is-disruptive-technology/#ixzz27VOhbqt1. For another excellent discussion of detective fiction, see Ben Yagoda, "The Case of the Overrated Mystery Novel," *Salon,* January 6, 2004, www .salon.com/2004/01/06/mystery_hype/. The genre is "devoid of creative or artistic interest," says Yagoda, who started as a fan, reading

Ross Macdonald and Chandler. Then he read his way through one series after another—Tony Hillerman, Sue Grafton, Lawrence Block, James Lee Burke, Jonathan Kellerman—but always ended up disappointed. He realized that two unvarying features of detective series kept them from being serious works of art: "The first is the main character, who is invariably romanticized or sentimentalized and who is always a combination of three not especially interesting things: toughness, efficacy and sensitivity . . . The second is the very formulaic quality that lets a book be part of a series. Similar things happen in similar ways, which is probably as apt a definition as you'll ever find of how not to make good literature." Check out also a podcast, "Culture Gabfest" No. 193, with Stephen Metcalf, Dava Stevens, and Julia Turner, *Slate*, May 30, 2012. www.slate.com/articles/podcasts/cul turegabfest/2012/05/literary_fiction_genre_fiction_atavist_new _york_times_weddings_celebrations_vows_on_the_culture_gabfest .html.

209 veritas *or gravitas*: "Drew Gilpin Faust: By the Book," *The New York Times Book Review*, May 27, 2012. "I am a detective story addict," she says, and mentions specifically the mysteries set in academia by Columbia professor Carolyn Heilbrun, writing under the name Amanda Cross. www.nytimes.com/2012/05/27/books/review/drew -gilpin-faust-by-the-book.html.

211 *"the vanity of human hopes"*: *Idler* No. 103 (1760).

Key West library book sale

214 *"To read fiction"*: Jane Smiley, "The Future of Fiction," *The New York Times*, June 6, 2012.

215 *re-create Shackleton's journey*: www.psfk.com/2013/01/shackletons-jour
ney-australian-explorers.html. www.intrepidtravel.com/shackleton
and http://intransit.blogs.nytimes.com/2012/10/25/going-with-the
-floe-a-shackleton-expedition/?ref=ernestshackleton and http://blog
.vantagetravel.com/blog/tips-trips-and-travel/shackletons-antarctica
-an-exclusively-chartered-voyage-small-ship-cruise.

## 11. IMMORTALITY

218 *"Last Tuesday a man"*: *Spies of the Kaiser*, introduction by Nicholas Hiley (London: Frank Cass, 1996).
   Another parody of the invasion genre, *The Swoop!*, by P. G. Wode-
house, was published in 1909. It tells of the invasion of Britain by nine
countries, including Switzerland. In the face of his complacent family,
which refuses to recognize the threat, young Clarence Chugwater
foils the invasion with the help of other members of his Boy Scout
troop.

218 *many more people believed Le Queux's fantasy*: Including Hudson, the
butler in *Upstairs, Downstairs*, who suspects the local baker because of
his German surname. In the televised version of *Parade's End*, Sylvia
Tietjens's priest and conscience, the Irish Father Consett, is hanged as
a German spy. We had seen him riding on his bike in the countryside,
suspiciously making notes.

219 *"Some may think it fitting"*: *Spies of the Kaiser*, Hiley introduction,
p. xxx.

220 *"Q"*: Might also stand for "Quartermaster," although "M" has no
such easily referenced job title. Ian Fleming's biographer John Pearson
interestingly points out that Fleming often called his mother "M."

220 *"The world has been remade"*: Arthur Rowe in *The Ministry of Fear*
(London and Toronto: Heinemann, 1943).

221 *"I am going to stay at Claridge's"*: *The Young Archduchess*, p. 156. Other
quotations from this book at pp. 9, 125, 113, and 177.

230 *the emotional logic of the narrative*: The chronological sequence is quite
different. In sequential order, the stories would read, "Taman" (what
happened on Pechorin's way to Pyatigorsk), "Princess Mary" (what happened in Pyatigorsk), "Bela" (what happened after he was exiled

from Pyatigorsk after the duel), "The Fatalist," "Maxim Maximych," and, finally, the foreword to Pechorin's diary, in which we learn that Pechorin died in Persia.

231 *Why does the Lermontov seem so different*:

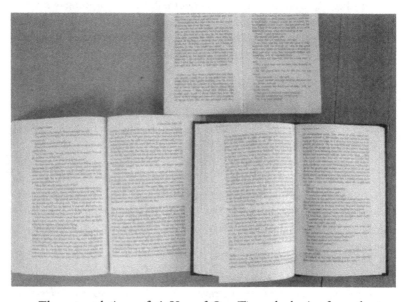

Three translations of *A Hero of Our Time*, clockwise from the top: Nabokov (note tiny type, cramped and yellowing pages), Randall (perfect type size, line spacing, and margins), and Schwartz (type a tad too faint; page too long; text too close to gutter on right-hand page; running head doesn't provide chapter titles). The typesetting and paper choice have as much to do with how I respond to each version as the translation.

The clarity I felt in Randall's translation proved hard to pin down.

> Today I was up late; I arrived at the well—no one was there anymore. The day began to get hot. White, shaggy rain clouds quickly sped down from the snowy mountains, promising a storm. The head of Mount Mashuk was smoking like an extinguished torch. Grey shreds of clouds twisted and crawled around it, like snakes, and they seemed to be held back in their strivings, as if they had been caught up in its prickly shrubbery. The air was filled with electricity. (Randall)

Today I arose late; by the time I arrived at the well, everyone was gone. It was getting hot; shaggy white clouds were scudding quickly off the mountains, promising a storm; Mashuk's dome was smoking like an extinguished torch; around it gray scraps of cloud coiled and slithered like snakes, clouds detained in their desire and seemingly caught on the thorns of its bushes. The air was saturated with electricity. (Schwartz)

It is true that in some ways Natasha Randall's translation is more forceful than Marian Schwartz's. Randall's preference for short sentences, the simple past tense, and monosyllables generates speed in her prose, whereas Schwartz's use of semicolons and participles ("was getting," "were scudding") slows hers. Both of them have a hard time with those gray shreds of clouds twisting and crawling around the top of the mountain like snakes. "They seemed to be held back in their strivings." What on earth does that mean? "Detained in their desire." Worse yet. I turned to Nabokov to see what he made of this puzzling phrase: "The top of Mount Mashuk smoked like an extinguished torch; around it there coiled and slithered, like snakes, gray shreds of cloud, which had been delayed in their surge and seemed to have been caught in its thorny brush." "Surge" makes sense of the image. The clouds are seen as sweeping up the mountain or across its top and held back in their movement, caught, torn to shreds by the underbrush. As I read more of the Nabokov translation—it happens to be a section of the book where Nabokov does not comment constantly—it seemed splendid, subtle and unobtrusive.

232 *"Enough people have been fed"*: Lermontov's introduction to *A Hero of Our Time*, in Nabokov's translation.

232 *"For all his genius, Lermontov"*: Quoted by Laurence Kelly, *Lermontov: Tragedy in the Caucasus* (London: Robin Clark, 1983), 240, n. 22.

233 *"Cousine, my darling"*: Kelly, *Lermontov*, 175.

235 *that one reward is worth it all*: John Updike spoke about this writerly goal in a *Paris Review* interview conducted by Charles Thomas Samuels in 1968: "When I write, I aim in my mind not toward New York but toward a vague spot a little to the east of Kansas. I think of the books on library shelves, without their jackets, years old, and a countryish teenaged boy finding them, and having them speak to him. The reviews, the stacks in Brentano's, are just hurdles to get over, to place the books on that shelf." Brentano's, it should be noted, used to be a

famous bookstore. It was absorbed into the Borders bookstore group, which filed for bankruptcy in 2011.

236 *anyone with eighty dollars*: To say nothing of audiobooks, which have evolved from Books for the Blind—cumbersome eight-track tapes that had to be mailed back and forth and played on a special machine—to electronic files you can download to your iPod and listen to on the subway.

# ACKNOWLEDGMENTS

Warm thanks to Jin Auh, Mark Bartlett, Michael Berman, Gabrielle Bordwin, Mari Brown, Laurent de Brunhoff, Max Byrd, Susan Chan, Wendy Gimbel, David Goldblatt, Molly Haskell, Adina Hoffman, Maya Jasanoff, Nancy Klingener, John Knight, Charles R. Larson, Bob Lerman, Rhoda Lerman, Lisa Lerner, Steve McGuirl, Nancy Nicholas, Marianne Noordermeer, Marjorie Perloff, Ted Rose, Eli Rose, Beckett Rose, David Schorr, Ileene Smith, and Krishna Winston for help that ranged from inspiration to forbearance and from useful remarks to generous participation and invaluable editorial readings. Special thanks to Annie Dillard, for a lifetime of friendship. Along with her husband, Robert D. Richardson, she is the "dedicated reader" who first led me into the stacks in pursuit of Nordhoff and Hall, so it's appropriate that she is the reader to whom the book is dedicated.

# INDEX

Printed in the USA
CPSIA information can be obtained
at www.ICGtesting.com
LVHW091139150724
785511LV00005B/421